Know who you are

Do all you can

Brent Crowe

2 Cor. 5:17-21

David Nasser / Brent Crowe

The
Call

David Nasser / Brent Crowe

The Call

INTERVIEWS WITH

WARREN WIERSBE

MATT REDMAN

FRANCIS CHAN

REBECCA ST. JAMES

CHRIS TOMLIN

VONETTE BRIGHT

LOUIE GIGLIO

PAT WILLIAMS
SENIOR VP / ORLANDO MAGIC

DARREN WHITEHEAD

ANNE GRAHAM LOTZ

LEELAND MOORING

DR. JAY STRACK

DR. HOWARD HENDRICKS

DR. BARRY C. BLACK
CHAPLAIN OF THE U.S. SENATE

DR. ERGUN CANER

ED YOUNG

MAC POWELL OF THIRD DAY

THE HARRIS BROTHERS

RON LUCE

DR. JOHNNY HUNT

DR. CHARLES RYRIE

AND MANY OTHERS

Redemptive art
PUBLISHING

Thanks

Brent and David would like to thank God for the humbling and exciting experience of being in ministry. It is our greatest joy to see people come to true repentance and faith in Christ. To You be the glory.

We would also like to thank the Gatekeepers who took time you didn't have to think about, pray through, and answer the questions in this book. May the wisdom you have gained be used by God to impact the lives of the ones who follow after you.

Thank you to the Crowe family and the Nasser family who lovingly encourage us to go and follow God's call on our lives.

A big thank you goes out to our editorial, graphic, and administrative team: LeAnn Gentry, Dana Davis, and Kevin Harvey. Your hard work and dedication to this project has not gone unnoticed.

Thanks to those whose lives and ministries have consistently been a testimony of God's truth and faithfulness. And to the thousands of students who are responding to "the call" and the tens of thousands who will soon answer.

Table of Contents

Introduction

By David Nasser

"When did you know that God was calling you to do this?" "How did you get started doing what you're doing?" And the inevitable follow-up, "Do you have any advice for me on how I can get started?" These are all questions that come my way frequently. Just about every week I get an email or a phone message from a young man or woman who wants to have coffee and get some advice about their "calling." The request is always primed with an, "I know you're super busy, but if I could ask for twenty to thirty minutes . . . " It always ends up being at least an hour, if not more. For years now, I have made it a point to try to make time for these meetings. After all, these eager men and women are the Christian leaders of tomorrow. I always think, *Could this be the next Lottie Moon, or the next Billy Graham; the scientist who finds the cure for AIDS, or a soccer mom who teaches Sunday school to my kids one day? What if this person becomes my pastor when I'm eighty? Is this someone who will one day be martyred in Sudan as a missionary, or even an author who will write children's books that have a redemptive message?*

Every one of these conversations is unique. Some people come in with a clear-cut game plan: website domain already reserved and marketing brochure already printed. Some have blurry visions and more confusion than conclusions. All, however, share a common thread: a zeal to see God use them. They sense an enlisting. A need to figure out how to get off the bench and into the game in order to make an impact. I love these meetings. It energizes and encourages me to see someone who has a burr in their saddle and can't wait to get started. In a world filled with indifference, it is refreshing to get to know those who are desperate to define and refine God's plan for their lives.

Once in a blue moon someone comes in who has an obvious agenda to be famous more than faithful, but they are few and far between. Most just want details, direction, or affirmation about what to do next. We sit and dream out loud together, we pray together, and on occasion, we've wept together. We shed tears for those whom God has called us to reach.

Let me be clear: these are not just conversations with people who want to be evangelists, Christian singers, or authors. No, this is about a life calling to use the gift. The one that has been specifically given for God's glory in just about every profession imaginable. For every conversation I've had with an aspiring author, or zealous evangelist, I've had another about the "everyday" callings and ideas to further the Kingdom of God.

I remember having a long conversation with a nineteen-year-old college student who wanted to own one hundred car wash franchises so that he could raise money for missionaries. He had a very specific idea that by having the best car wash centers ever, he could help "wash hearts." I realize it sounds corny to some, but I was thrilled to hear about his business plan and his branding concept. He had colors picked out for the logo, a Bible verse as a mission statement, and very specific details about what to do with the profits. God had given him the idea one summer as he worked as a cashier at a car wash. He realized how much money could be made in the car wash industry, so he used his job to learn the ins and outs. He then got a job the next summer at another car wash establishment in order to learn a different set of strengths and weaknesses. By the third summer (his senior year in high school), he was on a first name basis with dozens of reps and salesmen in the car wash industry, and had used his hands-on experiences to draw up his own business plan. I remember asking him if he was going to run his business as a non-profit, and he said, "Oh no, we will be full of profit all right. And we are going to evangelize thousands of people with all that money." Again, this is a nineteen-year-old man (notice I didn't say kid) on a mission. A man with a calling. He was passionate about finding the best window cleaner out there because he was passionate about the gospel. He was excited about carpet shampoo because he wanted to see God use carpet shampooing for His glory. Do you see it? He sure did.

On another occasion I sat with a girl who wanted to build an orphanage. She didn't have a clue where, or how, or when; she just knew that as a fifteen-year-old God had given her a burden for the 143 million abandoned children of the world. This was her calling—to look this need square in the eye and not flinch. It was an honor to encourage her in the genesis stages of her journey. I'll never forget her wide eyes bursting with excitement as she talked about Africa, and then China, and then India, and then Ukraine. She talked a hundred miles an hour, non-stop. Within ten minutes she had taken me around the world and back, telling me why this particular nation was where she wanted to go, and then another, and another. She finally stopped herself and said, somewhat embarrassed, "I just can't decide. Help me decide, please!" It was obvious to me that she was way past the, "Should I go?" or even the, "Can I go?" I simply leaned forward and said, "Who told you you have to decide on one? Why not have an orphanage in every one of them?" While this seemed obvious to me, it was a revolutionary thought to her. All of a sudden, the question changed. It was no longer, "Where do I go?" but it became "Where do I go first?" What a privilege it was for me to have a front row seat in her moment of discovery.

By the way, you are no different from her. Every person who has ever been redeemed by God has been given a specific calling that is unique. Even before we were born, God hard-wired this calling in us. It can reveal itself through a dream, a vision, a need, a holy frustration, or any number of ways. But when that call begins to ring louder and louder, you'll know that it's time to answer. Which brings us to another reason this book was conceived. We want to encourage and equip you in some small way in answering the call on your life. The intent of this project is to give you some biblically grounded, practical advice. The front half of this book is filled with common callings for all of God's people. Whether called to full-time ministry, or to work in the secular world, the principles found in these chapters can be applied across the board. For example, there is a chapter filled with wisdom on becoming a better communicator. Even if God doesn't call you to be a preacher, the advice in this particular chapter can help you as a future Sunday school teacher, or possibly in presenting a business plan to possible investors for your car wash idea. The second part of the book is meant to give you access to and insight from some of the most influential gatekeepers of our time. These are men and women whom God is using in tremendous ways. Some are preachers, some politicians, some musicians, and some are businessmen. But all are living out the dreams that God placed in them. Each of these men and women are wiser, more influential, and more experienced than Brent and I put together, so we figured a sit-down with them could have real value in widening your bandwidth for visioneering. Although you will see a lot of diversity in their answers, there are also many common threads. These heroes of the faith will inspire, challenge, confront, and most importantly, propel you to answer the call that God has specifically placed on you. Some of the questions are deep and serious, and some are purposefully designed to be more light and trivial. We wanted to show you that these are regular people just like you and me. People who watch football, drive minivans, and laugh at the same goofy things as you and me. All in all, these are ordinary people living extraordinary lives because they dared to answer the call. The deeper, more serious answers give us raw, unfiltered wisdom from people who are farther up the mountain of life. You will not only learn from the things they did right, but also by reading about their mistakes and shortcomings as well. As you read these interviews, remember that they're not designed to be an exhaustive list of the most important questions ever asked, or a to-do list for you to check off. As a matter of fact, reading these interviews in conjunction to one another reveals the opposite. They reveal that there's no *one* particular formula to doing ministry. Only common ingredients such as servanthood, humility, risk, and determination.

Our prayer is that each chapter will bring you to your knees in prayer and to the Word of God for ultimate revelation. We pray that God will use these pages to help you break free from the imprisonment of excuses and distractions. We pray that these words will help you truly trust the One who has placed the calling on your life, by offering all of you to His service. Can you hear Him? God is calling . . . are you ready?

CHAPTER 1

THE CALL TO GOD-CENTERED

Leadership

Quick, answer the following questions:

> Do you remember a time without a microwave, a DVD player, or VCR? . . .
>
> Do you remember when you didn't have a computer in your home? . . .
>
> Have you always had more than twelve channels to choose from? . . .
>
> Has your home telephone ever had a cord?

Chances are you have always had a microwave, DVD or VCR, a wireless phone, and more channels to choose from than there are flavors of ice cream. This is because we live in a digital age where the world is flat, and if you were born after 1982, then you are a "digital native." We are not talking about a small contingency of individuals either; this is the largest population segment in the history of the United States. If you find yourself in this category, then you have affectionately been referred to as a "millennial."[1] I like to refer to them as the "Joshua generation" because of the overwhelming potential that exists to lead a movement that would rival the Reformation in Europe, the Great Awakenings in America, and the Evangelical Awakening in Great Britain. The Joshua generation is more numerous, more affluent, better educated, and more ethnically diverse than any other in recorded history.[2]

What does Joshua's cultural DNA look like?

The following three statements capture the very essence or cultural DNA of this generation. It is important to understand the following realities whether you are part of the Joshua generation or another. And "Why?" you might ask—because it is in the process of preparation that we earn the right to speak into someone's life.

1. *Evolution is the norm.*

The Joshua generation has never known a time when the world around them wasn't constantly changing. Because of this they are very spiritual and prefer no normal or traditional institutional model of religion. In other words, they would prefer no standard of media, no standard of worship, no standard of reverence, and no standard of church. They are open to a multiplicity of truths believing that religion(s) do offer some reliable truth claims.[3] They choose to be very inclusive and pluralistic, following the modus operandi of "*co-exist and accommodate.*" In essence, they want to be spiritual without being religious.

2. *Entertainment is the means.*

For an entire generation, reality has been shaped by messages from culture, whether it is the Internet, music, or television. We are drowning in a sea of digital chaos; we jump up to read every text message, run to check our online profiles, rush to update the world on our latest comings and goings, only slowing down long enough to fall into hypnosis before a glowing screen. Each day there are more text messages sent and received than there are people in the world. The majority of them use their cell phones as media delivery tools. Therefore it is not hard to understand that the majority of information received is done so through the medium of entertainment.

3. *Experience is the goal.*

In the 1950s we questioned nothing, in the '60s and '70s we questioned everything, in the '80s we should have questioned our fashion sense, and in the '90s we questioned questions.[4] The Joshua generation has had enough with the questions because for them answers are not the destination of their life's quest. As a matter of fact, they are looking for community and relationships before they are looking for answers. This means they don't care how much you know; rather they want to know how much you care. Another interesting attribute is that they are primarily cause driven and not necessarily need driven. It is no secret that we live in a time when causes rule the day. Now, causes are by no means a bad thing, but it is important to remember that causes change from generation to generation while needs exist at all times and in any culture. Therefore the Joshua generation doesn't want to say something; they want to *do* something . . . they seek an experience.

Becoming Joshua

Joshua could not have become the spiritual champion or recognized his potential had it not been for the influence of Moses. Which leads us to an all-important question: *Who is your Moses?* Who is leading you and preparing you so that you may stand in your day and time and be "bold and courageous"? I think it is safe to say that had there been *no* Moses there would be *no* Joshua. The stories and accounts of the lives lived before us demand that we put ourselves through a process of leadership development. So go on a journey to become a spiritual champion. Not so you can say, "Look at me, I have arrived," but so you can help others to recognize their full potential in Christ. Become a Joshua so that you can be a Moses.

The life of Joshua was one that was born for the moment at hand. Just as Winston Churchill was born to defeat Hitler and will forever be known by his statement "Never give in!" so Joshua, the son of Nun, was born to lead the children of Israel into the Promised Land and forever be known for fulfilling the orders from God to "be strong and courageous." He first appears on the scene in Exodus 17, but prior to that, not much is known of his life or his family except that he was a prince in the tribe of Ephraim (Num. 13:8, 16; Deut. 32:44)[5] as the son of Nun, grandson of Elishama chief of Ephraim (1 Chron. 7:20-27). The name *Joshua* means "Jehovah is our help" or God-help, and it was given to him at the time he entered into Moses' service, either before or after the battle with the Amalekites.[6] Joshua's entire life was prepared for the moment in history when he would follow Moses as "the successor and the supervisor of Israel's conquest of Canaan and of the allotment of the land to the tribes."[7] For our purposes, attention will be given to the relationship between Moses and Joshua so a greater understanding can be gained as to how Joshua became a spiritual champion. How did Moses prepare his assistant for the task of leading a nation? Put more simply, how did one leader prepare another leader? Several events occur throughout their relationship that give great insight into how Moses developed his young assistant.

1. Joshua did war with Moses (Exodus 17:8-16).

For my own warfare, however, I am at a loss what course to pursue, what alliance, what word of wisdom, what grace to devise, with what panoply to arm myself against the wiles of the wicked one. What Moses did is to conquer him by stretching out his hands upon the mount, in order that the cross, thus typified and prefigured, may prevail. – Gregory of Nazianzus

The first event occurs in Exodus 17 just after the Amalekites had attacked Israel, when Moses said to Joshua, "Choose us some men and go out, fight with Amalek. Tomorrow I will stand on the top of the hill with the rod of God in my hand." This is the first mention of Joshua in Scripture. It is quite possible that Joshua had served as Moses' assistant for a short time prior to this, but now the leader of Israel called the young man's number to go into the game. Up to this point, God had fought for Israel, but now God was to fight through Israel. And the opponent was not one to be taken lightly. "The Amalekites, who appear here as the enemy of the Israelites, were a tough and aggressive Bedouin people who roamed the desert region of Sinai. Their nomadic existence led them to despise the settled and half-settled peoples who dwelt on the fringes of the desert, as the Israelites did. They thus robbed and harassed them, making themselves a serious threat to caravans and communities moving through the desert."[9]

The following morning after the initial attack Joshua did as Moses had commanded him and fought the Amalekites. During the battle, Moses, Aaron, and Hur went to the top of a hill overlooking the battlefield. There, Moses took his intercessory position holding the staff of God, praying with both hands raised toward heaven.[10] "Commentators, ancient and modern, almost unanimously consider this act of Moses as an act of prayer. As such, it expressed an attitude of dependence upon God that determined the outcome of the battle, and it served to demonstrate the reality of this dependence to all the people."[11] The Scriptures then say,

When Moses held up his hand, Israel prevailed; and when he let down his hand, Amalek prevailed. But Moses' hands became heavy; so they took a stone and put it under him, and he sat on it. And Aaron and Hur supported his hands, one on one side, and the other on the other side; and his hands were steady until the going down of the sun. So Joshua defeated Amalek and his people with the edge of the sword. Exodus 17:11-13

Following the battle Moses was to record in the book and recount to Joshua that God would utterly and completely destroy Amalek. Joshua was not to lose sight of what God was going to do to this people. Next, Moses built an altar, which he called "Jehovah my banner" or "The Lord is my Banner" to praise God for His help.[12] One could only imagine Joshua exhausted and covered in sweat, dirt, and the enemy's blood looking for praise and adoration upon his victory only to have the wise old leader immediately put the spotlight on the One who granted victory. It was only following this immediate focus upon what the Lord had done rather than what Joshua had done that the young warrior would learn that the battle was won on the mountain, not in the valley. It is in this first event that Joshua learned the battle and the victory are truly the Lord's.

There are three ideas that can be extracted at this point in Moses' relationship with Joshua and applied to developing spiritual champions today. Spiritual champions need:

- opportunities to lead that carry significant consequences;
- the mentality that true victory can only come from the Lord; and
- an understanding that prayer is a gateway to an *if-God-can-be-for-me-who-could-be-against-me?* attitude.

2. *Joshua walked with Moses (Exodus 24:13; 32:17).*

In Exodus 24 and then again in Exodus 32, Joshua accompanied Moses up and then back down Mount Sinai, the mountain of God. It is not believed that Joshua ascended all the way up the mountain but that he went a great distance with Moses and waited for him to come back down. No other individual is mentioned to have accompanied Moses up to Sinai but Joshua. The point to be made here is that Moses' leadership style was to teach as he went. Joshua is called Moses' "assistant" or "servant" in Exodus 24:13. It is safe to assume that since Joshua was Moses' personal assistant, where Moses went Joshua went. Therefore, Moses used his life as a platform on which to teach and develop Joshua.

Great leaders are constantly striving to be exhaustively intentional with their lives. To ensure they are a living sacrifice and that they capture the moments of life, they will have young leaders around them and use the commonality of everyday experiences and the decisions that leaders must make to train and equip. Most young men and women simply need someone to come alongside them and demonstrate before them that they can succeed. Moses had already demonstrated great belief in Joshua by commanding him to fight the Amalekites. Now he was taking Joshua and walking beside him on a daily basis using his life as a tool of encouragement, allowing his life to communicate to Joshua that God can use him to lead.

One of my favorite films of recent years is *Remember the Titans*. It is based on a true story of an African American coach being brought into a school district with a history rich in segregation. The movie portrays the struggles between the white and the black players and coaches as they attempt to become a team. Denzel Washington's character, Coach Boone, fills the role as head coach. This movie gives a unique perspective on how he attempts to bring coaches and players from many different backgrounds, cultures, and places on the economic scale so that they may become one unit. At one point in the movie, a conversation takes place over lunch about where the young men wanted to go and what they wanted to do following their high school career. Many wanted to go to college; many wanted to pursue other careers. One white young man, when asked if he was going to college, replies, "Coach, I'm just poor white trash, I'm a C student and I will never amount to anything." The camera angle shifts as Coach Boone pulls the young man aside and tells him to bring his grades and his upcoming assignments by his office at the end of each week so they can discuss them. Toward the end of the movie, there is a very moving scene in the locker room. All the players had taken the field for the upcoming game, and the C student and Coach Boone were all that remained. The young man was standing with his head held low and Coach Boone asked if there was anything on his mind. With tears in his eyes, the young man looked at his coach and stated, "Coach, I did it. I'm gonna graduate. I'm gonna go to college."

Coach Boone's leadership style reflects that of Moses. In the movie we have a young man who never really believed his life would amount to anything until one day, when an elderly leader looked at him and said, "I'm going to walk with you. We're going to do this together." The first leadership principle demonstrated by Moses to Joshua is that you can win in the valley because the battle has been won on the hilltop. If Moses simply had stopped there, he would have been an incomplete leader and mentor. Moses realized that he could not invest in Joshua properly only from the hilltop but that he would have to walk through the valley of life with him.

3. *Joshua worshiped with Moses (Exodus 33:11).*

The great Charles Haddon Spurgeon said, "God never permits His people to sin successfully."[13] Just one chapter prior, while Moses and Joshua were up on Mount Sinai receiving God's law, the nation of Israel, who had experienced God's provision and mercy so many times before, pleaded with Aaron to make a god for them to worship because in the absence of godly leadership, people will follow those who lead under the presupposition that truth is relative. This is what Aaron did because in

Exodus 32 he responded to the people by building a golden calf for them to worship. But Spurgeon is right and as a result of Israel's sin, God sent a plague, refused to go before them on their way to the Promised Land, and had Moses move the "tent of meeting" outside the camp.[14] It is in this punishment from the Lord that another insight is given into the relationship of Moses and Joshua. Now the "tent of meeting" was set apart from the rest of the nation of Israel. Moses and Joshua cared for this tent and when Israel would make camp, it was erected by one of the two and no other. This tent "was made into a temporary sanctuary by the fact that the pillar of cloud came down upon it, and Jehovah talked with Moses there, and which was called by the same name as tabernacle because Jehovah revealed himself there."[15]

The Bible says that "the LORD used to speak to Moses face to face, just as a man speaks to his friend. When Moses returned to the camp, his servant Joshua, the son of Nun, a young man, would not depart from the tent." What a phenomenal privilege for young Joshua to be able to sit in on that conversation. It is here that Moses demonstrates one of the most phenomenal leadership principles of all to Joshua: without God one cannot lead and with God one can lead anyone. Moses was now teaching Joshua that the only reason the battle could be won on the hilltop and the only reason he could walk in the valley every day is because he had met with God on a personal level.

I have often wondered why Joshua stayed behind in the tent after Moses returned to the camp. I mean, after God's presence left, it was just a tent. He could have packed it up and headed back to camp himself . . . so why stay? Could it be that Moses' worship was contagious? He had just witnessed conversational intimacy with the God of the universe and it probably blew his mind! I believe Joshua stayed in the tent because he wanted to experience God in the same way Moses had experienced God. The authentic nature in which Moses lived his faith out loud seems to have had a profound impact on the spiritual champion Joshua would become.

4. Joshua worked with Moses (Numbers 13:16-17).

Much had taken place leading up to Numbers 13. One gets the feeling that Israel may never enter the Promised Land as so much unbelief had characterized the children of God. And now they wanted to send a reconnaissance team to scout the land of Canaan before the entire nation went in to engage in battle (Deut. 1:22-23). The Lord allows them to do so, not so much because it was a great idea, but rather to teach them "to trust the Word of God and do the will of God His way and not their own way (Prov. 3:5-6)."[16] Spies are chosen, a leader from each tribe, and among them was Caleb and Joshua, to scout the land and report back to the people. They scouted the land forty days and then returned to report to Moses and Aaron and the children of Israel. Upon their return the spies painted a picture to Israel that the land "truly flows with milk and honey." The spies even brought back fruit to demonstrate how luscious and fertile the land was. Then in verse 28 the statement is made, "Nevertheless the people who dwell in the land are strong; the cities are fortified and very large; moreover we saw the descendants of Anak there." On and on the excuses and lack of faith in God flowed from their lips until the entire nation was weeping and complaining to Moses and Aaron how it was better off back in Egypt. Oh, but thank God for godly leadership, because in chapter 14, verses 6-8, the true leaders of God, Caleb and Joshua, stand up. Note the number of references to the Lord and His will:

> But Joshua the son of Nun and Caleb the son of Jephunneh, who were among those who had spied out the land, tore their clothes; and they spoke to all the congregation of the children of Israel, saying: "The land we passed through to spy out is an exceedingly good land. If **the LORD** delights in us, then **He** will bring us into this land and give it to us, a land which flows with milk and honey. Only do not rebel against **the LORD**, nor fear the people of the land, for they are our bread; their protection has departed from them, and **the LORD is with us**. Do not fear them." (emphasis added)

Through all the chaos and upheaval one can only imagine that at least in his mind Moses leaned back and thought, *That's my boy.* Joshua knew a simple yet profound truth that many lose track of so many times: this is all about God.

Only two men from that generation would be permitted into the Promised Land: Joshua and Caleb. What was the key to Joshua passing so great a test? How did he learn to stand for what God said when two million of his countrymen didn't believe? To find the answer we must look back to Numbers 13:16 after Moses had named the twelve men who assimilated the reconnaissance team, including Joshua. The Bible says, "These *are* the names of the men whom Moses sent to spy out the land. And Moses called Hoshea the son of Nun, Joshua." While this sounds like a very subtle change, upon further investigation the impact will prove to have quite an influence. Why was Hoshea's name changed to Joshua? The answer is found in the meaning of the names themselves. *Hoshea* in Hebrew simply means "salvation," while *Joshua* means "Jehovah is salvation." Moses knew that if Joshua was going to lead God's chosen people then everything about his existence must point to God; if he was going to be a strong leader then he must first be a passionate follower of God. Each success in his life must attribute to nothing less than the goodness of God. It is not simply that His provision is sufficient but rather without his provision there was no salvation.

The relationship between Moses and Joshua paints for us a picture of what it takes to develop spiritual champions. All of these same qualities can be seen in the ministry of Jesus. Just as Joshua learned the battle was won on the hilltop, so the disciples would live their lives in the shadow of the cross. Just as Joshua walked with Moses, so Jesus journeyed on a day-by-day basis with His disciples. Just as Joshua learned about worship from Moses, so the disciples learned what worship is from the One whom their worship was to be directed. And just as Joshua learned that all he does in life must point to the sufficiency of God, so the disciples learned that without Christ all is lost. So become the spiritual champion God has uniquely created you to be so that you may help others to do the same. Whether you are a father or mother, teacher or preacher, businessperson or military personnel, get busy becoming Joshua so that you can be a Moses.

1   Howe, Neil and Strauss, William. (2000). Millennials Rising. (Page 4). New York: Vintage Books.
2   Ibid., 4.
3   Denton, Melinda Lundquist and Smith, Christian. (2005). Soul Searching. (Page 74). New York: Oxford University Press.
4   Howe, Neil and Strauss, William. (2000). Millennials Rising. (Page 348). New York: Vintage Books.
5   Delitzsch, F. and Keil, C.F. (2001). Commentary on the Old Testament: Pentateuch. Vol. 1. (Page 371). Peabody: Hendrickson Publishers.
6   Ibid., 371.
7   Achtemeier, P. J., Harper & Row, P., & Society of Biblical Literature. (1985). Harper's Bible Dictionary. Includes index. (1st Ed.) (Page 508). San Francisco: Harper & Row.
8   Lienhard, Joseph T. (2001). Exodus, Leviticus, Numbers, Deuteronomy (Ancient Christian Commentary on Scripture: Old Testament. Vol. III. (Pages 91-92). Downers Grove: InterVarsity Press.
9   Mellor, Enid B. (1972). The Cambridge Bible Commentary: The Makings of the Old Testament. (Page 103). Cambridge: Cambridge University Press.
10 Delitzsch, F. and Keil, C.F. (2001). Commentary on the Old Testament: Pentateuch. Vol. 1. (Page 372). Peabody: Hendrickson Publishers.
11 Pfeiffer, C. F. (1962). The Wycliffe Bible Commentary : Old Testament (Ex 17:11). Chicago: Moody Press.
12 Keil & Delitzsch, p. 372.
13 Wiersbe, Warren. (2003). The Bible Exposition Commentary: Old Testament History. (Page 247). Wheaton: Victor Books.
14 Ibid., pp. 244-247.
15 Delitzsch, F. and Keil, C.F. (2001). Commentary on the Old Testament: Pentateuch. Vol. 1. (Page 473). Peabody: Hendrickson Publishers.
16 Wiersbe, Warren. (2003). The Bible Exposition Commentary: Old Testament History. (Page 332). Wheaton: Victor Books.

CHAPTER 2

THE CALL TO GOD-CENTERED

Marriage

Marriage provides the matrix or womb from which whole human beings can emerge to form whole human communities under God.[17]
– Dr. Dallas Willard

I recently had the amazing privilege to speak at a conference in Jericho, as in *the* Jericho where Joshua and the children of Israel marched around the city and the walls came crashing down, with a gentleman by the name of Dr. David Ferguson, one of the most respected voices in the country ministering to married couples. First of all, to be in that part of the world was beyond words. Everywhere you turn is rich in biblical history. Really, I was like a kid at Disneyland. But then second, to be able to serve alongside Dr. Ferguson was an honor I will never forget. After the conference we got in a taxi and headed back to Jerusalem for other business. During that forty-five-minute car ride I interviewed him on a subject he is more than qualified to speak about: *marriage*. Therefore the vast majority of what is shared in this chapter comes from that conversation, as well as resources his ministry has produced.

The Great Commandment Principle

As with everything in the Christian life, we must turn to Scripture to shape the big ideas on which our thoughts will marinate. One such thought for most is the idea of marriage. Now most books, seminars, and conversations focus on the pragmatics answering questions like: *How do I become the type of person someone would want to marry?* and *What is the list of characteristics I should seek in a mate?* The problem with these and others like it is they begin with the one asking the question, which is a recipe for disaster. So we will begin in the Scriptures and then build the practical applications on truth discovered.

To have an accurate view on the concept of relationships, we go back to the ministry of Jesus and what we will refer to as *Great Commandment Love*. Let me explain:

In one of the most defining moments of his ministry, Jesus was asked which commandment was the greatest. He answered, 'You shall love the Lord your God with all your heart, and with all your soul, and with your mind.' This is the great and foremost commandment. The second is like it, 'You shall love your neighbor as yourself.' On these two commandments depend the whole Law and the Prophets" (Matthew 22:37-40, NASB). This Great Commandment to love God and love people defines the true identity of those who are called his church. Great Commandment love is at the heart of who we are and what we do.[18]

While the Great Commission (Matt. 28:18-20) describes the mission for the followers of Jesus, the Great Commandment defines our identity. The Great Commandment Principle is the accomplishing of the Great Commission within the context of the Great Commandment.[19] What does this have to do with marriage? Everything, because this principle will positively impact every relationship we have, including our spouse. To further understand that we were created to love God and love people, we must go back to the very beginning.

Created Perfect but Needy

We all are familiar with the story of creation. If someone were to ask you what the first crisis was, you would probably point to Adam and Eve and the forbidden fruit. This is what throughout history has been called the "Fall of man," when sin entered the world. But did you know that even before the fall there was a problem? Adam was created in the image of God and placed in a perfect world. It was paradise and he had everything he could possibly want or possess. He was even "responsible for the fish in the sea, the birds in the air, the cattle, and, yes, Earth itself, and every animal that moves on the face of the Earth" (Gen. 1:26, The Message). And of course he had a perfect relationship with God. And yet something was "not good." To quote God: "It is not good for man to be alone." Even before sin the problem of aloneness existed.

God created us to need one another, and that has some very significant implications for our lives:

> First, none of us can rightfully say, "All I need is God." To do so is to reject other people as a channel of God's loving provision. Adam lived in perfection with a deeply personal knowledge of God. If anyone had grounds to think his intimate relationship with the Creator was all he needed, Adam sure did. . . . The second implication is closely related to the first. Just as we cannot claim, "All I need is God," we cannot truthfully convey the message, "You only need God." To do so is to communicate a message of condemnation: "You should be able to take care of yourself without needing other people. If you still have needs, you don't have enough of Christ. If you were more consistent in your quiet time, if you had more faith, if you loved God with all your heart, soul, and mind, you would not be needy." As important and necessary as faith and quiet times and loving God are, God has chosen to involve people in meeting the needs of other people.[20]

Notice that God did not create a "buddy" or just a "friend" to fix Adam's aloneness; He created an intimate partner, his wife. There are a lot of purposes and reasons for marriage, but in the beginning the great purpose of marriage was to fix aloneness with oneness. "The Man said, "Finally! Bone of my bone, flesh of my flesh! Name her Woman for she was made from Man." Therefore a man leaves his father and mother and embraces his wife. They become one flesh" (Gen. 2:23-24, The Message).

How does one seriously discern the will of God when it comes to marriage?

Begin with the understanding that this is a permanent decision and one that should not be entered into quickly. Really take the time, with the person you are dating, to make that a real, deliberate sensing of the Lord together. This is a generation that prides themselves on "reversible" being a good thing, which is why we place such a strong emphasis on a perspective of marriage as a decision that is irreversible and "till death do us part." Take the time to explore how God could be bringing us together *spiritually, emotionally, soulishly,* and one day possibly *physically.* Explore in that order as well.

How is God going to bring us together in a spiritual sense so that our walk with Him may strengthen and we can together make His Kingdom known? Wrestle with these big kinds of questions. How, in God bringing us together, would it be an additional blessing to each of us and an additional dimension of Christlike work in each of us? This is iron sharpening iron, and through the exploration of these Kingdom-type questions, many times clarity emerges. You ask big questions because on the other side of this part of the journey you want to be able to say, "I know that I know that I know that this is the one." Because it's been our experience in so many marriages, particularly those in vocational ministry, that you are inevitably going to go through some tough times, some darkness, some valleys, some challenges with kids, with rejections, with all kinds of things. Maybe the only thing you have to hold on to is to say, "We don't know whether we are supposed to be in church ministry or not," "We don't know if we're supposed to live in this city or not," "We don't know if we're supposed to have any or ten kids," or "We don't know whether I like your parents or if you like my parents," but the one thing that we do know is that God brought us together.

What ideas should our thoughts be marinating upon so that after fifty years of marriage we are more in love with each other, with Jesus, and more excited about Kingdom work than ever before?

I think we must go back to the spirit, soul, and body concept. In Genesis 2:7 God created man out of the dust of the ground and breathed in him the spirit of life. At that moment he became a living soul and soon God's going to make two into one. In light of how God created the first marriage, we should be asking: how are we cultivating, prioritizing, and deepening our spiritual walk together? The answer to this question has absolutely nothing to do with what church we're serving or whether we're in worship ministry or preaching ministry or evangelism . . . but rather, are we deepening our spiritual walk together?

Cultivate a Deep Spiritual Walk *Together*

For ten to twelve years, my wife and I struggled in our marriage to simply find a pattern that works for us on how we are going to come together from time to time and talk about how God is speaking to us through His Word. Part of the reason for this struggle is that we approach things very differently. For example, I am very meditative. I enjoy large portions of time to memorize large passages of Scripture. I can wander around outside and meditate on 1 Peter 1, having a wonderful time with the Lord, and when I come back in, my wife looks at me and says, "What did you write down?" You see, she is very organized and when she meets with God she has to write something down or fill in blanks. So it was through this struggle that we learned how we each processed differently, and in doing so we also learned how we have been uniquely created and crafted by Him.

We would also struggle with when to have that quiet time before the Lord and what we were going to study. I feel obligated to point out that by "struggle" I simply mean this holy desire to experience oneness with my wife in a very spiritual manner. For years I was a night person and she was a morning person and there was an ongoing tension concerning when we would spend personal time before the Lord. It may sound silly to some, but we wondered if we were growing together spiritually if we weren't sitting down at the same time with our Bibles open and a cup of coffee in hand. This healthy tension led us on a journey that greatly contributed to protecting each other spiritually.

We started by agreeing to study a chapter out of the book of Proverbs each day. I traveled a lot at that time, so there was a connectedness even if I was on the other side of the world knowing that on this particular day I was in Proverbs 14 and she was doing the same. It didn't matter if she read and studied that text in the morning and I at night. The idea here is to find what works for you, but you have to find something that brings you together spiritually. Always guard your heart against making assumptions. Don't assume that because you preach or teach the Scriptures, or are very involved in your church, that you are growing together spiritually. That is a false concept. There must be a great deal of initiative that you are going to nurture your spiritual life so that you connect and converse around spiritual things. It is obvious when this is happening because a natural part of your conversations will be statements like, "God spoke to me about this today" or "God pressed me with this today." This is critical because without these types of statements it becomes secondhand faith, which is characterized by statements like: "I think God wants us to do . . ." and "I think God wants me to be involved with . . ."

Cultivate a Deep Friendship

Certainly the first question revolves around spiritual oneness, but a second very practical question is "What are we going to do to cultivate and prioritize our friendship together?" We are not only going to have a spiritual life together, but there has to be a soulish and emotional connection. For us that typically boils down to a dedication to consistent, quality time together. Every Thursday for thirteen years my wife and I had lunch together from 11:00 to 1:00, and that was the first appointment I put on my calendar every week. I simply made it my priority to schedule everything else around that lunch with Teresa. We would also have a regular date night.

Now we are in a different chapter of life that doesn't allow us to keep that weekly lunch and date night so regimented. For this particular leg of the journey we have gone to a weekly "marriage staff meeting." That may not be the best title for everyone, but it helps us continue to build a healthy marriage. At this marriage staff meeting we sit down and talk about our schedules, how we are doing on our goals, and really life in general for at least an hour. Because of our busyness, we may lie in bed on Sunday night and say, "Well, we better have our marriage staff meeting Thursday night when you fly back in town or Saturday morning when we both get back in town." The idea is that we consistently have that time to talk.

We want to always have a marriage staff meeting, because I want Teresa to have in mind the next fun thing she is going to do with me, which we also discuss at this meeting. It is always my responsibility to give her that security so that she knows in four days (or whatever it may be), she and I are going to go to the beach to spend a couple of days together just being alone, chilling out or doing whatever. While we are just having fun together we will normally take turns choosing what to do. For example, on the first afternoon I will look at her and say, "What do you want to do?" And if she says, "Go shopping," then we are off to the mall. The next morning she will ask the same of me and I may say, "Lie beside the pool and read a book," so she gets some magazines and we go down to the pool. But we always try to say that every four to six weeks we plan and purpose those times so that we always have something we are looking forward to.

Cultivating this friendship takes a spirit of intentionality. Having said that, our ministry recommends the following:

1. Have a weekly marriage staff meeting where you connect on schedules, goals, and life in general. In many ways this time becomes iron sharpening iron. Through organizing the craziness of life, you can help each other run the race unto Jesus and also enjoy your friendship along the way.

2. Always have something to look forward to every four to six weeks. This can be getting out of town for a couple of days or sending the kids to the grandparents so you can be alone in your own home. Earlier in our marriage when we had a house full of kids, we would periodically ask ourselves, "When was the last time we were alone in our own house?" We were also in an accountability group with many people in the same stage of life, so once a month another couple would keep all the kids at their house in order to make that time possible. Each month every couple in the accountability group got an entire day to be alone in their house.

3. Annual goal setting. For twenty-five years we've taken the week between Christmas and New Year's to plan our goals. We have goals in eight different areas of life: spiritual goals, marital goals, family goals, financial goals, social goals, household goals, educational goals, and ministry goals. We will spend two to three days working through what we want to see God do in the next twelve months in each of those areas. What inevitably happens is that each of us takes the lead on articulating goals for different areas.

For example, Teresa may come to the table with a family goal to emphasize this in one of our children's lives over the next year. She may also take the lead with some of the household goals or what she calls her "nest," and she would say that in the next year we are going to do this with the nest. I typically bring to the table spiritual goals, ministry goals, and financial goals, and we take the next two to three days to talk and pray through the goals we have written down.

We usually get away for annual goal setting. So we may spend a couple of hours by the pool and then work on some goals . . . Go see a movie and then work on them some more. The idea is that we make this a fun quality time where we can work on our relationship. This year we came up with eighty-six specific goals in the eight areas of life. We may not get all eighty-six done; as a matter of fact we are on pace to probably accomplish seventy of our goals. But what I have discovered is if we didn't have eighty-six we would probably never get to seventy. Both Teresa and I have a copy of all eighty-six goals that we constantly review and pray for. One of the most critical reasons for our goal setting is that it helps us to stay focused and run the race that is set before us.

We have also discovered that goal setting better helps us to discern the will of God for our lives. One of the more beautiful aspects to the goal-setting approach is that if you are not yet married you can already begin to cultivate this lifestyle.

Cultivate an Intimate Affection

The third and last question we must ask is, how do you keep cultivating an affection for each other? My wife and I have submitted to the idea that "great commandment love gives first." God always gives first. We want to be a "giving first" people, so I think one of the things in the context of marriage is to develop this as a discipline. Yes, there is spiritual connectedness, friendship connectedness, and when it comes to affection we must startle one another in some "giving first" ways. I think one of the reasons these unexpected interventions are so important is that it helps keep the relationship fresh, and isn't that what God does for us? He doesn't consider our walk with Him as some kind of boring religious ritual, but rather *His mercies are new every morning.* Because our relationship with God is never boring, neither should our relationship with our spouse ever become mundane.

For example, we are having this conversation in a car driving from Jericho to Jerusalem and I, like you, am going to be without my wife for about seven days. She was with me in the Middle East a few weeks ago but decided to stay home and be with the grand kids this time. One of the things I felt impressed to do was write some notes to my grandchildren before I left, just to let them know I'd be thinking about them. I stuck a ten-dollar bill in each one of those envelopes and told them I was going to the land where Jesus had walked and looked forward to telling them about Jesus when I come back. I put the notes in the mail before I left so they will get them about halfway through my trip. As I am writing these notes I realized, *Hey, it has been a long time since I wrote my wife a note.* So I wrote her a letter as well and put it in the mail and she will also receive it about halfway through my trip, and I hope it catches her off guard. I want to constantly surprise her. I want her to know that wherever I go I am thinking of her. It could be a simple phone call from the office to say, "I love you, I miss you, and I can't wait to see you tonight."

I think the idea of taking initiative to give first, just to let the other person know you're thinking about them is obviously one of the things God does for us. He is thinking about us at all times and we need to keep that fresh among our marriages. God loved us first and in taking that initiative, which is the only hope any of us can have, He has given us a principle of "giving first." If this principle is implemented in marriages, then the option of boredom is removed from the table.

Therefore I think these three components:
Cultivate a deep spiritual walk together

Cultivate a deep friendship
Cultivate an intimate affection for each other
can lead to a marriage that is on a daring adventure of serving God and making His Kingdom known.

17 Willard, Dallas. (2005). Revolution of Character. (Page 152). Colorado Springs: NavPress.
18 Ferguson, David. (1998). The Great Commandment Principle. (Page 7). Wheaton: Tyndale House Publishers.
19 Ibid.
20 Ibid., pp. 21-22.

CHAPTER 3

THE CALL TO GOD-CENTERED

Finances

By Steve Richardson, C.P.A.

David and Brent asked me to write a chapter about financial accountability, but before I do that, I want to tell you about how God called me to be a CPA, an accountant committed to Him. The story of my call starts in high school almost forty years ago.

My mom and dad, my pastor, my youth group, everyone connected with me believed that I was going to be a preacher. They had every reason to believe that: I was an active Christian speaking to youth groups and rallies, ministering to people, preaching and teaching in church; I even traveled to different cities to minister in the name of our Lord. I was passionate and effective. I saw the Lord move in ways that still surprise me.

When it was time to go to college I chose a Christian university and planned to major in religion; my goal was to be a preacher. Everyone expected that I would and, frankly, I didn't have a better plan. For two years I studied religion and prepared myself for a life in ministry.

Sometime during those years my passion died. I became progressively more unhappy. I loved my academic training; it was first rate. I loved the people I was associated with, my professors and my fellow students who were called into ministry. I wasn't unhappy about that.

When I finally stopped long enough to think about my plans, I discovered three disturbing things. Sometime during my first year at school I stopped going to church. I didn't want to believe that at first; I mean, I'm getting Bible lessons every day and going to chapel services twice a week. I thought school was church; I was wrong. No school, even a religious school, is a church. I stopped going to church because I stopped anticipating the joy of worship in the presence of God! Somewhere, somehow, for reasons that I still do not understand, I stopped worshiping God.

The second thing I discovered was that I had stopped reading my Bible. At first I denied this to myself because I read the Bible every day in class and for homework. The Bible had become a textbook instead of the Word of God. I was learning a lot about the Bible, all facts and information, but I was not letting the Bible feed my soul. Ironically, I was starving for the Word of God even as I read the Bible multiple times every day.

The last and most shocking thing I realized was that I had stopped praying. I did not even remember it happened; I just realized I was not praying anymore. No wonder I was unhappy. Something had to change.

My personality is to always be proactive to attack a problem directly. With this stunning self-revelation, I did the most logical thing possible: I got on my knees and prayed. I vividly remember the prayer: *"Lord, I was a lot happier when I used to pray."*

God completely ignored what I had to say, and in an instant He clearly spoke to me and said, *I never called you to be a preacher.*

There was an abrupt end to that prayer. I was unhappy, distressed, and now angry. I had invested two years in training to be a minister. For the first time, I had a clear leading from God that told me I was never supposed to be a preacher.

I did what any depressed angry young man would do: I sulked and ignored the problem and became progressively more unhappy. About three weeks later I was so distressed that I had to do something, so I thought I would try to pray again. So I got on my knees and prayed the same prayer. *"Lord, I was a lot happier when I used to pray."*

Like the conversation was never interrupted, God spoke again. *I called you to be an accountant.*

In a split second I went from angry to furious. God had demoted me. He was telling me that He wanted me to be a technocrat—an accountant! God clearly did not understand me; I couldn't possibly be an accountant! If talking to God was going to be like this, then we were not going to talk. And I didn't for three months. However, I was obedient enough that I did take an accounting class as an elective.

I surprised myself; I liked the accounting class. It wasn't easy but it made sense and I enjoyed the material. The last semester of my sophomore year was one of my best academic years of my career. I took accounting, English lit from a brilliant older professor, and a course in New Testament letters and in Old Testament poetry. Academically it was a rich time. I learned more about myself in that one semester than I had learned all the preceding eighteen years, much of that I learned from my English professor—but that's another story.

On one level I was in my element enjoying school and doing well, but—there's always a but—I did not pray until the end of the semester. I went three months without praying and the lingering pain and frustration was growing.

In frustration and depression, with more than a bit of anger, I prayed for the third time in a year. There was no beating around the bush this time. I had a message that I wanted to give to God personally. So, on my knees, I prayed: *"Lord, I have decided to be an accountant, but I want You to know that I will never serve You as an accountant."*

Thankfully God ignored me. That wasn't really a prayer; it was a tantrum.

I ended up at the University of Alabama still angry, still a bit depressed; I was still in my self-imposed separation from God. I guess you could call it my time in the desert. I buried myself in my academic work to forget and discovered that I really loved accounting. I was good at it; it was fun. My spiritual life was a wreck, but I was doing well in school. Even still, God and I were not on speaking terms.

One evening, lonely and a bit depressed, I tried to pray thinking that maybe God and I needed a fresh start. So I prayed, again . . . the same prayer. *"Lord, I was a lot happier when I used to pray."*

And again God completely ignored what I had to say and immediately said to me: *You were a lot happier when you used to go to church.*

This prayer stuff was so very frustrating. I wanted to tell God what was going on in my life and He was not listening; instead He sounded like my grandmother giving me common-sense practical advice that I could get from anybody. I got angry with God. (Do you kind of sense a pattern here?) I got up off my knees and slammed the apartment door on the way out. If God wanted me to go to church, then by-God I was going to go to church. I walked to the closest church; it was during the week, about six or seven in the evening. I didn't think anybody would be in the building, but the college had some special thing going on. Still angry, still frustrated, I walked into the building . . .

The first person I met was my future wife. My first honest prayer in two years was prayed that night: *"Thank You, God; I think this is going to be a good church."*

I am more mature now; I wouldn't make the same mistakes again . . . I hope. But I clearly did receive a call from God. Maybe it isn't what most people think of as a "call"—I mean, accounting, how boring is that? No, not really; it is fun and exciting because I am living and working in my call.

As I retell this story I am sure you can see the pattern. Lacking a clear call I presumed upon God and decided that I was going to be a preacher. One thing you can see is "presumption." When God told me what I didn't want to hear, I got angry. I stopped my worship; I stopped my Bible time; I stopped praying—neglect. I neglected basic Christian spiritual hygiene. These are all hallmarks of immature faith, and I got depressed. My prayers weren't really prayers; they were immature tantrums. I didn't want to talk to God; I wanted to vent my frustrations.

Even in the midst of my immaturity, I did some things right. I recognized that I had a problem. Even in my depression I approached God—on my knees; at least there was some respect. Even in my anger I was obedient—sort of obedient anyway. I took an accounting class; I transferred to a major university with an outstanding accounting school; when God said go to church I went. I went in a pout; I went angry; but I went.

God's call into a life as an accountant, a CPA, has been rich. I currently work with over six hundred ministers and ministries in thirty-five states and twenty-five foreign countries. I've been active as a CPA working with ministries for over thirty years. Over the years I have worked with thousands of ministries around the world. This ministry takes up about 20 percent of my workday. I have had an impact on the Kingdom of God as an accountant that far exceeds anything I may have accomplished as a preacher. Well, that's how I was called.

That raises an important point: God can call you to a secular career. I believe that God calls all of us in some way or the other. He calls the lost to faith and eternal salvation. He calls the employee to work for his boss "as unto the Lord." He calls some to a life dedicated to the work of the Lord as whatever: missionaries, preachers, speakers, writers, musicians, the list goes on and on.

In thirty plus years of ministering to ministers as an accountant I have learned a few things.

The minister's personal finances are very important.

The person who is called must be financially secure. This is consistent with Scripture: "a laborer is worthy of his hire" and "those who preach the gospel should receive their living from the gospel."

The principle can be illustrated like this: if you are on an airplane holding an infant and the yellow oxygen masks fall down, you put yours on first. That is not selfishness or even self-preservation; it is making sure that you are strong enough to help someone else. Dealing with people from a secure position, especially a secure financial position, makes your job immeasurably easier.

The general wisdom is that ministries do not pay very well. Thankfully "general wisdom" or the "world's wisdom" is not even remotely related to God's wisdom. Here is a precept:

A financially secure minister can have a successful ministry.

The opposite is also true: a financially insecure minister is less likely to have a successful ministry.

To be financially secure a minister should do these three things:

1. Early, very early, in your ministry, you should get a trustworthy tax and financial advisor who understands ministry.
2. Immediately pay attention to your tax situation. Tax decisions you make during your first days of ministry—informed decisions or ignorant ones—will color your entire ministry and your relationship with the tax man.
3. Pay attention to your personal finances. We have many wonderful resources that you can draw upon to help tailor your financial situation. Dave Ramsey is only one, but he is a good one.

When you start a ministry, join a ministry, or take a call to a church or the mission field, one of the first considerations must be the pay. How much will you make? How can you stretch it? Is it enough to take care of your family? If the compensation is not enough for you to take care of you and your family, you must carefully examine your plan and your call. Think it through; pray it through very carefully. God could still be calling you there, but if He is calling you then you can bet He has a plan to make sure you have your financial needs met—soon!

I have an essay on family financial planning that I will be willing to share with you if you make the effort to contact me. I can be found on the Web at Steve Richardson, CPA, Tuscaloosa, Alabama.

The finances of the ministry are important.

Obviously the finances of the ministry must be stable too. Here is another precept:

A ministry is a business.

It's true; a ministry is a business. Hopefully it is going about the business of doing God's work, but it is still a business. Finances matter.

If you start a ministry, you must have a clear understanding of where the money to sustain the ministry is going to come from. Is the cash flow coming from a large and diverse donor base or a few wealthy individuals? Is the plan to have self-funding events such as camps and rallies? Will you simply rely on raw talent as a writer or musician to make your living? Are your plans to finance your ministry realistic?

The answer to these and other questions will give you a clear indication of the type of organization you need. Hear this loud and clear:

Most ministries do not need a not-for-profit corporation!

Some of the most important and successful ministries in America are profit-making entities such as S-Corporations and LLCs. Somewhere, somehow America has the notion that making a profit in ministry is somehow wrong. That's actually worse than ridiculous; it is sinful, carnal thinking, clearly contrary to the Word of God.

If you start a ministry, you have the advantage of choosing wisely the type of organization. If you join a ministry, the organization structure is likely predetermined for you. In any type of organization accounting is important.

The accounting must be sharp, accurate, clear, and, to the appropriate users, transparent. Simple things like bookkeeping matter. This is not and cannot be an afterthought. Do not mix personal and business transactions in your ministry accounting. There must be a wall of separation between the two.

The simple fact is that most people called into ministry are not good bookkeepers. If you are not a good bookkeeper, if you think that bookkeeping takes time away from your ministry, then don't try to take care of your own books; you will simply make a wreck of it. Hire it out if you have to; but whatever it takes, have good accounting.

Do not get in trouble with the Tax Man.

Tax compliance in ministry is essential. The single most common tax error made by ministers and ministries is payroll tax compliance. Once again, hire it out. There are a number of relatively inexpensive payroll services available to help. Use them.

Plan your cash flow.

You must always know how much money you have, how much you

are going to get and when, and how much you need. It's called budgeting and forecasting.

Here is an interesting fact: the most successful ministries in America all operate on budgets. An even more interesting fact is this: when these same ministries were just getting started, they were small, unstable, and often unsure of where the necessary cash was going to come from, but they still had budgets.

I've heard people say, "My ministry is too small to have a budget." Nonsense! If you are too small to budget, you are too small to make it to the next level of ministry and the next level of financial security.

Rely on professionals to help you.

You are not the Lone Ranger; there are people out there who have the tools and the desire to help you succeed. Find a trustworthy CPA and a good lawyer. Jim Baker said, "Never trust your CPAs and your lawyer; they will crush your vision." Of course Jim said that just before he went to prison.

The point I am making is obvious: get a good CPA and lawyer and trust them.

CHAPTER 4

THE CALL TO GOD-CENTERED

Health

Do you remember when you were a little kid? I mean just a little hulkster who could run around all day playing as many games as could fit into the daylight hours? It seems you were only held hostage by the clock and bedtime. Had it not been for those two things you would have surely ruled the world by age eight. What an amazing time it was to wake up full of energy and seem to have a source somewhere that refused to run out. And then something happened. Life played a dirty little trick that has haunted you ever since: you grew up. After enduring a multiplicity of hormonal changes that produced foreign feelings that almost drove you mad—physical changes such that you go to sleep one night only to awake the next morning to find the Normandy invasion has taken place on your face and your jeans are now too short; and relational changes where the opposite sex is someone you would rather kiss than punch—one would think the worst was behind them. But those were just the middle and high school years. Now on to the college years, where the word *complicated* seems to be the understatement of the decade when attempting to describe this time period.

Here you face a new world of opportunities accompanied with a whole new set of health issues. At one point it seemed that no matter what you ate or how much of it you consumed, you didn't gain weight. But by the time your freshman year is over you know how many pizzas you have consumed just by looking in the mirror. And if you're not careful, by the time you graduate a steady diet of hamburgers, pizza, sodas, and Mexican fast food has had a significant impact on your health, which is probably more noticeable in your energy levels than in your weight. But looking back on your graduation day photos you tell yourself it was worth it because it allowed you to spend more time studying or working to pay for the opportunity to study. Truth be known, it may have afforded you more time to conquer whatever video game had positioned itself as your arch nemesis at the time.

And there you are, ready to conquer the world, so you get a job or some more education to get an even better job. Maybe you marry and have a few kids; either way you are now the prime candidate for marketing campaigns for gymnasium chains all over the country. You get brochures and see commercials and finally realize that it is high time you did something about your health . . . so you join a gym. Now your life is going to be changed forever and ever as you begin a regimented routine of getting up early or going after work or taking a lunch break to exercise. The only problem is that "forever" turns out to be a few weeks and before long you are paying for a membership that you don't use but won't cancel because then you would have to admit your health is not central priority.

It may seem hard or easy to believe, but this is the predicament that millions find themselves in every day. The question that you must answer is this: will you fall victim to the cultural status quo when it comes to your health? In actuality, the word *victim* shouldn't be used because we all make the decision on how we live. As human beings we have our time, mind, and energy. We will always be putting a positive or negative charge to each of those areas with whatever activities we are involved in. I believe it is essential to health to put a plus charge to how we use our time, mind, and energy. If we don't, then life becomes a vicious circle of negativity. This in no way glorifies God! We must capture the moments of life in worshipful service to Him, and that means having a spirit of intentionality when it comes to taking care of our bodies.

The Basics

Living healthy is both a science and an art. It is a science because there are some activities that we know will produce certain results. For example if we eat X then we know it will produce a certain Y effect. But living healthy is also an art because you must find a strategy that works for you. Dr. James Rippe writes in *High Performance Health* that successful individuals must first master the basics:

1. ***Physical activity:*** Find a form of physical activity that is convenient for you and work your way up to accomplishing thirty minutes of this activity on most, if not all, days.

2. ***Weight control:*** People who successfully lose weight invariably incorporate four strategies into their weight management plan: regular physical activity, sound nutrition and calorie control, a long-term mind-set, and the support of other people.

3. ***Improved nutrition:*** Key recommendations for developing nutritional practices are: Consume a variety of nutrient-dense foods and beverages among the basic food groups, balance the calories you consume with calories you burn, emphasize your consumption of certain food groups such as fruits and vegetables, choose fiber-rich foods often such as whole grains and cereals.

4. ***Improved hydration:*** Water is part of every biochemical reaction in our body and is essential for every aspect of life. Therefore increase your consumption of pure water by having it available throughout the routine of your every day and it will make an enormous difference in your energy level.

5. ***Improved sleep and rest:*** Sleep and rest are both important to the healing and restorative processes of the body, both emotional and physical. If you get more than six and less than nine hours of sleep and you are not sleepy during the day then your sleep patterns are probably fine. Make sure that in addition to sleep you have disciplined periods of rest, which are key in achieving balance, rehabilitation, and recuperation.

6. ***Creating a positive environment for change:*** This is a practical consideration that makes mastering the other basics possible. This includes changing your physical, social and emotional environments.

7. ***Mastering the mind-set:*** While there are many aspects of mastering the mind-set, perhaps the most important fundamental trait is the ability to live in the moment. Focus on today, rather than regretting the past or fearing the future. Master the concept of "seize the day."

"We" Are the Temple

These are just the basics, and I hope you will go on to explore more of what it means to have High Performance Health. But why is this of any importance anyway? While there are several Bible texts we could point to, none are more relevant than:

> You realize, don't you, that you are the temple of God, and God himself is present in you? No one will get by with vandalizing God's temple, you can be sure of that. God's temple is sacred—and you, remember, are the temple. 1 Corinthians 3:16-17 (The Message)

> What agreement has the temple of God with idols?
> For we are the temple of the living God; as God said,
> "I will make my dwelling among them and walk among them,
>> and I will be their God,
>> and they shall be my people.
> Therefore go out from their midst,
>> and be separate from them, says the Lord,
> and touch no unclean thing;
>> then I will welcome you,
> and I will be a father to you,
>> and you shall be sons and daughters to me,
> says the Lord Almighty."
> 2 Corinthians 6:16-18 (English Standard Version)

In both of these texts Paul refers to believers as a temple and that God lives inside that temple. This description carries with it a sacred responsibility: the fact that we are the temple of the living God literally means that our lives are a sanctuary, the holy place or the most holy place of God.[22] Both of these texts are written to the church at Corinth, and in both cases Paul is not saying that each person or congregation is a separate sanctuary but rather God's people are one spiritual temple or sanctuary, and wherever God's people are, there that sanctuary is found.[23] The reason this interpretation is so important is because it means my life and how I am a steward of that life is a reflection on the larger community of Christ-followers.

"I have all the time in the world . . ."

Before we go any further I must confess that I am not a health nut who thinks that eating non-organic food is the same as taking the mark of the beast. I like pizza and Coke, french fries with a milkshake, watching football while eating chicken wings, and fried stuff with cheese. If you were to visit my house on Christmas or Easter you would not find granola and tofu in my kids' stockings and baskets. (I do control how much sugar they eat, though, on those holidays. When they aren't looking I eat half of their candy!) The idea here is that I have not gone off the deep end like some sandal-wearing yuppie with a fanny pack full of tasty organic treats. (By the way, if you wear sandals or a fanny pack then God bless you.) But I have realized that what I consume today and how much I consume of it will have lasting consequences on my life. I heard someone say years ago, "I have become what I ate—a lot of fat."

My encouragement to you is to see the big picture now and take a balanced approach to life. We have all said things like, "I have all the time in the world" or "I will diet and exercise later." I would encourage you to look at life like a seven-day week and each day of the week being a ten-year slot. Since most people die in their seventies the analogy fits. Therefore if you are fifteen years old, you have lived one and a half days and have five and a half to go. If you are thirty years old, then you have lived three days and only have four to go. Think about that—if you are thirty then your life is almost half over. Do you think the way you treat your body the first two or three days will have an impact on the last four or five days? It pays to see the big picture.

There Is Everything Right in Getting Help

There seems to be a great hesitancy from many to get help with their health. Take weight loss for example. If we can't fix the problem on our own then we either turn to surgery (which many times is only a temporary fix) or give up altogether. In the U.S. a majority of adults are either overweight or obese and child obesity has doubled in the last twenty years. "If we could eliminate overweight and obesity in the U.S., we could eliminate over 80 percent of all diabetes, over half of lipid (cholesterol) abnormalities, and between 40 and 70 percent of all high blood pressure."[24] So where do you turn if you need additional help in controlling your weight? Well, thankfully, there are quite a few options since weight control is something very few can do on their own. One such option is Weight Watchers. According to Dr. Rippe, this is probably the best commercially available program using sound scientific principles to help people in the area of weight management. The key to Weight Watchers is the supportive environment offered to help you stay focused on your goal, and these support groups can be found in most metropolitan areas through WeightWatchers.com. You often hear people say, "There is nothing wrong with getting a little help." The only problem with this approach is that imbedded in that statement is the idea of weakness as it relates to community. A more accurate statement is that there is everything right in getting help!

A Chemical Caution

As I write this I feel a bit hypocritical because I have at times taken a sleeping pill. In fact nearly fifty million prescriptions are filled every year for sleeping pills, which is up by almost 50 percent from ten years ago. I have several reasons for my caution against sleeping pills. First, they can enhance depression. Many sleep aid prescriptions warn against using their product if you have struggled with or are taking any medication for depression. Secondly, not all sleeping pills are created equal. I have some good friends who have taken them and then gone on to do and say things they were not even aware of. Next, many sleep aids can be addicting, or cause dependency, which require a caution whenever one would try to stop using. And finally, like most medication, sleep aids are metabolized by your liver; and the more chemicals the liver has to process, the more negative effect they have on this organ.

There is one simple step that can many times prohibit a doctor's office from prescribing you sleep aids. Simply speak to your primary physician first and ask him or her if there are any other steps you should be taking before popping a pill at night when you want to go to sleep. Some steps might include not having a television in your bedroom or watching media on your laptop before going to bed, not eating after a certain hour, exercising, and the list goes on. The point is, make sleeping pills a last option instead of a first one.

Living healthy is both a science and an art, and your approach to it will have either a negative or positive effect on every other aspect in your life. While it may be only day two or three, remember the lifestyle you engage in now will determine the quality of life you have later. When people outside the Christian faith observe those inside, they should witness a people motivated to be good stewards of the lives they have been given, because together we are the sanctuary of the living God.

21 Rippe M.D., James M. (2007). High Performance Health. (Pages 35-52). Nashville: Thomas Nelson.
22 Robertson, A. (1997). Word Pictures in the New Testament (1 Co 3:16). Oak Harbor: Logos Research Systems.
23 Lenski, R.C.H. (Second Printing 2001). Commentary on the New Testament. (Page 147). U.S.A: Hendrickson Publishers, Inc.
24 Rippe, M.D., James M., High Performance Health, p. 39.

CHAPTER 5

THE CALL TO GOD-CENTERED

Friendship

I ran back to my hut to collect all my possessions: my food bowl, a pair of torn mittens "inherited" from a dead typhus patient, and a few scraps of paper covered with shorthand notes (on which, as I mentioned before, I had started to reconstruct the manuscript which I lost at Auschwitz). I made a quick last round of my patients, who were lying huddled on the rotten planks of wood on either side of the huts. I came to my only countryman, who was almost dying, and whose life it had been my ambition to save in spite of his condition. I had to keep my intention to escape to myself, but my comrade seemed to guess that something was wrong (perhaps I showed a little nervousness). In a tired voice he asked me, "You, too, are getting out?" I denied it, but I found it difficult to avoid his sad look. After my round I returned to him. Again a hopeless look greeted me and somehow I felt it to be an accusation. The unpleasant feeling that had gripped me as soon as I had told my friend I would escape with him became more intense. Suddenly I decided to take fate into my own hands for once. I ran out of the hut and told my friend that I could not go with him. As soon as I had told him with finality that I had made up my mind to stay with my patients, the unhappy feeling left me.

I did not know what the following days would bring, but I had gained an inward peace that I had never experienced before. I returned to the hut, sat down on the boards at my countryman's feet and tried to comfort him; then I chatted with others, trying to quiet them in their delirium.[25]

Between 1942 and 1945 psychiatrist Viktor Frankl labored in four different Nazi prison camps, including Auschwitz, while his parents, brother, and pregnant wife perished. In *Man's Search for Meaning* he shares his experiences and stories of many of his patients. There may not be another account written that paints a more vivid picture of the Nazi network of concentration and extermination camps. The above excerpt takes place toward the end of Frankl's imprisonment when he had the opportunity to escape. Yet the idea of leaving a sick and dying comrade behind combined with the stinging words "You, too, are getting out?" seems to have caused him to discover something greater than escape . . . peace. In the midst of the most hellish situation imaginable there existed a relationship bound together by a common hope.

In the end accountability has at its binding agent that which existed between Dr. Frankl and his countryman patient so many years ago: *hope*. When we discuss the issue of accountability and one's inner circle, we must see ourselves in two very distinct lights: being both doctors and patients. An inner circle of people following Jesus and walking beside each other must recognize the need to care for each other's souls (the role of doctor) while also allowing their soul to be cared for (the role of patient). In other words if we understand accountability we are both doctors and patients.

What Is Accountability?

I don't know if it is arrogance or naiveté that keeps people from being transparently honest with others about their struggles, temptations, and life in general . . . maybe it is both. As we discovered in the chapter on marriage God did not create us to live life on our own, but rather He created us as relational beings. Now I realize that many of us reading this would dismiss such a statement because we prefer to be alone. Though your personality may tend to be more anti-social, it is not an excuse to retreat from having the right kind of relationships in your life. The ability to walk with others as we walk with Christ is a crucial part of our spiritual formation.

So what is meant by the word *accountability*? Though the word never appears in Scripture, the concept is oftentimes discussed within the context of friendship. Thus we will define it as follows: Accountability is an inner circle of friends who care for each other's souls as if they were their own for the purpose of helping each other be rooted and built up in Jesus and established in the faith. As with every group of people, a certain culture exists. The remainder of this chapter will focus on the cultural DNA that should exist in your inner circle. Remember that within this context, for accountability to exist, we must be willing to fulfill the role of both doctor and patient administering and receiving the following qualities.

Love

The soul of Jonathan was knit to the soul of David, and Jonathan loved him as his own soul. . . . Then Jonathan made a covenant with David, because he loved him as his own soul. 1 Samuel 18:1, 3

One of the more well-known and compelling stories of friendship in the Bible is that of Jonathan and David. David's friendship with Jonathan, Saul's oldest son, began when he killed Goliath and endured throughout Saul's persecution of David. What we know of their friendship is that Jonathan loved David as if he were his own soul. This is evidenced in that Jonathan made a covenant or a sacred agreement to be sworn brothers with David for life. The covenant was made official in a ceremony in which Jonathan gave his robe and even his armor to David. Do you catch what is happening here? Jonathan was the prince, heir to the throne, while David, up until just recently, had been nothing more than a shepherd boy. To receive any part of the dress, which had been *worn* by royalty, or his eldest son and heir, was considered in that culture to be the *highest* honor that can be conferred on a subject.[26] Jonathan was expressing that he loved David more than military strength, political power, and even his own life.

Guys reading this may be a little uncomfortable with where the application of this text might lead. I know in my own life it is a very difficult thing to tell another guy that I love him. I am not the type of friend who will end every phone call with "love you, man." I have friends like that and I am not saying they are wrong. In fact sometimes I say it back just so it's not awkward . . . yet saying it still feels that way. And yet there is a select *few* men in my life, my inner circle, whom I have told I love. And why? Because hopefully, I value their life as much as my own. C. S. Lewis said it this way: "Friendship is something that raised us almost above humanity. This love, free from instinct, free from all duties but those which love has freely assumed, almost wholly free from jealousy, and free without qualification from the need to be needed, is eminently spiritual. It is the sort of love one can imagine between angels."[27]

Oneness

Two are better than one, because they have a good reward for their toil. For if they fall, one will lift up his fellow. But woe to him who is alone when he falls and has not another to lift him up! Again, if two lie together, they keep warm, but how can one keep warm alone? And though a man might prevail against one who is alone, two will withstand him—a three-fold cord is not quickly broken. Ecclesiastes 4:9-12

Now this is a different kind of oneness than discussed in the marriage chapter. The two lying next to each other refer to those who travel together across deserts and would need to lie next to each other to stay warm during the cold nights. But it is verse twelve that demonstrates oneness in friendship by using the picture of three strands or individuals that have been woven together to create one cord or friendship for the purposes of being able to stand against evil. The picture that is painted in these verses is simplistic: if one falls the other picks him up (v. 10); if one is cold then together they can stay warm (v. 11); if one is attacked the other will have his back (v. 12); two is better than one and three is better than two (v. 12) because together they form *one* friendship. Friendship will revolve around an "If you go . . . we go" type attitude.

Are you the type of person who refuses to let your friends fall, feel cold, and even get beat down by all the demands of life? I am constantly amazed at the amount of people who attend church or stand in a crowded room of Christians and yet feel completely alone. One of my favorite sessions to teach at our Student Leadership University conferences takes place at SeaWorld and evaluates the cultural characteristics of the dolphins. Dolphins travel in family groups called pods and, like in Ecclesiastes 4:9-12, will protect other members of the pod at all costs. A friend of mine was visiting a navy base in Hawaii and observed the habitat that had been built there for dolphins. One dolphin in particular had been badly hurt and was being kept under constant supervision. A fishing boat had been dragging its nets and unfortunately the dolphin had gotten tangled inside, tearing its dorsal fin almost completely off in the process. Realizing it had little chance to live, the fisherman put the wounded, bleeding dolphin back in the water thrashing and making the most distressful noises. Of course this attracted two things: its pod and also many sharks. Knowing the navy had an interest in dolphins the fisherman called the base to let them know what had happened. In response the navy sent a rescue boat with divers to the coordinates that had been provided. Upon arrival, though, they observed the strangest sight they had ever seen: there were dead sharks everywhere in the water. The injured dolphin's cry had been heard by the pod and they responded by surrounding it and fighting any shark that dared to close in for attack. As a matter of fact, the divers had to tranquilize some of the male dolphins before they could enter the water because of how aggressive and protective they were.

Every time I tell that story I am reminded of the type of inner circle or community I want to be a part of. I believe that if anyone should have your back it should be your inner circle of friends. An essential component of friendship is that we don't leave each other behind. My fate and the fate of my friends should be one in the same. Can you look your friends in the eye and say, "If you go . . . we go"?

Loyalty

A man of many companions may come to ruin, but there is a friend who sticks closer than a brother. Proverbs 18:24

It is better to have one true friend than many casual acquaintances. It seems that this verse also indicates that true friendship may be thicker than blood. Matthew Henry states it this way:

In our troubles we expect comfort and relief from our relations, but sometimes *there is a friend*, that is nothing akin to us, the bonds of whose esteem and love prove stronger than those of nature, and, when it comes to the trial, will do more for us than a brother will. Christ is a friend to all believers that *sticks closer than a brother*; to him therefore let them show themselves friendly.[28]

There is a comfort in knowing someone is loyal and trustworthy. It is a trait that, potentially above all others, inspires and motivates. The story is told about two young men in the First World War who had been friends for their entire lifetimes. Being neighbors, they had played together, gone to school together, engaged in the same athletic programs, and finally enlisted in the army together. Fate determined they would eventually be in the same area of battle together.

After a particularly bitter battle one day, it was found that one of the boys was missing somewhere out in what is known as "No-Man's Land." The other boy, safe and unhurt, went to the commanding officer and requested permission to go out and look for his friend. He was told it was of no use for no one was alive out there after the withering fire of so many hours. After great insistence, he was finally given permission to go.

Some time later he returned with the limp dead body of his friend over his shoulder. The commander said, "Didn't I tell you it was no use to go?" to which the boy replied with radiance in his eyes, "But it was not; I got there in time to hear him whisper, 'I knew you'd come.'"[29]

Counsel

Oil and perfume make the heart glad, and the sweetness of a friend comes from his earnest counsel. Proverbs 27:9

When your friends think of you, there will always be a first thought, usually attached to a pattern of behavior. That first thought can be either positive or negative, depending upon the memories associated with the individual. The first thought then creates an expectation from the ensuing encounter. What do your friends expect when they see you coming? The writer of Proverbs uses an interesting analogy when describing what can be expected from a true friend. He says that *oil and perfume make the heart glad*, which speaks to how smell can invoke a certain emotion. Maybe that emotion arises because oil and perfume were reserved for honored guests or possibly because the smell was so pleasant that it caused one to feel a certain way. Either way the result is the same: a glad heart. The Message words it well: "Just as lotions and fragrance give sensual delight, a sweet friendship refreshes the soul."

Is the counsel that you give, the words you speak to your friends, refreshing their souls? They should receive that counsel and experience the same emotion that accompanies the smell of perfume and oil—a heart that is glad. We must be exhaustively intentional with the words we use when advising our friends. This can only be accomplished when our words are filtered through the truth of God's Word. Wise counsel is words that have weight because they are loaded down with God's truth.

Kindness

He who withholds kindness from a friend forsakes the fear of the Almighty. Job 6:14

Job is in the midst of discussing the manner in which his "friends" are treating him. He describes their kindness toward him as overflowing when everything is going well but empty when things are not. He goes on to describe them like a dry riverbed that once flowed with water but dries up in the heat of the summer. Their loyalty and kindness has dried up and they have treated him deceitfully. Here we are shown the importance of kindness as essential to friendship in that it wasn't demonstrated. Obviously the concept of kindness here is woven into the fabric of loyalty. In fact, kindness is the attitude demonstrated within loyalty. Think of loyalty as the outer bone while kindness and love are the marrow that run deep inside it. James takes a similar perspective on kindness when he writes: "For if you refuse to act kindly, you can hardly expect to be treated kindly. Kind mercy wins over harsh judgment every time" (James 2:13).

Honesty

Faithful are the wounds of a friend. Proverbs 27:6

The word *friend* in this passage could also be translated *one who loves*, and the wounds he inflicts are a result of rebuke and correction. True friendship, and therefore accountability, must love in such a courageous manner that one is willing to correct, even if it causes pain, for the purpose of keeping one's eyes fixed on Jesus. We do not edify by our silence when a friend needs to be rebuked or corrected. That word *rebuke* carries with it a harsh connotation at times, but when this word is understood it could be the most loving action demonstrated. To rebuke someone simply means to show the error of their ways by calling them back to a godly approach so that they will know their way will not work. This type of honesty is not easy, but it is essential. Remember that to take part in accountability means that we are both doctors and patients. If a doctor knows of a patient who has a disease for which there is a cure and does nothing about it, he is at best a deceitful liar and at worst the devil himself. To observe sin in another friend's life and do nothing about it, I would argue, is the equivalent to being that kind of doctor.

Sacrifice

Greater love has no man than this, than to lay down one's life for his friends. John 15:13

Jesus commands us to love one another in a sacrificial manner. In fact one of the ways we know we are abiding in His love is when we are willing to put our lives on the line for our friends. I find it quite interesting that Jesus was soon to lay down His life for each and every one of His friends, not to mention the entire world. But remember friendship is a two-way street . . . would the disciples in turn lay down their lives for Jesus if the opportunity arrived? According to tradition, all of the disciples died a martyr's death:

- Matthew suffered martyrdom by being slain with a sword at a distant city of Ethiopia.

- Mark expired at Alexandria, after being cruelly dragged through the streets of that city.
- Luke was hanged upon an olive tree in the classic land of Greece.
- John was put in a caldron of boiling oil, but escaped death in a miraculous manner, and was afterward banished to the island of Patmos.
- Peter was crucified at Rome with his head downward.
- James the Greater was beheaded at Jerusalem; James the Less was thrown from a lofty pinnacle of the temple and then beaten to death with a fuller's club.
- Bartholomew was flayed alive.
- Andrew was bound to a cross, whence he preached to his persecutors until he died.
- Thomas was run through the body with a lance at Coromandel in the East Indies.
- Jude was shot to death with arrows.
- Matthias was first stoned and then beheaded.
- Barnabas of the Gentiles was stoned to death at Salonica.
- Paul, after various tortures and persecutions, was at length beheaded at Rome by Emperor Nero.[30]

While there are larger amounts of supporting evidence for some of the disciples' deaths over others, both biblical and extra biblical, the idea remains true. They were friends of Jesus because they were willing to lay down their lives for His name's sake. Oftentimes the disciples' deaths are used, as well they should be, to support the idea that Jesus was in fact who He said He was. But let us not overlook the intimate friendship that existed between Christ and His disciples. He sacrificed His life and they sacrificed their lives because they knew that *this is the very best way to love. Put your life on the line for your friends.*

Obedience

You are my friends if you do whatever I command you. John 15:14

Upon the monumental statement dealing with sacrificial love, Jesus then delivers another targeted insight on friendship: that essential to friendship is obedience to the words of Jesus. The Greek word for *friendship* here means "a friend at court." It describes that "inner circle" around a king or emperor. (In John 3:29, it refers to the "best man" at a wedding.) The "friends of the king" would be close to him and know his secrets, but they would also be subject to him and have to obey his commands.[31]

So what does this have to do with accountability? Everything. You see, your inner circle is not a group of friends who sit around and look at each other asking tough questions. Your inner circle surrounds King Jesus and wants whatever He wants and does whatever He does. This is where most inner circles break down; they are egocentric rather than Christ-centric. They start with man's needs and thoughts instead of God's desires and thoughts. Part of friendship responsibility is ensuring that the other members of your inner circle are listening to the right voice and looking to the right person—Jesus.

Paul demonstrated this idea when writing possibly his most important letter: Romans. In the opening verses he writes: "Through Him we have received grace and apostleship for *obedience to the faith*" (Rom. 1:5, emphasis added). Then again in his closing statements he uses the same phrase from the opening of the book: "Now to Him who is able to establish you according to my gospel and the preaching of Jesus Christ . . . but now is made manifest, and by the prophetic Scriptures made known to all nations, according to the commandment of the ever-lasting God, for *obedience to the faith*" (Rom. 16:25-26, emphasis added). Now, call me naïve, but I believe the words of Scripture are inspired by the Holy Spirit. In fact, I go so far as to believe that the order of the thoughts of the writers of Scripture are also inspired and therefore it is not happpenstance that Paul uses this same phrase both in the beginning and final words of the most important letter he would ever write. Could his message to us be that by the power of God we can have an *obedience to the faith* beginning and an *obedience to the faith* finish?

Communication

The Lord spoke to Moses face to face, as a man speaks to his friend.
Exodus 33:11

The phrase *face to face* refers to a oneness and friendship within which clear communication takes place. Moses' meetings with God provide for us a basic insight into friendship: communication. Now the Bible doesn't tell us, but I seriously doubt that Moses spent the majority of his time with God talking. I mean, after all, a meeting with God is a pretty good time to basically shut the ol' yapper and listen. In fact, it is a good rule of thumb to listen twice as much as you talk. Most people want to speak or maybe they just want to be heard; either way it elevates their ego. Filling silence with stories or conjecture is not communication. In the context of friendship communication is conversation in which each individual is heard and the one not talking is an interested listener. For our purposes these conversations at times need to be plain talk, while other times they can take place in a more relaxed atmosphere. But make no mistake, the ability to care for one another's soul will require face-to-face segments of time in atmospheres that allow open and clear communication to take place.

Self-control

Make no friendship with a man given to anger, nor go with a wrathful man, lest you learn his ways and entangle yourself in a snare.
Proverbs 22:24-25

This text gives us a strong warning against being friends with someone who has a hot temper they cannot control. The writer of Proverbs speaks of a man given to anger. This is an individual who is not in control over his own moods but rather his moods master him. Because these types of people have no control over their temperament and words, they attack and destroy others as they go. The last part of the text warns that whoever is friends with this person may become entangled and also be mastered by their moods. I have discovered in my own journey that those who let their emotions rule them are contagious individuals. If good or bad attitude is in fact contagious, then we are to place ourselves around those who have their emotions in check.

Paul speaks of self-control when he writes, "God gave us a spirit not of fear but of power and love and self-control" (2 Tim. 1:7) The word *spirit* means one's demeanor or attitude, thus part of that which characterizes the follower of God should be the ability to control oneself. It is a discipline to not be the type of person who is held hostage by feelings or circumstances. The consequences for being ruled by your emotions are numerous, but in the context of friendship they can be almost unforgivable. Let me show you what I mean. You will always have the inside information on your inner circle. It is expected that what is said or shared stays in the inner circle. If one does not control their emotions, then it is an impossibility to control one's words, which will inevitably lead to a divulgence of confidence and will, therefore, tear down instead of build up friendships.

Character

Iron sharpens iron; so a man sharpens the countenance of his friend.
Proverbs 27:17

When a piece of iron is rubbed against another piece of iron, it shapes and sharpens it. Your friends should make you better and you should make them better. The writer of Proverbs makes the above statement when discussing money and mutual help. Bible commentator John Phillips describes how this verse deals with character:

Underlying all true prosperity is integrity of character and scrupulous honesty in dealings with other people. Our friends and partners are important. We learn from one another; we take character and color from one another. Our character eventually shows in our faces.[32]

There are two pillars to being a person of influence: skill and character. While skill can be learned and acquired, character can only come from knowing Christ and being filled with the Holy Spirit. The Bible is the only book ever written that demonstrates for us how God-like character is to be embodied in our own lives. To ensure that you become the person you were purposed to be in the mind of God, you must have friends around you who are close to the heart of God. And that can only happen when we are allowing the Bible to impact our lives in the manner the writer of Hebrews discusses: "For the word of God is living and active, sharper than any two-edged sword, piercing to the division of soul and of spirit, of joints and of marrow, and discerning the thoughts and intentions of the heart" (Heb. 4:12).

Doctors and patients . . . caregivers and caretakers of each other's souls so that we may be rooted and built up in the faith. While accountability is important, and at times overrated, friendship is even more important. And as we have seen, when true friendship occurs so does accountability. Build friendships in which you minister and are ministered to with the hope of seeing Jesus one day and may we never look at each other and utter those haunting words that Viktor Frankl heard in a concentration camp so many years ago: "You, too, are getting out?" Instead let us make the decision he made: never leave a countryman behind.

25 Frankl, Viktor E. (2006). Man's Search for Meaning. (Pages 58-59). Boston: Beacon Press.
26 Jamieson, R., Fausset, A. R., Fausset, A. R., Brown, D., & Brown, D. (1997). A commentary, critical and explanatory, on the Old and New Testaments (1 Sam 18:4). Oak Harbor, WA: Logos Research Systems, Inc.
27 Lewis, C. S. (1990). The Quotable Lewis. (Page 237). Wheaton: Tyndale House Publishers.
28 Henry, M. (1996, c1991). Matthew Henry's Commentary on the Whole Bible: Complete and unabridged in one volume (Pr 18:24). Peabody: Hendrickson.
29 Tan, P. L. (1996, c1979). Encyclopedia of 7700 Illustrations: A treasury of illustrations, anecdotes, facts and quotations for pastors, teachers and Christian workers. Garland TX: Bible Communications.
30 Tan, P. L. (1996, c1979). Encyclopedia of 7700 Illustrations: A treasury of illustrations, anecdotes, facts and quotations for pastors, teachers and Christian workers. Garland, TX: Bible Communications.
31 Wiersbe, W. W. (1996, c1989). The Bible exposition commentary (Jn 15:12). Wheaton, IL.: Victor Books.
32 Phillips, John. (1996). Exploring Proverbs Vol. 1. (Page 415). Grand Rapids: Kregel Publications.

CHAPTER 6

THE CALL TO GOD-CENTERED

Teachability

As we begin this chapter I hope you will indulge me as I share a poem I wrote sitting in some airport somewhere as my flight was delayed late into the night. My mind was tired and therefore I wasn't up for reading. I had been speaking all day and so I didn't feel like talking to anyone on my phone. Having spent a lot of time in airports, naturally I have experienced quite a few delays and canceled flights. Most of the time airports are busy with people coming and going and acting all kinds of crazy over delays and cancellations. I have watched as people cried and begged, cursed, and slammed their fists on the ticket counter, and other times simply threaten to not move until a resolution to their liking had been found. But despite all the emotions, I have never witnessed a delayed or canceled flight suddenly be able to leave on time as a result of tears, curse words, or standoffs. And yet this particular night the airport was virtually empty, which is a very unusual sight, even for someone like me who's on the road almost every week. As I reflected upon how God is allowing me to live out the calling He placed on my life, I jotted down the following words:

Empty airports and late nights
Cheap meals and expensive flights
Long days and little respect
Careful choices and a few regrets
Late night meals and lonely hotel rooms
The smiles are real but so is the gloom
Tires wearing thin and so is my soul
No one cares but no one knows
Front of the line, back of the bus
This, my friends, is the story of us
A league of oddballs with a burden to bear
Gaining weight and losing hair
Standing each night with a Bible in hand
The ancient message and a want-to-be band
Pleading, hoping, beckoning for some
That sins would be realized and heaven would come
Jesus moves in and sets up shop
Changing everything and saving the lost
Knees bent and a head bowed
Our Father in heaven *cover me now*

My reason for sharing this is that as I wrote these words I realized that while life was a daring adventure it was also a lot of hard work. That for every mountaintop moment there were days, weeks, months, and even years spent in the valley. For example:

- Noah's ark that would hold two *of every living thing of all flesh* probably didn't get built overnight.
- Moses spent forty years on the backside of nowhere herding sheep before he would utter the words "Let my people go."
- Jeremiah preached one single message his entire life—*repent*—only to see no fruit (which is partly why he wrote Lamentations).
- Simeon held on to a promise that he would see *the Lord's Christ* until the fourth quarter of his life when a young couple came walking into the temple.
- Paul would travel weeks and sometimes longer just to preach in a city.

I hope that doesn't depress you but rather is, in some small way, helpful in understanding the sobering reality of what it means to be a living sacrifice. *A living sacrifice is one who captures the moments of life as if the present moment being experienced were the last.* To be a capturer of the moments of life takes, as Winston Churchill has already put it, "blood, toil, tears and sweat"[33]; after all, running a race is hard.

I am still somewhat early in my ministry years but have been greatly blessed to have a lot of wisdom spoken into my life. What I wish to share in this chapter is the essential wisdom that is helping me to seek Jesus with all of my existence as I run this race. I will do my best to give credit to those who shared with me the following wisdom, realizing that some of the following realities my mind and heart awakened to gradually or through experience or reading. Thus where I cannot site the person I ask for grace.

1. Know God; don't settle for knowing about God.
2. If God be for me, who could be against me?
3. In the end, it's all about relationships. *(Dr. Jay Strack)*
4. There is always a way.
5. An invaluable question: Can you help me?
6. Under promise . . . over deliver.
7. Never go one place and do just one thing.
8. Have a clear understanding on the front end so there isn't a mis-understanding on the back end.
9. Love God and do as you will. *(St. Augustine)*
10. Preparation is easier than course correction.
11. Character precedes vision.
12. Feel your muscle, not your pulse. *(Dr. Jay Strack)*
13. Don't allow yesterday's crisis to become tomorrow's cross.
14. Do everything humanly possible you can do and trust God to do what only He can do.
15. One cannot move forward while looking backward.
16. The questions that matter in life are remarkably few, and they are all answered by the words—"Come to me." Matt. 11:28. (Oswald Chambers in *My Utmost for His Highest*, June 11)
17. Tell on your sins or your sins will one day tell on you. *(Dr. Johnny Hunt)*
18. Look at the calendar, not the clock. *(Dr. Jay Strack)*
19. Every day read, every day file. *(Dr. John Maxwell)*
20. Shut your yapper (I think that is Greek for mouth) and develop the art of listening.
21. Communicate truth that is difficult for people to hear as if it pains you. *(Doug Fields)*
22. There are only two days in life that matter . . . this day and that day. *(Martin Luther)*
23. Right belief and right action is not a substitute for love (*Observation after reading on the Church of Ephesus in Revelation 2*)

24. Let your view of God determine everything about you. *(Dr. Bill Bright)*
25. Obedience to God is liberating. *(Dr. Bill Bright)*
26. Never pretend something hasn't happened . . . with yourself or with God.
27. Make sure your enemies could tell your story. *(Sir Michael Hobbs)*
28. Make sure your pain can lead others to God. *(Sir Michael Hobbs)*
29. You can fail and still move closer to Jesus.
30. Laugh at yourself.
31. Be transparently ordinary.
32. Journal the journey.
33. The community is not always right and sometimes you must stand alone.
34. The need to have position and status are for the insecure.
35. If you want to see the power of God, pray, pray, and then pray some more.
36. Have a vision that will last longer than your life.
37. Vision attracts reality. *(Dr. Jay Strack)*
38. The difference between success and failure is energy. *(Vince Lombardi)*
39. Moral courage is unseen and you don't get medals for it. *(Sir Michael Hobbs)*
40. Make a fool of yourself every day. *(Sir Michael Hobbs)*
41. Live as if the blood of Jesus matters most.
42. Roll until the wheels fall off.
43. I never said it would be easy, I only said it would be worth it. *(Vince Lombardi)*

33 Lukacs, John. (2008). Blood, Toil, Tears and Sweat. New York: Basic Books.

CHAPTER 7

THE CALL TO GOD-CENTERED

Communication

By David Edwards

"How hard could it be? To be a speaker that is. I mean, fly from place to place, stand on a stage in front of a lot of people, and speak for a half hour. What a life!"

This is what I heard a guy in his twenties say to me standing backstage while I was getting ready to speak. He continued. "That's what I want to do, but I only want to speak in big rooms. I've got a powerful testimony that needs to be heard by lots of folks." With that he followed, "Hey, how do I get a schedule like yours? Is there a list I can put my name on that will make me a famous speaker and get me bookings?" To which I replied, "Let me know when you find it. We'll both put our names on it!"

I realized that this guy was speaking from inexperience and a lack of knowledge of what is really required to do ministry well. Without some direction, that attitude can keep him from great opportunities.

It is true that what you don't know can hurt you in ministry.

Whether traveling or speaking, or doing ministry of any kind, one thing is sure: it takes work. After fifteen years of traveling and speaking to more than five hundred thousand people a year, I still haven't found that list. But through my own observation and personal field-testing, I have discovered the list that all of us need to apply to our lives.

1. *The smaller the room, the bigger the stakes.*

Most people assume that you should be more nervous the larger the room is; however, the stakes are much higher the smaller the room gets. Typically, the fewer the people there are in a room, the weightier the decisions. When you are speaking in a smaller room, everything that happens is amplified. Every gesture and nuance about you is seen. This is why you have to be aware of everything you are doing in these situations.

It is important to consider the impact of your message and to understand the importance of managing every aspect of your presentation style. It is a proven fact that 55 percent of your impact comes from what your body is doing while you are speaking. Knowing this will encourage you to focus on how you can best express commitment to, and enthusiasm for, what you are saying through your facial expressions, posture, and gestures.

What you don't know can hurt you, as you may be projecting an image that is counter to what you feel or what you want to present.

Consider these eight things:
- *Eye contact.*
  Even if you find it uncomfortable to look others in the eye, train yourself to do it. Be careful to not stare, but looking into the eyes of others conveys self-confidence and shows that you're listening and engaged in the conversation.
- *The handshake.*
  Keep your handshake firm, but not aggressive. If your handshake is too limp, you'll come across as insecure and passive.
- *Hold your head up.*
  Nod your head frequently to signify agreement, and vary your facial expressions in response to what is being said. Tilting your head sideways signifies interest, while lowering your head generally means you're suspicious of what you're hearing. If you want to convey a neutral attitude, keep your head centered.
- *Mirroring.*
  If it's a one-on-one meeting, mirror your posture with the other person. Gently mirroring the pose, tone, and facial expressions of the other person will put him or her at ease. Keep it subtle. Don't change your pose every time the other person does so, and don't mirror someone who appears defensive. Conversely, when you no-

tice someone mirroring your posture and gestures, it's a good idea to move toward the goal of your talk or conversation.

- *Be still.*

  If your eyes wander, your foot swings, or your fingers drum, you'll give the impression that you are not interested in the conversation. Fidget, but don't be rigid. Take a few notes, and leave your laptop at home because you won't influence anybody by staring at the screen. Use gestures, but minimally.

- *Speak up.*

  Make sure you communicate your words well and pronounce them correctly. Be careful to not speak too quickly. If it feels slow to you, it feels normal to the listener.

- *Watch your posture.*

  Don't slump. It is not a sign of being cool. Good posture is a sign of confidence.

- *Keep your body language open.*

  Crossed legs are fine, but folded arms or hands in your pockets convey protectiveness. Keep your hands still and casual at your sides, in your lap, or on a table. Use open gestures to others often and lean forward to show your interest. Be careful about appearing too casual. Leaning back in your chair with your hands clasped behind your head may even be taken as an arrogant stance.

2. *Love your listeners.*

Sometimes the most well-crafted presentations fall flat because the audience perceives an arrogant attitude, insincere motives, or a judgmental spirit. No matter who Jesus was talking to, the audience always knew one thing: that He loved them. Because of His love it didn't matter how deep the message; the truth always changed them.

You cannot hide what you really think about your audience. It will show up in your body language and tone of voice. Your love or lack of love will show through. If your day has been tough and you are emotionally drained, don't take it out on your audience. When I have had a rugged day and have to speak that night, I have to check myself and ask if I have enough love for the room. Before you give any kind of presentation, the last thing you need to ask yourself is: am I doing this because I love the people God has put in front of me?

Whether in a boardroom or one on one, focus on the other person's needs first. As you begin the discussion, ask what the other person wants and needs before you state your own goals. By demonstrating that, you don't make it all about you or just getting what you want. Listen to what they say; ask questions about their needs and goals; show respect.

3. *You will be heard before you speak.*

When you walk into a room people make assumptions about what kind of person you are based on how you are dressed. When someone is dressed well the knowledge and feeling of it has a positive effect. It gives them more confidence, increases credibility with their message, and heightens their self-respect. Many have said that when they had the look of success they found it easier to think success and to achieve success. This is the effect clothes have on the wearers themselves.

What effect do they have on an audience? I have noticed time and again that if a speaker looks sloppy and has made little effort to be properly dressed, an audience has little respect for that person. They are very likely to assume that his or her preparation and presentation is just as sloppy as their unkempt hair and wrinkled clothes.

There is a paradigm shift that takes place when you walk into a room with people outside of your ministry. As a youth worker you have to move into a professional zone and dress one level above the other people in the room. For instance, if everyone else is wearing nice shirts, you need to wear a nice shirt and a coat, taking it up one level. Dressing like a kid in an adult setting will not help your influence. Make every effort to present yourself like an expert in your field.

Here are some things to keep in mind: Wear light colors for day events. Wear dark colors for evening events. If you reverse the two, you look like a vampire at a Martha Stewart event. Flip flops are for beach ministry only. Speaking without shoes does not make your talk more spiritual. Unless you're a Samoan, lose the Puka Beads. Tank tops: if you are built like a tank, don't wear the top. No ironic T-shirts and when in doubt, tuck your shirt in. Remember, you never want your clothes to speak louder than your content.

4. *Read the room, not your presentation.*

As the speaker you have to have a sense of what is going on in every part of the room. When you know what to look for, it will guide you to know what approach to take for your presentation.

- Is what you're going to say supportive to the theme? Just because your face is on the poster doesn't mean it's about you. Every conference has a theme, and as a speaker you want to integrate that theme into your talk. It conveys that you care about the event.
- Is the size of your Bible appropriate for the situation? If you are speaking at a large conference, don't use a tiny pocket Bible. It makes it look like a caricature.
- Does your audience have their own Bibles? If you are the only one in the room with a Bible, then you'll have to simplify your talk so that the audience can stay with you.

- How are the chairs set out? What is the distance from the front of the stage to the first row? Seeing this will help you determine what you are going to do during the invitation. What's the furthest chair from the stage (the back corners)? This will determine the volume that you will speak at because you have to speak to the back row.
- What is the temperature of the room? If the room is hot, you won't have long to speak.
- How is the room lit? Typically, when the lights are on in the entire room, the crowd will be more distracted. The stage should be the brightest thing in the room. The lights should keep their same setting through the entire program. For instance, some places turn all the lights on when it's time for the message. This subconsciously communicates that the event is over.
- What is happening before you speak? The more stuff that is going on before you (music, video, drama, testimonies, games, interpretive dance, Fear Factor competitions, emcees), the more you have to do to win the room back. If it is at all possible, you want to follow music. This helps set your talk apart from everything else.
- If possible, don't use videos. It takes away from the intensity of your message. It disengages your listener from you by placing their attention on the screen. As a speaker, you should be able to hold the attention of a crowd by holding a Bible and a microphone.
- What is the posture of the kids? Are they standing up? Looking forward? Engaged? Or are they leaning on the chairs? Slumped over? Are there sections of kids sitting down, slumped over in that brooding jock pose? How are they responding to what is happening on stage? All of these things are indicators of what direction you need to go as a speaker. Leaning forward with their hands in their pocket can be a sign that they have never really experienced worship before. Slumped over can be a sign of apathy. This requires some spiritual warfare on your part to deal with this. Likewise, if they are singing, clapping, or laughing, it will be easier to guide a room like this.
- Where are you in the room? It's good to locate yourself on the front row, far side, so that you can glance over your shoulder to get a read on the room until it is time for you to speak. Even in a conference room, never sit at the head of the table or in the middle unless you are offered those seats.
- Where are you going to speak from? It is good to take an inventory of the platform before you get up to speak. Check for cables, clutter, music stands, etc. For you to communicate clearly, you need

an uncluttered place to stand. Studies have shown that the stage to the left of the audience is the strongest place to stand. It is always good to know and make friends with the tech guys. You want them to be your friends.

5. There is a difference between just saying something and having something to say.

Anybody can download talks from the new, popular speaker of the moment and get up and deliver it with precision. That's being a mimic. It is just being an echo of what has been said before. Lifeless presentations use the same predictable phrases, outline the obvious, and use words that everyone has heard hundreds of times before to the point that people in the audience start to finish your thought before you do. As a presenter, it takes real work to have content and to speak with authority. Here is a list of suggestions to help your presentations be more engaging:

- *Use relevant introductions.*
  The goal of the introduction is to get people to want to listen to you. Use questions to create interest; use real-life situations to create tensions; use stories to connect with the audience emotionally.
- *Use Scripture with integrity.*
  Learn the rules of interpreting Scripture and use them well. Using Scripture to highlight your stories will hinder your effectiveness. However, using stories to highlight the meaning of a passage produces power.
- *Know your takeaway.*
  After hearing you speak, what is your audience going to walk out with? Will it be a principle about a subject? A strategy about how to handle a situation? Takeaway means that you have made your presentation both understandable and doable.
- *Speak out of your heart and not off the page.*
- *Don't read your talk.*
  Spend time internalizing the talk so that you don't just know it; you feel it. The effectiveness of your talk is in direct proportion to how much of it has been absorbed into your heart. It is important to remember that we don't just have a message; we are the message.
- *Don't forget to smile.*
  Being a powerful communicator doesn't mean you have to be somber. Smiling lets people know that you are glad to be there.
- *As you speak, let your impulses drive your gestures.*
  Don't be mechanical or repetitive.

- *Make sure you pause after important words or statements so that the thought hangs in the air.*
  You will create an impact by varying your volume. Try moving from loud to soft.
- *Close well.*
  Don't just drift out of your talk with a random statement or prayer. Summarize what you have said, then follow with a call to action. Tell people what you want them to do with what you've said.

6.   Less is best.

In communicating your message or vision to your leaders, often it comes across as too complex or even cluttered. We think that adding more to our presentations will make them more successful, when in reality the clutter leads to confusion. If it is unclear, it is unsuccessful.

We have to be able to simplify our message. There are some questions we have to ask about anything we are doing or any presentation we are to give:

1.   What is the one thing I want to accomplish?
2.   At the end of the day, what is the one thing that must be done?
3.   What do I want people to know?
4.   Why do I want them to know it?
5.   What do I want them to do with it?

The first step is to write out your answers fully, and then reduce them so that they can be articulated on a square paper napkin. If you can fit your strategy or your message on a napkin, you will find that it is understandable, doable, and reproducible.

7.   Stick your landing.

Just as it is important for a gymnast to land squarely on her feet after ending her routine, it's the same with communicating. You have to be able to land your message into the lives of your listeners. Not all listeners process what you are saying the same way. Knowing your audience will help you tailor your message.

Communicating to Parents

When speaking to parents, there are six concerns that parents want you to address. Knowing what they are will help you gain their trust and support.

1.   Will you love my child?
2.   Will you provide memorable experiences and encounters with the Lord?

3. Will they be discipled?
4. Are you in tune with the Lord?
5. Will you help me in the transitions of their life?
6. Tell me how I can be involved.

When you address these six things, you draw your parents in and their receptivity to you and your ministry begins to increase.

Communicating to Students

Communicating to students can be volatile—you never know if they are going to laugh, cry, or open fire. No matter the setting, there are three things you always want to do.

1. Be Authentic.

   Students can detect if you are genuine in your pursuit of God. Your ability to be transparent is what connects with students.

2. Be Clear.

   When trying to gain the attention of students, don't get caught up in gimmicks, trying to be clever or shocking, and lose sight of your message.

3. Use Concise Groups of Scripture.

   It is important to get all of what you want to say out of one section of Scripture. Too often we can be guilty of skipping around, using too many verses, many times stripping them from their real meaning and context.

Communicating to Adults

All adults generally fall into one of three categories. Knowing these three categories will help you identify the approach you take with adults.

1. Those that are for what you are for.

   They are for your cause or particular ministry, though they might be resistive to your method. Continue to teach them and cast vision to them to gain their buy-in.

2. Those that are for you.

   These are people who have a personal connection to you because of an investment you've made in them or their family. They will use their time and resources to help you and your ministry out of gratitude.

3. Those that are for what you're for and for you.

   These are people who are deeply committed to you and your cause; they are willing to do whatever it takes to make the ministry work.

8.   Leverage the power of honor.

There is authority and a chain of command in the Kingdom that is reflected in the order of the church. To the extent that we can recognize the authority of the senior pastor determines the kind of success we will have in that ministry. Every successful youth pastor stands in the shadow of a successful pastor. Even in itinerant work, you serve under the authority of the pastor. Of the many student pastors I have worked with over the years, the ones who have had the greatest success are the ones who honored their senior pastor.

There is one thing you can do that will blow a pastor's mind and cause him to invite you back over and over: ENCOURAGE HIS PEOPLE! So many times young ministers come into churches with self-serving agendas and a bloated view of their significance in ministry. The pastor has read more books than you, he has attended more conferences than you, and he has more experience in the mud of ministry than you. He doesn't need you to come in with any condescension. He needs you to encourage his people. He needs encouragement. Most pastors know that the church, at least the Western church, has gotten some major things wrong. Buzzwords like "relevant" and "post-modernism" and "contemporary," etc. will get you nowhere with a pastor. Treat him and his people with dignity. I hate sports analogies, but you are the kicker, he is the quarterback. He is on the field sweating it out, getting beaten up the entire game. You come in all shiny and new and limber and add the extras, and leave the field until you are called upon again. The kicker doesn't run on the field like he will ever be the MVP. He gets out there and adds the extras—the encouragement, the edification—and he leaves.

9.   You can be right or you can be friends.

If you are a guest speaker somewhere, don't offer criticism unless you're asked. If you do, here are some things to remember.

Identify your motive for criticizing.

Positive reasons for criticizing include commitment to and concern for another person and a sense of responsibility to have things done "right." Negative reasons for criticizing include poor self-esteem and the resulting attempt to build yourself up at someone else's expense or as a defense or excuse for your own failures. If those two statements can't help you sort out your motives, try the following, more detailed checklist:

- Will this criticism make you look better?
- Will you enjoy or dread giving this criticism?
- Do you want to demoralize the other person?
- Do you want to condemn or guide?

- Do you want resolution or more conflict?
- Is the issue a personal matter with you?
- Do you criticize habitually?
- Are you open or manipulative in your comments?
- Do you feel critical simply because you're in a bad mood or feeling depressed?
- Are you the best one to give this criticism?
- Are you giving the criticism to appease some third party?
  If you don't like the answers to any of these questions, consider waiting to give the criticism until your motives are clear.

Assume some of the blame yourself.

If you can do so honestly and if you have the ego-strength to meet the other person more than halfway, this approach will certainly generate a welcomed response. Let the receivers of the criticism save face by your sharing any blame that needs to be assessed. It takes the pressure off them to defend themselves and make excuses.

Recognize when enough is enough.

After you've made your point, illustrated your point, asked for and discussed the receiver's response, and identified specific actions to be taken or behavior to be changed, stop. There is nothing but resentment to be gained by repeating yourself.

Receive criticism.

Receiving criticism can be tougher than giving it. When people are faced with criticism, the two most common responses are "fight" and "flight." Fighters react by counterattacking. "It's not my fault," they might protest. Another response is to blame others: "I'm not the only one who's at fault here. I could have done better if I had gotten more support." Your own experience probably shows that fighting with your critics seldom persuades them to back down. If your purpose is to argue with their answer, you'll only escalate the situation. But if your purpose is to learn from their comments, you'll present yourself as a reasonable, self-assured, open individual.

10. *Just because you work for God doesn't mean you are God.*

We always have to keep our attitudes in check. Here are three things to keep in front of you as you follow God's call.

Stop trying to be famous.

One of the most common misconceptions in ministry is that the success you achieve is connected to your ability to promote yourself. If we concentrate on being excellent in our gift as speakers or any other office, for no other reason that it honors God, then God will make a way for us to continue in our ministry. After all, true and lasting promotion comes from God. If we make a big deal about God, He will make a big deal about us. So stop trying to be famous and be faithful to the task God has given you.

Protect your life by how you live.

Keep your life clean. Your ministry must be protected by how you live in your personal life. It does matter how you live. Momentum to do ministry comes from keeping our lives morally clean and pursuing purity as a way of life. That will put us in a place of constant readiness to minister to others. In every situation we have two choices: we can either do whatever we want to do or we can keep our life in a place where God could show up at any moment and demonstrate Himself through us.

Serve your way in; serve your way up.

Excellence is contagious and so is the lack of it. As ministers we have to always do our best with every opportunity we are given no matter what size the crowd or the kind of venue. Nobody starts out at the top. The currency of the Kingdom is service and we are servants of God and His purpose. In any type of ministry, whether it be church or itinerant, we serve our way in and we serve our way up. Opportunities will open for you if you are willing to serve somebody else's vision before your own.

CHAPTER 8

THE CALL TO GOD-CENTERED

Preaching

By Dr. Daniel Akin

How to Begin Well: The Introduction

Sermon introductions and conclusions have been compared to the takeoff and landing of an airplane. The analogy is appropriate. Almost all airplane crashes occur either on takeoff or when the plane is coming in for landing. The same is true for most sermons.

The importance of the introduction is self-evident. Those are the first words that your audience hears coming out of your mouth. It is the first impression you make. If you start poorly, it will be a struggle to regain their attention and receive a hearing. John Stott says, "A good introduction serves two purposes. First, it arouses interest, stimulates curiosity, and whets the appetite for more. Secondly, it genuinely introduces the theme by leading the hearers into it."[34] The burden is on the preacher to make the argument that what he has to say is important. Now of course we know that what we say is important. We know it has eternal consequences and that the souls of men and women are at stake. Nevertheless, we must convince the people who come to hear us that this is so. We dare not assume they come convinced.

An introduction also sets the tone for your message. It is important that the tone and theme of the message match up. To start a message on the doctrine of hell and eternal judgment with a joke or funny story is doomed from the start. Your introduction will determine whether you gain or lose credibility for your message. It will determine whether or not they will lend you their ear, open their mind, and expose their heart.

Finally, the introduction is the preface to the body of your sermon and your exposition of the Word of God. A good introduction is something of a map. It guides the audience into the message showing them both where we are and where we are going. To do this well takes careful thinking and precise planning. A good introduction will not happen by accident.

Preparing a Good Introduction

Haddon Robinson says, "I believe it is absolutely essential that a minister have his introduction clearly in mind when he stands to speak. While other parts of the sermon may be outlined [we still believe it is wise to write out a full sermon manuscript], the introduction ought to be written out. It is in the introduction that the preacher establishes contact with the people in the pew. . . . If there is ever a time that the mind will go blank, it is in the first moment or two you get on your feet."[35] We'd like to suggest some careful and simple steps you can follow that will enable you to craft interesting, engaging, and attractive introductions:

1. Pray over and through your introduction. Commit this aspect of sermon development to God seeking the assistance and guidance of the Holy Spirit. As a faithful Christian herald, I believe there should be a Theocentric/Christocentric component to the introduction regardless of the text, its genre, or the theme you will develop. Help your people see that God has a word about the subject you will address and that Christ will be the key to its resolution.

2. Keep before your mind's eye (and ear!) the truth that this is one of the most, if not the most, important parts of the sermon. God deserves, and the sermon demands, excellence at this point.

3. Write the introduction out word for word. Script it for the ear, asking the question, "How does this sound?" Your goal is to get your audience's attention, grab their interest. You want to show them why they want to hear what you have to say. You want them to see the wisdom of giving you their undivided attention for the next thirty to forty minutes. This is no easy task! You must work hard at it.

4. Write the introduction, as a general rule, toward the end of your

sermon preparation. Your exegesis and exposition of the text should shape and guide your introduction, not the reverse. However, there can always be an exception to this rule. If the Lord brings the right introduction to your mind, then write it down and do so immediately! Do not let it pass just because it does not come in sequence with your normal pattern of sermon preparation.

5. Remember the value and impact of a powerful illustration, pointed and specific information, and a compelling question. Keep in mind that the delight is often in the details. Work at being a creative and interesting storyteller.
6. Keep your introduction brief. Far too many sermons falter at this point. An introduction should never be longer than the body of your message. It should not be longer than any one of your main points or movements. In a thirty- to forty-minute message, a five- to seven-minute introduction is about right.
7. Memorize your introduction. Know exactly and precisely what you want to say and how you want to say it. Know it so well you can deliver it naturally and freely.
8. Build in a smooth and logical transition to the text of Scripture and the body of your sermon. Scripting your transition is a wise strategy to consider.

Haddon Robinson cites a wise Russian proverb when it comes to a sermon's introduction: "It is the same with men as with donkeys: whoever would hold them fast must get a very good grip on their ears!"[36] The proverb is right. When we stand to proclaim "the unsearchable riches of Christ" or as the HCSB translates it, "the incalculable riches of the Messiah" (Eph. 3:8), it is imperative that we get a good grip on our audience's ears from the beginning. It is essential that we begin well.

Proverbs 25:11 reminds us that, "A word aptly [the NKJV says 'fitly'] spoken is like apples of gold in settings of silver" (NIV). In other words the right word spoken at the right time and in the right way is a beautiful and valuable thing. We believe this is true anytime we speak. It is especially true when we introduce the Word of God to people who need to hear from the Lord.[37]

How to Land the Plane Safely: The Conclusion

As we noted earlier in the chapter, a number of teachers of preaching have likened the conclusion of a message to the landing of an airplane. It requires planning, skill, and timing. Haddon Robinson, using this analogy, writes, "An experienced pilot knows that landing an airplane demands special concentration, so an able preacher understands that conclusions require thoughtful preparation. Like a skilled pilot, you should know where your sermon will land."[38] The point we are trying to make is crystal clear: a wonderful sermon can be destroyed by a crash landing, a poor conclusion. In fact Stephen and David Olford believe, "More sermons are ruined by a poor conclusion than for any other reason."[39] It has been our experience and observation that this is true. Therefore, if the introduction is the most important part of the sermon, the conclusion runs a close second in our judgment.[40] A good preacher will not short-change this vital component of his message because of time constraints, fatigue, or laziness. He will take to heart the wise words of E. K. Bailey: "A great sermon not only starts well, it ends well."[41]

Preparing a Good Conclusion

Ramesh Richard says, "Faulty conclusions are notoriously discouraging."[42] Hershael York and Bert Decker are even more adamant in their concern: "We will go so far as to say that the *greatest error* most otherwise good preachers make is in their conclusion—or lack thereof."[43] Taking to heart what these excellent practitioners of preaching say about the conclusion, what guidelines can help us in bringing our message home safely and effectively?

1. As with all parts of the sermon, pray. Ask the Holy Spirit to direct you as you put your conclusion together. Be careful to exalt Christ and avoid mere moralisms that gut the power of the gospel.
2. Let the body of your message dictate how you craft your conclusion. You do not have a great conclusion in search of a sermon and a text. The conclusion should flow clearly and naturally from your exposition of God's Word. Plan your conclusion carefully after your work of exposition.
3. Remember this is a crucial component of your sermon. It must not be prepared in haste or with minimal attention.
4. Think in terms of how your conclusion can naturally flow from the body of the message as well as into the Christ-centered invitation.
5. Briefly summarize your major idea.
6. Highlight your points of application.
7. Keep it brief. Three to five minutes sets wise parameters.
8. Remember the value of a powerful and memorable story.
9. Challenge your audience to act, decide, respond.

10. Ask and answer the question, "What do I want my people to leave with and do in response to this message?"
11. Work at developing a clear and concise statement that captures the essence of your sermon.
12. Script the conclusion, at least as it pertains to its overarching structure, so that you will end your message exactly like you want.

Our friend E. K. Bailey is now with the Lord, but he understood the necessity of ending well. He would affirm, without hesitation, these twelve principles. And yet, he would encourage us to always have an ear for the voice of the Holy Spirit as we bring the message to a close.

"As I approach the end of the sermon, I'm watching and reading the congregation. I've been here before, many times, but I know that God may want to do a new thing today. So I watch my people and listen for the Spirit, even as I'm speaking. In some African-American traditions, when a preacher strikes a chord with the congregation, he'll not only get a verbal response, but the body language of the congregation changes. The Spirit may then lead me to develop a thought, because that's where the Spirit is dealing in the hearts of people. But other times I've sensed, it's time to shut it down and land."

John Broadus says well, "Preachers seldom neglect to prepare some introduction to a sermon, but very often neglect the conclusion; and yet the latter is even more important than the former."[44] It is difficult to over-state the crucial nature of the conclusion. It is your last words, and last words should be lasting words. A conclusion brings things to an end with the goal of making a lasting impression on your listeners. You do not want to let them off the hook. Like men and women in a juror's box, they have heard the final argument and they must render a verdict. They cannot escape. They must decide. So, what should we do at this critical moment that is of eternal weight and significance? The invitation provides the natural opportunity for a decision to be made and confirmed. It is to that important component of the sermon that we now turn.

Developing the Main Ideas of the Text and Message

We believe there are three key questions that help us identify and clarify the Main Idea of the Text (MIT). They are:
1. What was the main point then? (Idea)
2. What was the biblical author talking about? (Theme)
3. What was the biblical author saying about what he was talking about? (Complement)

At the heart of a text, usually a paragraph should be one cardinal thought: the "main idea of the text" (MIT). This proposition is made up of two components: the theme and the complement. The main idea, as noted above, is sometimes called by other names: "textual thrust," "central idea," "exclusive emphasis," or the "big idea."

The main idea is the single idea around which the details of the text are woven. Since we want to communicate one major point for the people to hear, understand, and obey, we seek to communicate the major idea of each Scripture text in contemporary terms. Charles Simeon writes, "Reduce your text to a simple proposition . . . illustrating the main idea by the various terms in which it is contained."[45] The main idea of the text is the single unit of thought that binds together and gives meaning to all the particulars of a text. In some manner it should relate to your title.

It should always be in the form of a full grammatical sentence, stated clearly and concisely. It places a laser beam focus on: 1) what the author is talking about; and 2) what the author is saying about what he is talking about.

The Purpose of the Message

We find the purpose of the message (constructing the purpose bridge) by asking and answering the following two questions: *On the basis of the main idea of this text, 1) what does God want His people to know, and 2) what does God want His people to do?* As you ask and answer these crucial questions, two others must be on the table as well:

1. Can I make an exegetical or theological case that my message's purpose is compatible with the purpose of the text?
2. Can I make a pastoral case that my message's purpose is compatible with the needs of my audience? This question is clearly secondary, but it should still be asked. You will be guilty of ministerial malpractice if you ignore the needs and conditions of your audience. You are both liberated and limited by the main idea of the text. You must identify the text's purpose and then fine-tune it to the audience to whom you minister. Thus, two purposes are legitimately drawn from most texts. The first is content oriented; the second is behavior oriented. This now leads us to five questions you should ask of every text. This will solidify your purpose and guide you in sermon development.

Five Crucial Questions for Every Sermon to Raise and Answer

1   What does God want His people to know? Every exposition of

Scripture will have a knowledge element. There will be biblical and theological content. Biblical and theological illiteracy is rampant in our churches. It is a malady that afflicts far too many congregations. A faithful expositor will always strive to teach the "stuff of Scripture."

2. *What does God want His people to do?* Doing follows knowing. Having immersed people in God's Word as to what does it say/mean, I will now craft an action plan that paves a clearly marked road for obedience. If we answer the knowledge question but fail to follow up with an outlet for concrete and specific action, people will become confused and frustrated. They may not see the relevance and practical nature of the Bible for how they should think and act today. Our goal is to make disciples of Jesus who will think and act in a "Christian worldviewish" kind of way. People who do not think like Jesus will not act like Jesus, and people who do not act like Jesus are not really thinking like Jesus.

3. *What does this text teach about God and His character and ways?* This question is related to question number one but is more direct and specific. It is intentionally theological and God focused. It may actually be the first question you should ask. This question looks for the "vision of God" in the text. It probes the text to discover what it teaches about God's person, character, and attributes. It seeks to discover what we learn about God's purposes and ways. We are trying to learn more about the God who has made us and redeemed us, the God who tells us to call Him Father.

4. *What does this text teach about fallen humanity?* This question naturally follows number three, and it should always follow number three. It will keep us from being man-centered in our preaching. Bryan Chappell has a wonderful word in this context. He speaks of the "Fallen Condition Focus" (FCF). He defines this concept as "the mutual human condition that contemporary believers share with those to or about whom the text was written that requires the grace of the passage for God's people to glorify and enjoy him."[46] In other words, what does this text reveal and teach about human persons made in God's image who now bear the curse of sin and a depraved nature? Here is wisdom and balance. We are made in God's image. That is good. We are sinners by nature and choice. That is bad.

5. *How does this text point to Christ?* This is central in the sermon construction process and therefore we locate it "under the

bridge" to support the entire structure. Jesus is the hero of the Bible. The Old Testament anticipated Him and the New Testament explains Him. This is not a novel idea. The church fathers were thoroughly Christo-centric in their preaching. After all, they got it from the apostles, and they got it from Jesus. Jesus teaches us in Luke 24 that all of Scripture is about Him . . . all of it. In John 5:39 He says, "The Scriptures testify of me." Therefore we dare not treat the Old Testament, for example, like a Jewish rabbi. To gain just a taste of what Christo-centric hermeneutics and homiletics can do, listen to the insight of Tim Keller as he scans the redemptive storyline of the Old Testament. This will say it better than we can.

It's All about Jesus (slightly revised)

Jesus is the true and better <u>Adam</u> who passed the test in the wilderness, not the garden, and whose obedience is imputed to us.

Jesus is the true and better <u>Abel</u> who, though innocently slain by wicked hands, has blood that now cries out not for our condemnation but for our acquittal.

Jesus is the better <u>Ark of Noah</u> who carries us safely through the wrath of God revealed from heaven and delivers us to a new earth.

Jesus is the true and better <u>Abraham</u> who answered the call of God to leave all that is comfortable and familiar and go out into the world not knowing where he went to create a new people of God.

Jesus is the true and better <u>Isaac</u> who was not just offered up by his father on the mount but was truly sacrificed for us. And when God said to Abraham, "Now I know you love me because you did not withhold your son, your only son whom you love from me," now we can look at God taking his Son up the mountain of Calvary and sacrificing him and say, "Now we know that you love us because you did not withhold your Son, your only Son, whom you love, from us."

Jesus is the true and better <u>Jacob</u> who wrestled and took the blow of justice we deserved, so we, like Jacob, only receive the wounds of grace to wake us up and discipline us.

Jesus is the true and better <u>Joseph</u> who, at the right hand of the king, forgives those who betrayed him and sold him, and uses his new power to save them.

Jesus is the true and better <u>Moses</u> who stands in the gap between the people and the Lord and who mediates a new covenant.

Jesus is the true and better <u>Rock of Moses</u> who, struck with the rod of God's justice, now gives us living water in the desert.

Jesus is the true and better <u>Joshua</u>, who leads us into a land of eternal rest and heavenly blessing.

Jesus is the better <u>Ark of the Covenant</u> who topples and disarms the idols of this world, going himself into enemy territory, and making an open spectacle of them all.

Jesus is the true and better <u>Job</u>, the truly innocent sufferer, who then intercedes for and saves his stupid friends.

Jesus is the true and better <u>David</u> whose victory becomes his people's victory, though they never lifted a stone to accomplish it themselves.

Jesus is the true and better <u>Esther</u> who didn't just risk leaving an earthly palace but lost the ultimate and heavenly one, who didn't just risk his life, but gave his life to save his people.

Jesus is the true and better <u>Daniel</u>, having been lowered into a lion's den of death, emerges early the next morning alive and vindicated by his God.

Jesus is the true and better <u>Jonah</u> who was cast into the storm so that we safely could be brought in.

Jesus is the <u>real Passover Lamb</u>, innocent, perfect, helpless, slain, so the angel of death will pass over us. He's the <u>true temple</u>, the <u>true prophet</u>, the <u>true priest</u>, the <u>true king</u>, the <u>true sacrifice</u>, the <u>true lamb</u>, the <u>true light</u>, and the <u>true bread</u>.

The Bible really is not about you is it? – It really is all about him.[47]

Getting at the Main Idea of the Message (MIM)

The main idea of the message is the heart and soul of your sermon. The MIM is derived from the MIT and channeled through the Purpose. It is then contemporized in the main idea of the message. The MIM takes you into the homiletical aspects of the sermon preparation process. The importance of this step is crucial to the success of your message. Stott notes, "For the sermon, as a living word from God to his people, should make its impact on them then and there. They will not remember the details. We should not expect them to do so. But they should remember the dominant thought, because all the sermon's details have been marshaled to help them grasp its message and feel its power."[48] John Broadus says, "The subject [MIM] answers the question, what is the sermon about? . . . Whether a sermon has two points or ten points, it must have one point, it must be about something."[49] John Killinger adds, "The first thing in making a sermon, the sine quo non, is the idea. There can be no sermon that was not first preceded by an idea or a theme."[50] Finally, and in a famous and much quoted statement, J. H. Jowett states, "I have a conviction that no sermon is ready for preaching, not ready for writing out, until we can express its theme in a short, pregnant sentence as clear as crystal. I find the getting of that sentence is the hardest, the most exacting, and the most fruitful labour in my study."[51]

The Main Idea of the Message

Theme: What am I talking about?
Complement: What am I saying about what I am talking about?

Six guidelines guide us in honing in on the MIM:
1.   Develop the MIM with your audience in mind.
2.   State the MIM in the most memorable sentence possible.
3.   State it positively, not negatively, if possible.
4.   State it in the active voice, not the passive voice.
5.   State it in words or phrases that are precise, concrete, and familiar to your listeners.
6.   State it so that the truth is readily seen as relevant to your audience and their needs.

What are the characteristics of a good MIM?
1.   It is derived from the main idea of the text. The MIT determines the MIM.
2.   It is what the preacher will be talking about in his message.
3.   It is a carefully worded statement.
4.   It is geared to the audience.
5.   It has a subject and a complement.
6.   It is a complete sentence that is memorable.

Now let us sound a word of warning in closing this chapter. Identifying the MIT/MIM does not give one license or permission to ignore the supporting ideas of the text. The supporting ideas must be allowed to support! Allen Ross addresses well just what we are talking about:

Too many so-called expositors simply make the one central idea the substance of their message. The narrative may be read or retold, but the sermon is essentially their central expository idea—it is explained, illustrated, and applied without further recourse to the text. This approach is not valid exegetical exposition. In exegetical exposition, the substance of the exposition must be clearly derived from the text so that the central idea unfolds in the analysis of the passage and so that all parts of the passage may be interpreted to show their contribution to the theological idea.[52]

Faithful exposition will honor the whole text, big ideas and little ideas. This will allow the whole as well as the parts to fulfill their divinely inspired assignment. Key points will support the main point, and minor points will support the key points. Text-driven preaching will be our guide and compass every step of the way.

The Work of Exposition: Structuring the Message

Engaging exposition requires the preacher of God's Word to develop a comprehensive and structured method for moving from his study notes and research to the completed sermon. He must bring order and logic, what Martyn Lloyd-Jones called "logic on fire" to the work done in the study. The goal is that the end product will have unity, cohesion, and form. It will be fit for passionate delivery to people who need to hear a word from God. In closing, the following is a summary of the basic principles for effective sermon outlining:

1. Use concise, complete sentences, not single words or phrases.
2. Use, when possible, a key word or phrase to assure consistency and symmetry in your division statements.
3. Craft your statements so that they stand alone as universal principles of biblical truth. Your points should contain that which is true anywhere, any place, any time, under any circumstances.
4. Follow a logical progression of thought in the arrangement of the outline statements.
5. Use present tense, contemporary language suitable for the particular audience you will address.
6. State your sermon points as sound theological principles that encourage faith and obedience in the hearer.
7. If additional development is needed under a particular point, work to make it simple.
8. Outline the sermon with your audience in mind.
9. Do not let the points stray from the main idea.
10. Alliteration is okay for some, but is not a requirement for effective preaching. If you are not good at it, then don't do it!

Why is sermon outlining helpful and important? Several quick observations:

1. It is important because it assists effective communication.
2. It is important because it is helpful for understanding.
3. It is important because the human mind seeks order and unity.
4. It is important because it helps you see how you have arrived where you plan to go.

5. It is important because it helps you gain a proper perspective on the text you are studying.
6. It is important because it helps you discover the pattern, order, and logic of the original author.
7. It is important because it helps you highlight the main points or thoughts in the text and the sub-points that explain and amplify those main points.

34 John R. W. Stott, Between Two Worlds: The Art of Preaching in the Twentieth Century (Grand Rapids: Eerdmans, 1982), 244.
35 Haddon Robinson, source unknown.
36 Haddon Robinson, Biblical Preaching: The Development and Delivery of Expository Messages 2d Ed. (Grand Rapids: Baker, 2001), 166.
37 "You must remember that you come to the pulpit having spent hours in the study pouring over the passage on which you are to preach. You have been thinking over your subject for days, or weeks, perhaps even for years. But your people have probably not thought about it at all. Indeed, they may not even know what it is going to be before you stand up to speak. (Pray that they will know after you have finished.) The chasm separating their thoughts from biblical ideas may be vast. In the introduction you must enter their world and persuade them to go with you into the world of biblical truth, and specifically the truth that is the burden of the sermon." (William L. Hogan, "It Is My Pleasure to Introduce...," The Expositor 1,3 (August 1987): 1).
38 Haddon Robinson, Biblical Preaching, 2nd Ed. (Grand Rapids: Baker, 2001), 175.
39 Stephen and David Olford, Anointed Expository Preaching (Nashville: Broadman and Holman, 1998), 78.
40 Interestingly, Walt Kaiser would go even further. He says, "I would urge God's ministers and teachers of the Word in every type of ministry inside and outside of the Church to severely limit their work on the introduction and to devote that time and those energies on preparation to an expanded and clearly-thought-out conclusion." From Toward an Exegetical Theology (Grand Rapids: Baker, 1981), 103.
41 E. K. Bailey, "Smoothing Out the Landing," Leadership, Fall 1997, 39.
42 Ramesh Richard, Preparing Expository Sermons (Grand Rapids: Baker, 2001), 127.
43 Hershael York and Bert Decker, Preaching with Bold Assurance (Nashville: Broadman and Holman, 2003), 185.
44 Broadus, 277.
45 John R. W. Stott, I Believe in Preaching (London: Hodder & Stoughton, 1998), 226.
46 Bryan Chappell, Christ-Centered Preaching: Redeeming the Expository Sermon 2d. ed. (Grand Rapids: Baker, 2005), 50.
47 Tim Keller, "It's All about Jesus" (Theology and Quotes, 12-4-06).
48 John R. W. Stott, I Believe in Preaching, 225.
49 John A. Broadus, On the Preparation and Delivery of a Sermon, 38.
50 John Killinger, Fundamentals of Preaching, 44.
51 J. H. Jowett, The Preacher: His Life and World, 133.
52 Allen P. Ross, Creation and Blessing, 47.
53 D. Martyn Lloyd-Jones was a tremendous preacher in Great Britain who emphasized passion, logic, and theology in the act of biblical preaching. Without it, he said, one was not fit to enter the pulpit. "What is preaching? Logic on fire! Eloquent reason! Are these contradictions? Of course not. Reason concerning this Truth ought to be mightily eloquent, as you see it in the case of the Apostle Paul and others. It is theology on fire. And a theology which does not take fire, I maintain, is a defective theology; or at least the man's understanding of it is defective. Preaching is theology coming through a man who is on fire. A true understanding and experience of the Truth must lead to this. I say again that a man who can speak about these things dispassionately has no right whatsoever to be in a pulpit; and should never be allowed to enter one. What is the chief end of preaching? I like to think it is this. It is to give men and women a sense of God and His presence." From Preaching & Preachers. (Grand Rapids: Zondervan, 1971), 97.

CHAPTER 9

THE CALL TO GOD-CENTERED

Service

It was called the oddest game ever played in high school football history. Two teams, Grapevine Faith versus Gainesville State School, who under normal circumstances would never share the same field. Maybe it is because Gainesville is a maximum-security correctional facility that has to play every game on the road and Faith is a private Christian school in a very affluent part of Dallas, Texas. Maybe it was because Faith had seventy players, eleven coaches, all the latest equipment, and involved parents. All Gainesville had was a lot of kids with a lot of convictions for drugs, assault, and robbery—many of whose families had disowned them—wearing seven-year-old shoulder pads and ancient helmets. Now in virtually every other football game, success is determined by little light bulbs that line up on scoreboards in the shape of numbers. And if your team has a higher number than the other team at the end of the game, you win. In other words, you were successful in your venture for victory. But on this particular fall night, success was not determined by flickering lights and how many times a little leather ball was navigated up and down a 120-yard-long rectangle with goal posts. As a matter of fact, success on this night had already been predetermined some time earlier.

It all started in the mind of Faith's head coach Kris Hogan, who saw his role as football coach as an opportunity to serve God and make His Kingdom known. The idea was as follows: What if we prepared more to serve them rather than to beat them? As Coach Hogan's thoughts marinated around the concept of service, the evolution of an idea began to take place that would make a statement far greater than one more win. He thought, *What if half of our fans on this particular night cheered for the other team? What if a parent of a player for Faith learned the name of a player from Gainesville and sat and cheered on the opposing team's side?* So Hogan sent an email out asking the Faith parents and fans to do just that. He wrote, "Here is the message I want you to send: You are just as valuable as any other person on planet Earth."

Of course some fans and players asked, "Coach, why are we doing this?" Hogan would respond, "Imagine if you didn't have a home life. Imagine if everybody had pretty much given up on you. Now imagine what it would mean for hundreds of people to suddenly believe in you."

When game night finally arrived, the outpouring of response from parents and fans was overwhelming—and a bit confusing to Gainesville. A large banner was constructed for the Gainesville players to run through that said "Go Tornadoes," and more than two hundred Faith fans sat on the Gainesville side cheering players on by name. Alex, a Gainesville linesman, said, "I thought maybe they were confused, they started yelling 'DEE-fense!' when their team had the ball. I said, 'What? Why they cheerin' for us?'" Isaiah, Gainesville's quarterback and middle linebacker, commented, "I never in my life thought I'd hear people cheering for us to hit their kids. But they wanted us to." One of the more illuminating comments came from Gerald, a lineman who will wind up doing more than three years in prison. He said, "We can tell people are a little afraid of us when we come to games, you can see it in their eyes. They're lookin' at us like we're criminals. But these people, they were yellin' for us! By our names!"

The outcome of the game would have caught no one's attention if they were just looking at flickering lights. Faith won by a score of 33-14. But something much greater was taking place in the hearts and minds of those on the field, which became evident after the game when both teams gathered at the fifty-yard line for prayer. It was here that Isaiah caught everyone off guard by asking to lead. He prayed the following:

Lord, I don't know how this happened, so I don't know how to say thank You. But I never would've known there was so many people in the world that cared about us.

At this point even the head football coach couldn't hold back the tears. The Gainesville coach saw Hogan wiping his eyes, grabbed him by the shoulders, and said, "You'll never know what your people did for these kids tonight. You'll never, ever know."

Soon after, this reality would paint a somber picture with her sobering brush as the Gainesville players were lined up by police officers two by two and put back on their bus. Before leaving they were given a bag for the ride back to their prison that contained a burger, some fries, a soda, some candy, and a Bible. As the bus pulled away that night, all the Gainesville players crammed to one side of the bus and pressed their hands against the window as they disappeared into the dark night. All of the Faith fans stood smiling and waving until they could see the bus no more.[54]

They say in Texas football is king. That the Friday night lights burn bright and everything else is put on hold. At the end of that night one team will raise its helmets in victorious celebration while the other will hang its head in defeat. This night, though, was different. This night the love of Jesus had made everything go topsy turvey. Think about it: the winning coach cried while the losing coach was given a Gatorade bath by his players and everyone was able to raise their helmets in victory. And why? Because this night football wasn't king; Jesus was King. While others have called it the oddest high school football game ever played, it could accurately be called Friday Night and the Light of Jesus.

Coaches, players, and parents who all viewed their roles as opportunities to serve the obviously overlooked. That is the heart of ministry. Whether you're a coach or a carpet cleaner; whether you fly an airplane or just ride one; whether you deliver pizzas or deliver the mail; whether you teach in a classroom or build houses; whether you work the graveyard shift or punch a nine-to-five, you are a servant of Christ.

Servant: From Slavery to Slavery

What then? Are we to sin because we are not under law but under grace? By no means! Do you not know that if you present yourselves to anyone as obedient slaves, you are slaves of the one whom you obey, either of sin, which leads to death, or of obedience, which leads to righteousness? But thanks be to God, that you who were once slaves of sin have become obedient from the heart to the standard of teaching to which you were committed, and, having been set free from sin, have become slaves of righteousness. Romans 6:16-18

I was once a slave to Satan, and so were you. The word *slave,* or *ser-*

vant, is derived from a Greek word that means "to bind." In the Greek, the language used to write the majority of the New Testament, there are two words that refer to a person in slavery. One word refers to one taken captive in war, while the other refers to one born into slavery. It is the latter definition that is used in Romans 6.[55] Though it flies in the face of a "man is basically good" culture, we are all born into sin and thus slaves to sin and Satan. And this bondage to Satan is a relationship that can only be broken by death. The very definition of slavery to sin should stir within every Christian a holy desperation for the redemptive work of Jesus Christ. For it was His death that broke our relationship with Satan, placing us in permanent relationship with Him. "But praise God, because He lives, we live, and since He never dies, we will never die."[56] We were born from slavery to slavery, which may sound counter-productive at first glance, but follow this train of thought:

A slave to Satan is born into sin.
A slave to Jesus has been reborn.
A slave to Satan is a slave to sin.
A slave to Jesus is a slave to obedience.
A slave to Satan is consumed with serving only a prince.
A slave to Jesus is consumed with serving the King of kings.
A slave to Satan is devoted only to self-interests.
A slave to Jesus is completely devoted to God's interests.
A slave to Satan has only death as his destination.
A slave to Jesus has only life that is everlasting.

If that isn't enough for you, consider this: we were created not to be slaves to Satan but to know and enjoy God. And because we were created for a relationship with God, only in knowing Him can we experience true freedom.

The apostle Paul was an incredible example of understanding freedom. As a matter of fact, in every major treatment on the subject of "freedom in Christ" Paul wrote, his favorite reference for himself was "a bond slave of Jesus Christ." Let us now turn our attention to what a life looks like that has moved from slavery to slavery. To put it another way, the qualities of one who is a servant of Christ.

A Servant of Christ:

Serve with the right motivation

The highest for every Christian must be love of Jesus. To remove oneself from the shadow of the Cross of Christ is to begin down a pathway that leads to life motivated only by selfish desires. Service for us only makes sense in the light of God's grace and mercy toward us. Romans 12:1 says, "I urge you therefore, brethren, by the mercies of God, that you present your bodies a living sacrifice, holy, acceptable to God, which is your reasonable service." God's mercy should bring about one reasonable service in our lives: to be a living sacrifice. But what does it mean to be a living sacrifice?

If you have been exposed to this verse a lot, then you probably read over the words *living sacrifice* with no hesitation. But if you were in a house church in first-century Rome hearing this verse read, you would probably say, "Hold the phone!" After all a sacrifice was typically an animal whose entire purpose in life was to die. They were born, raised, and sold for the purpose of being placed in front of a priest who would take a knife and drain their blood. So for Paul to say, "That is how you are to serve God" could cause some confusion. Could it be that Paul was saying to live every moment as if that moment were the last you would ever have on planet Earth? Martin Luther said it this way: "There are only two days in life that matter, this day and . . . that day." "This day" of course means the present day you are currently experiencing; after all, it is the only day you have control over. By "that day" Luther was referring to the day we will stand before God and give an account of the life we have lived. Therefore, motivated by God's mercy toward us, we are to capture the moments of today with profound sense of mission and intentionality. In other words, we are to be a living sacrifice.

Serve knowing God doesn't need you

The God who made the world and everything in it, being Lord of heaven and earth, does not live in temples made by man, nor is he served by human hands, as though he needed anything, since he himself gives to all mankind life and breath and everything. Acts 17:24-25

God doesn't need our service. He doesn't benefit from us having served Him, and we are not meeting His needs. Dr. John Piper phrases it this way in his book *Brothers, We Are Not Professionals*:

All other so-called gods make man work for them. Our God will not be put in the position of an employer who must depend on others to make his business go. Instead He magnifies His all-sufficiency by doing the work Himself. Man is the dependent partner in this affair. His job is to wait for the Lord. . . . What is God looking for in this world? Assistants? No. The gospel is not a help-wanted ad. It is a help-available ad. Nor is the call to Christian service a help-wanted ad. God is not looking for people to work for Him but people who let Him work mightily in and through them.[57]

What God is looking for are those who will serve Him in such a way that demonstrates our desperation and dependence and highlights His all-sufficiency.

Serve so that God has complete control

The apostle Paul spoke the above words in Acts 17 while ministering in the city of Athens, a city he said was "given over to idols." In an earlier chapter we highlighted that we live in a very cause-driven culture. It seems as though every aspect of our culture is baptized in one or more causes. You can buy a certain color cell phone and a portion of your money will go to fight AIDS in Africa. You can buy a pair of shoes and the shoe company will donate another pair to a third-world country. You can even buy cleaning products with the promise that the chemicals in that product will not harm the environment. Whether your cause is green, red, or pink I believe it to be a good thing. There is a word of caution here for Christians, though: *don't make idols out of causes*. While the doors of opportunity for service have swung open all around, this truth still remains: "No servant can serve two masters. Either he will hate the one and love the other, or he will be devoted to the one and despise the other" (Luke 16:13). Make sure your causes do not control you and your service falls under the full Lordship of Jesus Christ.

Serve happy . . . and don't be a South Pole elf
Serve the LORD with gladness! Psalm 100:2

One of my favorite Christmas movies is *Elf*. It ranks right up there with *It's a Wonderful Life* and *Ernest Saves Christmas*. It is a story about an orphan who wakes up on Christmas Eve to find Santa visiting and somehow climbs out of his crib and into Santa's big bag of toys. This mishap is not discovered until Santa arrives back in the toyshop the next day and the little tike comes crawling out right there in the middle of the workshop. Since the baby had no known family or name, Santa allowed him to stay in the North Pole and be raised by a four-hundred-year-old elf whom he would affectionately call "Papa." He was given the name "Buddy," and as the years passed by he grew up in the land of Christmas carols living by the code of the elves. Now he wasn't the sharpest crayon in the box because he never noticed that he was twice the height of all the other elves and had to have special shoes made to fit his enormous feet. Then one day he overheard two of his fellow elves discussing the fact that he was human. It was then that his snow globe of a world was turned up-side down. Buddy soon set off on a long adventure to find his biological father, who lived in New York City. Throughout the entire movie Buddy navigates through a culture of business, short tempers, and cabs that will run over you if you step out in front of them. One day Buddy meets a successful writer who happens also to be a little person. Buddy, with no ill will in his heart, refers to the writer as an elf, asking him, "Does Santa know you left the workshop?" Of course the writer takes great offense and proceeds to give Buddy the beat down of his life. Buddy—confused, bloody, and bruised—can only come to one conclusion: "He must be a South Pole elf!"

"Serve the LORD with gladness" is not a suggestion. The Christian, above all else, should be characterized by joy in his service. The well of gratitude should run deep yet not be able to contain the happiness and excitement over the Lord and His salvation. There is nothing worse than seeing a Christian with a negative disposition. There are no excuses, be-cause our attitude is in fact our decision. By the way, your attitude is the single most important decision you will make each day. A Christian with a bad attitude should be as foreign as the world outside the North Pole was to Buddy. You and I are not citizens of this world; as the old saying goes, "This is not my home, I'm just passing through." Serve as a citizen of heaven would serve, and always remember: don't be a South Pole elf.

Serve without segregating the love of Jesus

Now by chance a priest was going down that road, and when he saw him he passed by on the other side. So likewise a Levite, when he came to the place and saw him, passed by on the other side. But a Samaritan, as he journeyed, came to where he was, and when he saw him, he had compassion. . . . Which of these three, do you think, proved to be a neighbor to the man who fell among the robbers?" He said, "The one who showed mercy." And Jesus said to him, "You go, and do likewise." Luke 10:31-37

We have all heard the story of the Good Samaritan. A man goes on a journey from Jerusalem to Jericho and gets mugged along the way. They leave him lying in the ditch on the side of the road bleeding and dy-ing. The best he can hope for is that he would bleed out and die before sundown, before the wild dogs came and ripped him apart. Anyways there he lay, with the sun beating down on him and the flies buzzing around his wounds. With his vision going and his lungs filling with fluid he hears the shuffling of sandals along this rocky terrain called a road. Maybe through his blurred eyesight he could make out the fact that the figure moving in a now swift fashion was a priest. If so he would have most certainly thought, *If this guy won't stop, then there really is no hope.* Closing his eyes a tear cut through the dirt and dried blood slid down the side of his face. At this point he tried to remember happier times with his wife and kids. Then during his trip down memory lane, he hears another pair of shuffling sandals approaching him. He opened his eyes to see the priest's helper looking at his mangled body in disgust. With every ounce of strength he had left he tried to utter, "Help me, help me!" But like the priest before him the passerby avoided real service at all cost. By now death would be a relief that couldn't come soon enough. Trying to resurrect a memory of a better time and place, he heard, yet again, the sound of shuffling sandals, and this time they were slowing down. He would soon feel a hand and hear a strong and comforting voice say, "Fear not, I will take care of you." The sweet sound of mercy! Compassion had broken through his prison of pain and torment. Light had driven out the darkness making room for hope. Whoever this Samaritan was—really he is the Christ figure—had made a way for life.

Has anyone ever thought of you in that way? It is impossible to understand Christian service without first understanding two concepts: who is my neighbor and what does it mean to have compassion? The word for neighbor in this text simply means "the near ones." Whoever is near you is your neighbor. That means your neighbor could be a sibling or a spouse, a coworker or a teammate, the guy who takes your ticket at the theater or the person working the register at a fast-food restaurant. Francis Schaeffer defines it this way:

All men are our neighbors, and we are to love them as ourselves. We are to do this on the basis of creation, even if they are not redeemed, for all men have value because they are made in the image of God. Therefore they are to be loved even at great cost.[58]

The word *compassion* paints for us a much more vivid picture. It is a picture of someone who sees another in pain and hurts with that person. Notice I said "hurts with" and not "hurts for." The pain is felt deep into one's stomach and will not leave until something is done about the person they are hurting with. Maybe that is what the apostle Paul meant when he said, "Weep with those who weep" (Rom. 12:15).

Care for the obviously overlooked

"I was hungry and you gave me no food, I was thirsty and you gave me no drink, I was a stranger and you did not welcome me, naked and you did not clothe me, sick and in prison and you

did not visit me." Then they also will answer, saying, "Lord, when did we see you hungry or thirsty or a stranger or naked or sick or in prison, and did not minister to you?" Then he will answer them, saying, "Truly, I say to you, as you did not do it to one of the least of these, you did not do it to me." Matthew 25:42-45

It is impossible to be a servant of Christ without understanding the principle of "the least of these." God is overwhelmingly clear that He will judge based on our service. Now there are quite a few basic needs mentioned in this one text: hunger, thirst, warmth, clothing, health, and aloneness. Yet with an ever-growing list of needs, and for our culture we would also add causes, one reality must dominate our thinking: a failure to serve others is a failure to serve God. The act of serving is the outworking of our identity, and as you serve don't miss the obviously overlooked. James, the half brother of Jesus, said it this way: "Anyone who sets himself up as 'religious' by talking a good game is self-deceived. This kind of religion is hot air and only hot air. Real religion, the kind that passes muster before God the Father, is this: *Reach out to the homeless and loveless in their plight*, and guard against corruption from the godless world" (James 1:26-27, The Message, italics added).

54 Reilly, Rick. (2008, December 12). "Life of Reilly." ESPN Magazine. Retrieved January 14, 2009, from http://www.espn.com
55 Wuest, Kenneth. (1973). Word Studies in the Greek New Testament Vol. III. (Page 45). Grand Rapids: Wm. B. Eerdmans Publishing Company.
56 Ibid.
57 Piper, John. (2002). Brothers, We Are Not Professionals. (Page 40). Nashville: Broadman & Holman.
58 Schaeffer, Francis. (1970). The Mark of the Christian. (Page 9). Downers Grove: InterVarsity Press.

CHAPTER 10

THE CALL TO A GOD-CENTERED

Ending

One of the most significant and influential historical figures in the Anglican Church is Thomas Cranmer. His life echoes through the ages one revolutionary truth: *it is not how one begins the race but rather it is how one crosses the finish line.* Cranmer attended Cambridge in the early 1500s, where he was ordained as a priest. There he immersed himself in his studies and soon became an outstanding and well-respected theologian who was particularly fascinated with Luther and committed himself to understanding the theological significance of the Reformation. In August 1529, King Henry VIII and Thomas Cranmer's paths happened to cross and both their lives were changed forever. King Henry found himself in a quagmire as he was trying to dissolve his first marriage to Catherine of Aragon so that he may marry Anne Boleyn. Henry appointed Cranmer to write a treaty that allowed him to divorce Catherine and then selected him to act as one of his European ambassadors. When the archbishop of Canterbury died, Henry immediately appointed Cranmer to the position. His first act as archbishop was to declare the king's marriage to Catherine of Aragon as void. From this point on, Thomas Cranmer's life was wrought with both compromise and success. While he would annul marriages for King Henry, he also fought for believers who had fallen out of grace with the king, and he also opposed the king when he wanted to take the country back toward Catholicism.

Eventually Henry died and King Edward took the throne for a short time ushering in a fresh wave of religious liberty. During Edward's rule, Cranmer wrote his most famous work, *The Book of Common Prayer*. Following Edward's reign, Mary Tudor, the daughter of Henry VIII and Catherine of Aragon, took the throne. Mary was a staunch Catholic and sought to restore Catholicism to England. During her time in power, almost three hundred protestant clergymen were burned at the stake, while many more were imprisoned, earning her the nickname "Bloody Mary." Cranmer was sent to Rome where he was tried and found a heretic and sentenced to join those who had gone before him at the stake. Before his death, Mary wished to achieve a moral victory over the Protestants by having Cranmer recant. The former archbishop was placed in an Oxford cell and forced to watch as two of his closest friends, Latimer and Ridley, were put to death. Despondent and disillusioned, Cranmer eventually signed the recantation saying, "I confess and believe in one, holy, Catholic visible church, I recognize as its supreme head upon earth the bishop of Rome, pope and Vicar of Christ, to whom all the faithful are bound and subject." Before his death, he was taken to the Church of St. Mary where he would publicly retract thereby completing Mary's victory over what was left of the Protestant leaders. As he waited his turn to speak, one could only imagine that he pondered over his life and so many of the decisions he had made as so much compromise and hypocrisy stained this life he had lived. Sure, he had some successes, but in such a moment as this, it is what one did wrong that weighs heavy on the soul. It may have been while waiting his turn to speak or somewhere in the sleepless night before his execution that Thomas Cranmer decided he would end his journey not by trying to save his life but by trying to be committed to the One who saved his soul. So when it was his time, he stood to a wooden podium and began to speak of his weakness and sins. Then his speech took an unusual and sharp turn as he declared this of his recantation:

> They were written contrary to the truth which I thought in my heart, and written for fear of death, to save my life if it might be. . . . And forasmuch as I have written many things contrary to what I believe in my heart, my hand shall first be punished; for if I may come to the fire it shall first be burned.

He was immediately dragged outside the church where he was burned at the stake. As the fires began to grow beneath him, he kept the vow he had made just moments earlier and put his right hand in the flame stating, "This hand hath offended." He removed it but once to wipe his brow and immediately return it to the flames. With the last bit of breath in his lungs he prayed, "Lord Jesus, receive my spirit!" Then he died.[59]

It is difficult for me at times to relate to certain heroes from the Word of God. For example:
- I have never killed a giant. (In fact, I have never killed anyone.)
- I have never built a boat and survived a flood that destroyed the remaining population of the world.
- I have never put a stick in a body of water only to see the water divide.
- I have never spent the night with lions (though I did stay at a Holiday Inn Express last night).
- I have never been a king or even met a king.
- I have never walked on water.
- I have never been shipwrecked, snake bitten, or stoned (in the "we are going to kill you" sense).
- I have never been to jail (except as part of a class I took in college).

You see, there is a lot I have *never* done and will *never* do that certain characters throughout the story of redemption experienced. Thank God, though, that our cup runneth over with examples of characters I can relate to. Characters who:
- got it right on some days and wrong on others;
- were *obedient to the faith* one moment and falling on their faces the next;
- compromised and were corrupt;
- started well, removed themselves from the protection of God, and finished poorly;
- started well, removed themselves from the protection of God, repented, and by His grace were still able to finish well.

When I read the story of Thomas Cranmer's life, my thoughts are not consumed by the compromise that seemed to litter his path, but rather the manner in which his chest hit the tape. His was a life that crossed the finish line *looking unto Jesus*. His was a life that finished well. Could the same, one day, be true of us? You see, there is one inevitable reality that we all must one day face: unless Jesus returns in our lifetime, we are going to die. The question of when we have no authority over. The question of how is a different matter altogether. Let us now turn our attention to stuff that finishers are made of.

This may seem like an odd topic to those beginning life's journey. Some of us may think, *Finish well? I am just trying to get started!* It is my conviction that these are one in the same. Those who want to begin well have enough competence and foresight to realize that they must begin with their eyes on the finish line. This is the great lesson we learn from Hebrews 12 when the author says, "Let us run with endurance the race that is set before us looking unto Jesus, the author and finisher of *our* faith, who for the joy that was set before him, endured the cross, despising the shame, and has sat down at the right hand of the throne of God." How does one finish well? What is the finish line for a follower of God? In a word . . . Jesus. We live, we breathe, we strive, we run, because one day we will cross the finish line and when we take our last breath in this life, our eyes will be opened into the face of God. Thus, we begin the way we finish and the way we run in between: with our eyes fixed on Jesus, always considering Him.

Bob Buford's book *Finishing Well*, a phenomenal read for anyone serious about how they will finish their journey in this life, is built around this premise: "It's never too late (or too early) to begin finishing well." "If people see their best years behind them, they're probably not going to finish very well, because you can't finish well when you're going backwards."[60]

The writer of Hebrews may offer the greatest insight in all of Scripture on the subject of finishing well. Hebrews 12:1-3 is essential to understanding the key to running well and finishing well. Below is an exposition of this text that I believe will be very helpful in understanding how to have longevity and to cross the finish line as faithful as we began the race.

How to Finish Well:

Those who finish well learn from our predecessors in the race (v. 1)

We are surrounded by so great a cloud of witnesses.

Experience is not the best teacher; someone else's experience is the best teacher. What does it mean that we are surrounded, and who is this cloud of witnesses? In the previous chapter the writer of Hebrews shares with us an eclectic group of characters whose lives all had one thing in common: they were characterized by faith. And as such their lives serve as an example and source of encouragement for all those who seek after Jesus. They were part of how God, in His sovereignty, aligned the events of history for the day that a *Child is born . . . a Son is given.* Therefore if we are serious about finishing well then we must tap into the lives of *these pioneers who blazed the way, and all these veterans cheering us on.*[56]

Those who finish well take preparation for the race seriously (v. 1)

Let us lay aside every weight and the sin that so easily ensnares us.

There are two ideas never far from the finisher's mind. First, *I must rid my life of anything that would slow me down from exhaustively pursuing Christ.* The idea of laying aside every weight has to do with that which is unnecessary in our life. It is a difficult concept for those in digitally cluttered cultures to understand. And yet this one little concept can facilitate a sacred simplicity for life's journey by always asking of any decision: does it help or does it hinder? Second, *I must rid my life of the sin that addicts.* You know the sin I am talking about. The one that seems to have that addictive power over you when committed. The great danger in the sin that addicts is that it becomes the sin that is worshiped. The best definition of addiction is that it is simply misplaced worship. And it is an impossibility to run a race from the prison of addiction.

Those who finish well understand our participation in the race (vv. 1-3)

Notice the use of the words us, we, *and* our *seven times from verses one through three:*

- *we* also
- *we* are surrounded
- let *us* lay aside
- the sin which so easily ensnares *us*
- let *us* run with endurance
- the race that is set before *us*
- the author and finisher of *our* faith

Do you think the writer of Hebrews is trying to send us a message? "Be doers of the word, not just hearers only" (James 1:22). In other words, read your Bible and live your Bible; we have a responsibility to run.

Those who finish well understand our pace in the race (v. 1)

Let us run with endurance.

When I was in middle school I tried out for the track team to run the 800-meter and the one-mile. There were probably twenty or thirty other guys who were trying out that day, and the coach lined us all up and said, "Well, let's see what you've got." He blew his whistle and off we went to run sixteen hundred glorious yards. One guy acted like he was being shot out of a cannon when the whistle blew, and before long he was a good two hundred yards in front of the rest of us. I remember thinking, *This cat is a world athlete in the seventh grade and probably can already grow a mustache (and I mean a real mustache, not the kind that takes an entire summer vacation to grow).* You probably already know what happened next. Before he hit the half-mile marker, his world-wind pace was reduced to a decrepit pace that resembled an elderly person pushing a walker. Living exhaustively intentional does not mean living exhausted. Finishers know the value of a well-balanced life providing them the ability to have a well-balanced pace.

Those who finish well have a proper perception of the race (vv. 2-3)

Looking unto Jesus. . . . For consider Him.

The phrase "consider Him" carries with it a mathematical connotation in the original Greek. In a very practical sense, it means to always consider the sacrificial love of Jesus in light of any circumstance. I can think of nothing else that provides perspective better than Isaiah 53:4-5:

Surely He has borne our griefs
And carried our sorrows;
Yet we esteemed Him stricken,
Smitten by God, and afflicted.
But He was wounded for our transgressions,
He was bruised for our iniquities
The chastisement for our peace was upon Him,
And by His stripes we are healed.

Those who finish well are motivated by our prize having run the race (v. 2)

To finish well we must live with the end game in mind. What a reassuring thought it is that we can finish strong because Jesus finished strong. Think about this idea for a moment: He is both the author of our faith and the finisher of our faith . . . He begins this revolutionary journey and takes us hand in hand to the finish line. And our reward for walking faithfully is that we get to see Him. If the very idea of seeing Jesus one day is not enough for you, then there are some very serious questions you must ask of yourself.

In his book *Finishing Strong*, Steve Farrar outlines what he calls four stays that enable us to anticipate and avoid ambushes. These four stays will help us stay the course by willfully and purposefully remaining under the protection of Jesus Christ.

1. Stay In . . . The Scriptures
2. Stay Close . . . To A Friend
3. Stay Away . . . From Sexual Temptation
4. Stay Alert . . . To The Tactics Of The Enemy[62]

Thomas Cranmer at times did not live his life well. The compromise that littered his path I have also seen in my own journey. Even though he didn't choose when he would die, he certainly chose how: *looking unto Jesus*. You see, in the end he discovered that Jesus was more than enough. The tragedy of Cranmer's life is that while he had made that discovery much earlier in his theological studies, his heart had probably never awakened to Christ's all-sufficiency. For you and I the relentless grace of God seen in the sacrificial love of Jesus can capture both our affections and imagination today. To finish well, we must start now, for the race is as Eugene Peterson has already said: "a long obedience, in the same direction."

59 Gonzalez, Justo. (1985). The Story of Christianity Vol. 2. (Pages 72-78). San Francisco: HarperCollins.
60 Buford, Bob. (2004). Finishing Well. (Inside Cover). Nashville: Integrity Publishers.
61 The Message.
62 Farrar, Steve. (1995). Finishing Strong. (Pages 63-64). Sisters: Multnomah Publishers.

CHAPTER 11

A CONVERSATION WITH

Matt Redman

Someone who loves life, loves his family, and has a brilliant sense of humor, Matt Redman is one of the foremost voices in the modern worship movement. With a catalog of songs that are more like modern-day hymns and are sung in churches all over the globe, Matt writes from a place of passion and certainty. He urges the body of Christ to trust in a God who is stable, unshaken, and sovereign. In addition to writing songs, he has also written several books centered around the theme of worship. Matt has been one of the main voices in the Passion movement and the One Day world tour, has lead worship at various conferences and festivals all over the world, and is now helping lead worship at Passion City Church. Matt, his wife, Beth, and their children, Maisey, Noah, Rocco, and Jackson, have recently moved from England to Atlanta, Georgia, where the tea is served iced, not hot.

———

INTERVIEWER: Describe the experience or moment when your calling became evident to you.

MATT REDMAN: When I was sixteen years old I definitely had a moment when something changed and my thoughts about worship leading became more of a lifetime pursuit than just a temporary hobby. A small group of musicians and pastors took time to pray for me at a conference, and it was a very affirming and powerful moment, which I walked away from different. I think a sense of calling always must go beyond "self-affirmation"— *a true calling will always be affirmed by pastors, leaders, and others around us* (not just our mothers!). I've met so many people trying to "self-affirm" by trying to convince everyone around them that "this is my calling" . . . but no one else is seeing it. The most healthy scenario is when others are constantly encouraging us in the gift God has trusted us with.

INTERVIEWER: After you sensed this calling what were your first actions? How did your life change immediately after your calling?

MATT REDMAN: I remember the very next week I started a study on the Psalms and tried to write down every single phrase I could utilize for a song. I was fired up! I also felt I needed to focus on worship leading more, and in particular to give up acting, which I'd been into in a big way. This was so costly at the time—many of my un-churched friends thought I was being ridiculous, and I took some stick for it. But something in me had changed, and I started to rearrange my life accordingly.

INTERVIEWER: When did you get a vision for your present ministry?

MATT REDMAN: I'm always hesitant to label anything "my ministry." I always try to remember that I don't own any of it; it's simply an entrustment. I've had a vision to worship lead and song-write for over half of my life, but more recently have tried to capture what it is in words. I landed on three words: amplify, multiply, and exemplify. I want to amplify the name of Jesus through music, train others in doing the same, and aim to make my life exemplify what I sing about (that's always the tough one!).

INTERVIEWER: What has been the biggest shift as you look back on the landscape of your journey? How has your calling matured or evolved?

MATT REDMAN: I think the biggest shift has been learning to love and embrace many different streams of the church. When I first started out I had a bit of a narrow outlook—I wasn't really interested in connecting with anyone who didn't express worship or church in the same way I did. But over the years I've had the privilege of being involved in some very different streams of the church—all of them evangelical and sticking to the key points of faith in Christ, yet very different expressions of worship. And I have come to love that! I still have a strong sense of vision and value for the way I might do things, but at the same time I am realizing that there's so much to learn from all these streams of the church.

INTERVIEWER: Who have been the most influential people (*that you know personally*) in your journey? How did they influence or impact you?

MATT REDMAN: I'd have to say Bishop David Pytches from Chorley-wood, England. I was in his church from age four, right through to my twenties. He's a great leader, and I observed him time after time make some brave and humble decisions. But more than anything I look at him, now in his seventies, and see that he and his fantastic wife, Mary, are still running the race of faith. They have not fallen, or fizzled out, or compromised character and that inspires me. I've had too many disillusioning moments in ministry—when a gifted friend or peer "loses the plot" and opts out or is removed from ministry. I don't say that as a judge—for we all need be humble and alert. But in light of these disappointments, people like my friends David and Mary Pytches, and their long walk of faith, passion, and integrity, inspire me.

INTERVIEWER: What is the greatest single theological theme that seems to come out in your songs?

MATT REDMAN: I think it's the glory and the grace of God. As a songwriter I'm always looking to find a new way to speak about that mystery. It's the majesty and mercy, the fear and the friendship, the Lion and the Lamb, creation and the cross. If we could paint a big picture of the glorious God we worship through the way we express church, and then onto it project His unfathomable grace, we will draw people into a life-changing mystery.

INTERVIEWER: How have you stayed focused on what God has called you to do? What role have spiritual disciplines, such as Bible study, played in keeping that focus?

MATT REDMAN: I find I suffer greatly without the input of the Word in my life. I see it in every area of life—I'm a better husband, father, friend, songwriter, and leader when I'm spending time in the Word and presence of God. Of course, that's easier said than done . . .

INTERVIEWER: What makes you laugh?

MATT REDMAN: Usually word play—like the fact that "Presbyterians" is an anagram of "Britney Spears."

INTERVIEWER: What has been your greatest temptation?

MATT REDMAN: To "go through the motions" in ministry. After a while it's easy to get into an autopilot mode. Even after years of experience we may have a rough idea of how to lead people without thinking about dependence on God. Oswald Chambers said that "Weakness and dependence will always be the occasion for the Spirit of God to manifest His power."

INTERVIEWER: What resource (book, ministry, place, etc.) has had the most significant impact on your life?

MATT REDMAN: It's hard to narrow it down to one thing. I've been blessed to be around such exciting movements such as Passion [in the USA] and Soul Survivor [in the UK]. Seeing a generation of teenagers and students rise up in Christ and live for Him is massively impacting.

INTERVIEWER: If you were on a deserted island and allowed a certain number of books, what would be your top five?

MATT REDMAN: *The Dangerous Duty of Delight* by John Piper; *My Utmost for His Highest* by Oswald Chambers; *Worship: The Missing Jewel* by A. W. Tozer; *The Treasury of David* by C. H. Spurgeon; and *Under the Unpredictable Plant* by Eugene Peterson.

INTERVIEWER: What is the single most influential piece of advice someone ever gave you?

MATT REDMAN: A leader once told me, "Maturity is aiming for the ideal, whilst living with the actual."

INTERVIEWER: Is there one particular quote that has always stuck with you?

MATT REDMAN: I read an interview with John Wimber, the leader of the Vineyard church movement, who has since passed away. He commented that the real test in these days isn't going to be in the writing and producing of new and great worship music—the real test is going to be in the godliness of those who deliver it. That's a great reminder and challenge.

INTERVIEWER: What concerns you most about the church right now?

MATT REDMAN: As someone who writes and leads worship songs, it's been interesting to see things go "wider," in terms of how this expression of worship music has become more and more popular. But I'm passionate to see it go "deeper" too—particularly that we pursue the quest to paint the biggest and fullest picture of God that we can.

INTERVIEWER: What encourages you most? What is the church doing right?

MATT REDMAN: I'm encouraged that the church is beginning to be known for what it is "for," and not just what it's "against." Social justice and expressions of compassion have been a big part of this.

INTERVIEWER: When I say the word *accountability*, what or who comes to mind? Why?

MATT REDMAN: "Team." So much of it is about team—this is no time to be a lone ranger.

INTERVIEWER: On the following subjects what nuggets of wisdom come to mind that you would want to pass on to this next generation desiring to serve God, beginning with marriage?

MATT REDMAN: Find someone who will pull you up when you're down, and pull you aside when you're wrong! I love so many things about my wife, and the fact that she won't let me get away with a bad attitude is a blessing from God.

INTERVIEWER: On raising children?

MATT REDMAN: When you're spending time with them, be with them one hundred percent. That's easier said than done, but leaving the cell phone inside (rather than answering it every two minutes) when you're outside playing basketball with your kids can communicate greatly.

INTERVIEWER: On communication?

MATT REDMAN: Whether it's a song or a sermon, I love the thought of trying to express a universal theme in a unique way. There's nothing new under the sun really—we're just trying to find fresh, relevant, and powerful ways to express the beautiful truths of God we live in.

INTERVIEWER: With your permission I would like to ask some light questions that have some pretty short answers . . . beginning with what is your favorite sports team?

MATT REDMAN: The England soccer team.

INTERVIEWER: Favorite movie?

MATT REDMAN: *The Sound of Music*—phenomenal songwriting!

INTERVIEWER: Greatest band ever?

MATT REDMAN: U2. They write about the big themes of life.

INTERVIEWER: Dream vacation?

MATT REDMAN: My wife and kids, a book, some sun, and a pool.

INTERVIEWER: Favorite hobby?

MATT REDMAN: Reading the *Times of London* newspaper.

INTERVIEWER: Favorite TV show as a kid?

MATT REDMAN: *The A-Team.*

INTERVIEWER: If you could give just one piece of advice to this generation, what would it be?

MATT REDMAN: In the words of Hudson Taylor, "God's work, done in God's way, will never lack God's supply."

CHAPTER 12

A CONVERSATION WITH

Anne Graham Lotz

Just like her father, Anne Graham Lotz is known for the sacred simplicity of her message: Jesus. She teaches the Word of God all over the world in stadiums and arenas with a laser-like focus and somber determination. The ministry she founded, AnGeL Ministries, is dedicated to rightly dividing the Word of God in a way that will affect people in all aspects of their lives. Anne and her family live in North Carolina.

INTERVIEWER: Describe the experience or moment when your calling became evident to you.

ANNE GRAHAM LOTZ: Since God has no grandchildren, I knew I was responsible for making my own decision to confess my sin and ask Jesus to be my Savior, which I did when I was a young girl. I then invited Him into my life as my Lord. And I knew, from what my parents and grandparents taught me, that God's will for my life from that point on was to glorify and enjoy Him.

Years later, when I was a young mother with small children, God used the stress of my circumstances to give me a longing to know Him better. This desire led me to establish a Bible class in my city, which I agreed to teach, just so that I could be in it and learn. I taught that class of over five hundred women for twelve years without ever missing a class, because I wanted to learn all I could. Looking back, I can see clearly that my desire to know Him prompted by my own need was indeed His call to ministry outside of my home.

After twelve years of teaching the class, God distinctly and specifically called me from Acts 26:15-18 into an itinerant ministry. I obeyed, and used my initials to name the ministry—AnGeL Ministries. Angels in the Bible were messengers who go where God sends them, speak to whoever God places in front of them, and never give out their own ideas or opinions, but always deliver God's Word. I believe God has called me to be His messenger in much the same way.

INTERVIEWER: When did you get a vision for your present ministry?

ANNE GRAHAM LOTZ: Actually, in the over thirty years of being in ministry, I have never had a "vision" for my ministry. From that early time of committing my life to be available for service to Him, I have been on a personal journey of faith, seeking to know God better today than I did yesterday. When I focus my sight on establishing a personal relationship with God through faith in Jesus Christ, then—like Abraham—follow Him in a life of obedient faith, one day at a time, my "ministry" has naturally unfolded. The journey has been a thrilling adventure of getting to know God outside of my own comfort zone. And it has led increasingly to a sense of fulfillment in God's unique purpose for my life. Had I limited my ministry to that which I envisioned for myself, I'm sure I would have wound up with a lot less than God has given me: teaching God's Word on every continent, meeting with various heads of state, as well as international Christian leaders, speaking to thousands of people in overflowing arenas around the globe, and authoring award-winning and best-selling books.

INTERVIEWER: What has been the biggest shift as you look back on the landscape of your journey? How has your calling matured or evolved?

ANNE GRAHAM LOTZ: After more than ten years in itinerant ministry, during a two-year period, all three of my children were married within eight months; four weeks before his wedding my son was diagnosed with cancer and underwent major surgery and follow-up radiation; my mother had over ten serious hospitalizations and surgeries; my father also had surgery; my husband's dental office burned to the ground; our property was devastated by several hurricanes in which we lost over 102 trees; and through it all, I kept up my intense speaking and writing schedule. When I went to church, I didn't want to be entertained or given a formula or go through more rituals or be placed in a program. In the midst of the stress, pressure, and weariness, I knew I didn't want to quit ministry or to escape life; I didn't want a vacation. I didn't even ask God for a miracle. The cry of my heart was, "Just give me Jesus." Because even if all my problems were not solved or questions answered, I felt I could endure if I just had a fresh touch from heaven.

God in His grace led me to the Gospel of John. As I studied the encounters Jesus had with various people, I felt I had a personal encounter with Him too—and God answered the cry of my heart. I wrote down what He taught me in that personal study, and it was published as the book *Just Give Me Jesus*. God then used my own need, once again, to open my eyes to the fact that there are a lot of people like me—raised in a Christian home who have attended church all their lives—who need a fresh, personal encounter with Jesus. And so I have offered attendees an opportunity for that fresh encounter in arenas throughout the world, in a two-day event we call Just Give Me Jesus. Hundreds of thousands have received a fresh touch from heaven as a result.

INTERVIEWER: Who have been the most influential people (*that you know personally*) in your journey? How did they influence or impact you?

ANNE GRAHAM LOTZ: Ever since I was a child, the Lord has blessed me with *many* strong Christians who have been wonderful sources of wisdom and advice. Certainly, my parents top that list, as they influenced me from birth and still today. From my mother, I gleaned her love for God's Word, her commitment to take everything to God in prayer, and her fierce loyalty to family. From my father, I have gleaned a strong commitment to be faithful to God's call in my life. Like my father, I have an enormous sense of urgency to use the time God has given me wisely, and to work while it's day, because I believe the night is coming.

INTERVIEWER: What is the greatest single theological theme that seems to come out in your sermons and books?

ANNE GRAHAM LOTZ: Jesus. Regardless of the question, He is the Answer. Regardless of the problem, He is the Solution. He is everything.

INTERVIEWER: How have you stayed focused on what God has called you to do? What role have spiritual disciplines, such as Bible study, played in keeping that focus?

ANNE GRAHAM LOTZ: A compass is an essential piece of equipment used by many travelers, hikers, and outdoorsmen. The needle on the compass has a magnetic tip that is designed, regardless of which way the compass is turned, to always point north.

In order to live out my Christian faith every day, all day, I need to set my "compass." Every morning I rise early and spend a few minutes in Bible reading and prayer. When I read my Bible, I do so expectantly, listening for God to speak to me through it. When He does, I obey what He says. When I pray, I talk to Him about what I have just read, applying it to myself as well as others on my prayer list. For me, this is like setting my spiritual compass. No matter what happens during the day, it's as though my thoughts, attitudes, and actions automatically turn towards God and how I can please Him because I started my day by focusing on Him.

INTERVIEWER: Without sharing anything too specific or private, what has been your greatest temptation?

ANNE GRAHAM LOTZ: Actually, my greatest temptation is the one I face each day in my ministry and also in my personal life—the temptation to let busyness or tiredness keep me from maintaining consistency, concentration, and meaningful content in my daily prayer time.

INTERVIEWER: What is the single most influential piece of advice, for better or worse, that someone ever gave you?

ANNE GRAHAM LOTZ: One of the best pieces of advice I've received came just as I was beginning to step out into itinerant ministry. It was given by a dear friend and mentor, Stephen Olford, who told me that if I went around giving my opinions or ideas or insights, people would be bored, and I would soon pass from the scene. On the other hand, if I learned to dissect the Word of God, and give it out so that others could hear God speaking through me, people would sit up and take notice, and there would always be a place for me in ministry.

His advice confirmed my aim to consistently, clearly, and simply give out God's Word so that others can hear His voice and be drawn into a vibrant, personal relationship with Him.

INTERVIEWER: Is there one particular quote that has always stuck with you?

ANNE GRAHAM LOTZ: One from the Lord through the prophet Jeremiah:

> "Let not the wise man boast of his wisdom or the strong man boast of his strength or the rich man boast of his riches, but let him who boasts boast about this: that he understands and knows me" (Jeremiah 9:23-24).

Jesus confirmed the importance of knowing God when He defined it in His prayer of John 17 as "eternal life."

INTERVIEWER: What concerns you most about the church right now?

ANNE GRAHAM LOTZ: Generally speaking, I believe the message for the church today is the same as it was in the first century as recorded in Revelation 2-3, which is to repent of sin. Second Chronicles 7:14 says, "If my people, who are called by my name, will humble themselves and pray and seek my face and turn from their wicked ways, then will I hear from heaven and will forgive their sin and will heal their land." The primary problem with our world is not war, economic recession, famine, or disease—though these are all serious problems. The primary problem in our world is sin. And specifically, I believe sin in the church among God's people. The bottom-line reason that the church has not had a greater impact on our culture today is because we are not right with God. Praise the Lord that His Word promises that if we will come back to the cross, confess our sin, and turn from our wicked ways, then He will hear us, forgive us, and heal us. The message for the church is therefore primarily not to be busier with Christian activity, not to get politically involved in order to reverse some of the disturbing trends, not to offer more programs and worship styles and conferences, etc., but to return to the cross, repent of sin, and recommit to proclaiming the gospel of Jesus Christ and to living a life of selfless, obedient service to the glory of God.

INTERVIEWER: On the following subjects what nuggets of wisdom come to mind that you would want to pass on to this next generation desiring to serve God, beginning with marriage?

ANNE GRAHAM LOTZ: Marriage is not a union, civil or religious. Marriage is an institution established by God at creation for the successful functioning of society. Marriage is God's idea. It is not open for redefinition. And God has clearly stated that it is between one man and one woman for life.

INTERVIEWER: Raising children?

ANNE GRAHAM LOTZ: My mother once quipped that we would never get our children to eat their spinach if every time they saw us eating ours we gagged! In other words, the example we set is much more powerful than the words we say. Who we are and what we do, especially when we are in private, behind closed doors, or when we are experiencing pain and pressure, are teaching moments that impact our children for a lifetime.

INTERVIEWER: Living healthy?

ANNE GRAHAM LOTZ: Many times, people use the word *life balance* when talking about living healthily. Honestly, my aim is to be obedient to the lordship of Christ. I do not try to achieve "balance." I simply have surrendered all my life and all of my time to Him. Therefore, the biggest challenge for me personally is discerning how He wants me to spend what is really His time by making sure that in the busyness of ministry I make time for Him—in His Word, in prayer, and in stillness—that I might hear my Shepherd's voice. I have long believed that, rather than trying to take matters into my own hand to find balance and relaxation in my schedule, I would just trust the Lord to provide opportunities. As I have been about His business, He has been so good to be about mine.

INTERVIEWER: If you would permit I would like to ask you some light questions that will have some pretty short answers. What is your favorite sports team?

ANNE GRAHAM LOTZ: University of North Carolina Tarheels. Men's and women's teams. All sports, but especially basketball. Go 'Heels!

INTERVIEWER: Favorite movie?

ANNE GRAHAM LOTZ: As a result of watching Cecil B. DeMille's *King of Kings* when I was a little girl, I confessed my sin, asked God to forgive me, and claimed Jesus as my personal Savior, inviting Him into my heart. So I would have to pick that movie as my all-time favorite.

INTERVIEWER: Dream vacation?

ANNE GRAHAM LOTZ: A month on a warm, sunny beach anywhere, but a North Carolina beach in particular.

INTERVIEWER: Favorite hobby?

ANNE GRAHAM LOTZ: Hobby? Who has time for hobbies?

INTERVIEWER: Favorite TV show as a kid?

ANNE GRAHAM LOTZ: Any show with a dog or horse in it.

INTERVIEWER: If your own child were graduating from high school, what would be the main piece of advice you would offer to them on graduation night?

ANNE GRAHAM LOTZ: My main advice would be to get serious about God. I would challenge them to establish a personal relationship with Him that He would acknowledge. Then develop it daily through prayer, Bible reading, obedience, and fellowship with other like-minded young people. And I would tell them to seek His wisdom and will for all of their decisions: school choice, marriage partner, college major, career track, etc. He has a plan and purpose for their lives that is far richer, broader, and more wonderful than they could possibly imagine or plot out for themselves. But they may miss it if they don't intentionally seek Him.

Also . . .

When I was a teenager, it occurred to me that one day I would stand before God and give an account to Him for my life. I realized that He would not give me credit for what my father or my mother had done, but would ask me what I had done for Him. And at that point, I had done nothing. So I knelt on my bedroom floor, and offered Him in prayer my life from that day forward. I told Him I wanted my life to count in a way that would be eternally significant. God took me up on my offer. There was an immediate difference in my life as I did begin to care about others and their relationship with God. Over the years my heart has enlarged progressively, both in my love for God and also in my love for others. I live with a strong sense of compulsion to tell others that God loves them, that He has given His own Son Jesus Christ to be their Savior, and that when they place their faith in Him they will not only have their sins forgiven and receive eternal life, but they will have their eyes opened to see themselves and their world from God's perspective.

Also . . .

First, never forget that God loves you and deeply desires to know you in a personal, permanent love relationship through His Son, Jesus. I would urge any new graduate to do two things: One, make sure they themselves are right with God by deliberately, consciously confessing their sin, asking for forgiveness, placing their faith in Jesus Christ alone to make atonement, and invite Him into their hearts, surrendering their lives to Him as Lord. Two, if they are sure that when they step into eternity they will step right into heaven because they have made the above transaction by faith and thus been born again into God's family, then I challenge them to tell others about Jesus and the heavenly home He is preparing for His loved ones, and how they can be sure they will go there when they die.

CHAPTER 13

A CONVERSATION WITH

Francis Chan

The son of Chinese immigrants who both died before he was twelve years old, Francis has seen God do miraculous things in and through his life. As one of this generation's most compelling and dynamic speakers, Francis is pastor of the Cornerstone Community Church in Simi Valley, California. He is also the founder and chancellor of Eternity Bible College and author of the best-selling book Crazy Love: Overwhelmed by a Relentless God. *He spends much of his time speaking to high school and college students and inspiring them to know God, sacrifice their lives, and invest in eternity. Francis and his family reside in sunny California so that Francis can spend some of his off time surfing the waves.*

INTERVIEWER: Describe the moment or experience when your calling to become a minister of the gospel and pastor became evident to you.

FRANCIS CHAN: Yeah, I think there was a process that actually started when I was in high school. Because, I mean, it was during my high school years when I really began to have a passion for the lost. That was when I really understood my relationship with Jesus, and out of that grew a concern and my heart broke for the lost. And so I spent a lot of my time sharing Jesus with my friends out of concern for their eternal destiny. But it really wasn't preaching as much as it was I didn't want my friends to go to hell. So, I just would share the Word with them. After graduating from high school, I still just wanted to tell them about Jesus, and so my youth pastor Stan allowed me to work with the youth ministry focusing on high school students, with my friends that were still sophomores and juniors, you know. And then eventually Stan asked me to intern for him. Seeing that I had a heart for ministry, he discipled me as I'd share my faith on campus. He would answer my questions and worked with me in the context of ministry. I think at one point I said to him, "There is nothing else I want to do in life." It was at this time that I had the belief and desire to communicate in front of a crowd. So I began speaking to our youth group. I would record myself so I could go back later and realize how bad I was, and yet there was something in me that kept saying, "I'll figure this speaking thing out."

INTERVIEWER: When did you get a vision for your present position in ministry where you are a pastor of a local church?

FRANCIS CHAN: While I have a vision for the church I pastor, it is also presently undergoing a lot of change. Looking back, this vision has grown out of an ongoing discontent for anything unbiblical, and as we were faithful there is this ongoing clarity that also grew. For example the elders would notice something we are doing wrong that is not as biblical as it could be. So then we change it and suddenly we notice something else. It kind of snowballed from there once we started changing these things. Then you experience so much blessing in it and so much joy with just simple obedience. You start changing more and more and taking bigger and bigger jobs, you know, like the Lord does with our faith. And I think, yes, there was probably a point two years ago where I realized how much I was holding back and how much I hid a lot of what I believed for years and never expressed. Maybe there was a new boldness at that time to just verbalize it and then speak up, and I think it has been a very healthy thing for our church. That was the attitude of my heart, and there wasn't any exact moment when everything changed because it's been a process, like our sanctification. It started to grow and I'm learning new things every week. There is more clarity every week. There is more that God reveals to me in His Word. But what's changed is the willingness to speak up in the context of my biblical community, my board of elders, discussing with them, and there's been strength because I'm not alone in this. The elders board studies passages of Scripture for a week and then gather to see if the Spirit of God is leading in a certain direction. And it's still being done that way. I think years from now in our church, we will have a more developed vision because of the additional scriptures that we're considering.

INTERVIEWER: I want you to talk a little bit more about Stan, if you will. What was it about him? I have heard you mention from stage that he was probably one of the most influential individuals in your life as your youth pastor. What was it about him that had such an impact on you?

FRANCIS CHAN: Yeah, it was . . . his faithfulness and availability and his priority in me, you know. For me, I didn't have a dad, so Stan was the first guy I heard share the gospel. He's the first guy that explained the gospel in a way that I could understand every word because he's a youth pastor. And so that started it off, just listening to his teachings every week and then him befriending me. I remember he used to come on the high school campus and he took like some of my friends to lunch and then invited me along. And I thought, *Cool!* I was just excited to be in the group that got to leave campus and go out to lunch. Then he took an interest in me and got to know me, and out of that relationship I became interested in just learning the Word. He was available to teach it to me and anyone else who would listen. Even if other people dropped off, he didn't go, "Well, we only have three people coming, so let's just can it." Even when it ended up being just me, as long as I wanted it, he was going to keep teaching and stretching my faith, directing and challenging me. Whether it was evangelism on campus or eventually when I graduated from high school, he was saying, "You know, you can take this group of freshman guys and disciple them." He gave me whatever I needed and said, "Go for it and I'll be alongside if you need help." Next he started putting me in charge of whole events. It was over my head but I went for it anyways, confident in his consistency and faithfulness. I met with him for four years every week. He certainly rubbed off on me and was always available for me, and I just never had that type of mentoring before. I can summarize Stan's influence by saying that he was relationally authentic, biblically consistent, and he called me out. Twenty-five years later he is still a mentor and a friend.

INTERVIEWER: You know, Stan kind of helped you understand that if God is for you, who could be against you?

FRANCIS CHAN: Yeah, you know, he simply believed in me. He believed there was a future for me and yet, he was wise enough to keep me from getting arrogant by not giving me too much too soon. There was part of me that just wanted to get up in front of the whole crowd and speak. And there was a part of him that kept me sitting in a chair, which frustrated me at times, and yet he would stretch me in other areas. He called it the real stuff of discipleship.

INTERVIEWER: What has been the greatest theological theme woven throughout your preaching, teaching, and writing ministry?

FRANCIS CHAN: The holiness of God. We are way too casual about Him.

INTERVIEWER: I want you to talk just a couple of minutes about how that theme of being committed to the holiness of God is woven throughout the thread of your preaching, teaching, and writing, but also, is very consistent with the idea of making the Kingdom of God known.

FRANCIS CHAN: Well, it is an interesting topic and there are Scriptures that immediately jump out at me when dealing with this fear of the Lord and evangelism. To me they go hand in hand. Take 2 Corinthians 5:11, where it says, "Since, then, we know what it is to fear the Lord, we try to persuade men." God has every right, because of His holiness and greatness, to send my friends to hell! So, I must preach the gospel in light of that. To me it's kind of interesting to hear some leaders talk about fearing God and getting away from events or moments when we call people to a relationship with Jesus. It's kind of shocking to me.

I think also of 2 Thessalonians 1:7-9: "This will happen when the Lord Jesus is revealed from heaven in blazing fire with his powerful angels. He will punish those who do not know God and do not obey the gospel of our Lord Jesus. They will be punished with everlasting destruction and shut out from the presence of the Lord and from the majesty of his power." You know, it's just hard.

I mean, what does one do with that? Do you just sit there and sing another worship song? Or will it scare the crap out of you to think, *I need to go to all my friends and tell them about the Lord Jesus who is being revealed with His mighty angels, in flaming fire dealing out retribution?*

INTERVIEWER: How have you stayed focused on your calling? What role have spiritual disciplines, such as Bible study, played in keeping that focus?

FRANCIS CHAN: The only thing that keeps me focused is my time alone with God. Listening to sermons is great, but nothing compares to my time alone with Him. It's during that time that I am most deeply convicted and moved to action. I can't quote it verbatim, but Oswald Chambers in essence said, "Don't turn your experiences into principles, allow the Holy Spirit to be as original with others as He was with you." I want to be very cautious, because there is both a commonness and uniqueness in the way the Holy Spirit leads and directs and the way God speaks.

INTERVIEWER: Talk a little bit about what makes you laugh.

FRANCIS CHAN: I must admit I am a humor snob and don't give courtesy laughs. I don't like gross or shock-value humor that is involved with a lot of reality television. I love to laugh, and loud, though when people are genuinely funny. I mean, there are certain people that just crack me up. My kids crack me up. Kids tend to crack me up, little kids. But I love laughing and you know one of my favorite things is when people can laugh at themselves for doing something really stupid. And my kids are able to laugh at themselves. I love that quality in people, and of course I like to laugh at myself. I laugh hysterically with some stupid things I do, and I like it when other people laugh at me when I do some stupid things.

INTERVIEWER: What has been your greatest temptation?

FRANCIS CHAN: Simply put: pride, lust, and laziness.

INTERVIEWER: If you were on a deserted island and allowed a certain number of books, what would be essential for you to have?

FRANCIS CHAN: *Foxe's Book of Martyrs*, *Desiring God* by John Piper, and *Holiness of God* by A. W. Tozer.

INTERVIEWER: What resource (book, ministry, place, etc.) has had the most significant impact on your life?

FRANCIS CHAN: I would have to say John Piper's ministry. He's just real to me and has lived the message of Jesus so faithfully. He's one of these guys that could take life easy, make a ton of money, live in excess, but he doesn't. He always makes Christ shine while he sacrifices for the gospel. He is one of the first scholars that I have met whose knowledge actually led him to a deeper passion. Whereas most scholars I've met, their knowledge led them to arrogance and deadening of their soul. I have been privileged to talk with him a couple of times, and whether I have talked with him or listened to a message or read one of his books, I have always thought, *Wow, this guy really loves God.* I can see it jump out of the pages. And on top of it all he is extremely smart.

INTERVIEWER: What concerns you most about the church right now?

FRANCIS CHAN: You know, my major concern is that so many attendees are lukewarm and will be rejected by God. I am also concerned, and this stems from my first concern, of what church leaders are teaching about true belief and faith. Some have taught that to believe means you give intellectual assent to the fact that Jesus died on the cross for our sin and He rose from the grave. The Biblical definition, however, teaches that *belief* means you buy into Him with all of your existence. Not just intellectually, but with your heart, soul, and strength as well. Jesus said, "You will lose your life for My sake and you'll find it." So, for you to truly believe in Jesus, you must lose your life in Him fully by denying yourself, taking up your cross, and following Him.

INTERVIEWER: When I say the word *accountability*, what or who comes to mind? Why?

FRANCIS CHAN: I'm not a huge fan of accountability. Personally, I've found that we can all stretch the truth. I think about our need to have a deep fear for God—the only One who sees through our lies every time.

INTERVIEWER: On the following subjects what nuggets of wisdom come to mind that you would want to pass on to this next generation desiring to serve God, beginning with marriage?

FRANCIS CHAN: Don't let marriage become an idol. It was meant to be a picture of something far greater. We've idolized marriage in American Christianity by giving it too much focus. You see everything we do is to put the gospel on display, and that's what Ephesians 5 is about, not how to make a marriage work. We make that a marriage passage, but God is making it clear we're talking about Christ and the church. We're not just talking about a man and a woman being together. In effect that passage paints a picture of Christ and the church. So it needs to take its proper place . . . that I've lived for the sake of the gospel and I live to put the gospel and Christ on display. So I do that through the way I love my wife. I sacrifice for her. But it is bigger than her or her deserving it, because loving a person is really secondary to my passion for Jesus. I mean, if you think about it and go back to the Old Testament, God is so much bigger than our wives. Read Ezekiel when God basically said, "Hey, I want to strike her dead tomorrow, and I don't want you to mourn for her because I want it to be a picture to Israel." We would probably call that blasphemy today and say that God was not being fair. And it's not just that passage in Ezekiel. I mean, even the way God does it, and He goes, "I'm going to strike the delight of your eyes." Not even that woman that he doesn't get along with anyway, you know. It means the woman you're madly in love with, the delight of your eyes, I'm going to take her from you and I don't want you to mourn. That's the commitment God called us to. It's so much bigger than our marriage. I read a great quote this morning, so it's good timing. Charles Spurgeon said, "We should love but we should love with the love which expects death." You see, I should love my wife. But when you love her in the light of knowing that she's going to die and our relationship is going to end, in light of that, knowing she's going to die and stand before God, how do I as a husband love her? I want to prepare her for that moment when she sees God, and that's the greatest love I can show her—to prepare her for that moment.

INTERVIEWER: That's a great word. Now a word on raising children?

FRANCIS CHAN: Remember that our job is to raise soldiers in the Kingdom of God. Too often parents get into protection mode and raise kids that are weak or have no influence in the world because they are so sheltered.

INTERVIEWER: Finances?

FRANCIS CHAN: We live in such a self-centered and greedy society that we have to be careful that we don't think too highly of ourselves for being above the norm. Look into Scripture for the standard.

INTERVIEWER: Communication?

FRANCIS CHAN: Don't teach what you haven't lived. There are too many speakers and not enough doers.

INTERVIEWER: Just one- or two-word answers on the following light subjects: Favorite sports team?

FRANCIS CHAN: Lakers.

INTERVIEWER: Favorite movie?

FRANCIS CHAN: *Cinderella Man*.

INTERVIEWER: Greatest band ever?

FRANCIS CHAN: U2, but I hate their message!

INTERVIEWER: Favorite hobby?

FRANCIS CHAN: Surfing.

INTERVIEWER: Favorite TV show as a kid?

FRANCIS CHAN: *The Brady Bunch*.

INTERVIEWER: If you could give just one piece of advice to this generation, what would it be?

FRANCIS CHAN: Stay close to God and Scripture. Re-evaluate everything you've been taught in light of Scripture. You are going to face God one day, and it'll be sooner than you think. Be ready.

CHAPTER 14

A CONVERSATION WITH

Chaplain Barry C. Black

On June 27, 2003, Rear Admiral Barry C. Black (Ret.) was elected the 62nd Chaplain of the United States Senate. Prior to coming to Capitol Hill, Chaplain Black served in the U.S. Navy for over twenty-seven years, ending his distinguished career as the Chief of Navy Chaplains. He has received numerous personal decorations and awards over his long and distinguished career. Chaplain Black is married to the former Brenda Pearsall of St. Petersburg, Florida. They have three sons: Barry II, Brendan, and Bradford.

INTERVIEWER: Describe the experience or moment when your calling became evident to you.

CHAPLAIN BARRY C. BLACK: There was no "one moment," but I cannot recall when I did not know that I should be a preacher. My mother was pregnant with me when she was baptized and asked God to anoint the child in her womb. So my earliest impressions, as it pertains to my calling, are probably prenatal.

INTERVIEWER: After you sensed this calling, what were your first actions? How did your life change immediately after your calling?

CHAPLAIN BARRY C. BLACK: There was no dramatic change because I always had the belief that I was called. This belief motivated me to strive for exemplary living. I knew that I could not just do everything that my peers thought might be fun.

INTERVIEWER: When did you get a vision for your present ministry?

CHAPLAIN BARRY C. BLACK: It was eighteen months before I retired from the navy. I suddenly became fascinated with the U.S. Capitol building. I wondered why I felt such a magnetic pull toward a building. Looking back, I believe it was God preparing me for an appointment that was still nearly two years in the future.

INTERVIEWER: What has been the biggest shift as you look back on the landscape of your journey? How has your calling matured or evolved?

CHAPLAIN BARRY C. BLACK: My calling was nurtured initially by biblical revelation. My mother encouraged me to memorize the Bible and insured that I matriculated at Christian schools. The second phase came through general revelation. One night under the stars in Pottstown, Pennsylvania, my heart strangely warmed, and in a mountainous village in Peru, I heard the voice of God through nature's beauty.

INTERVIEWER: Who has been the most influential person *(that you know personally)* in your journey? How did they influence or impact you?

CHAPLAIN BARRY C. BLACK: My mother has been the most influential person in my life. She repeatedly reminded me of the prayer she prayed before my birth: "You have been set apart by God." I heard her say that more times than I can remember. I was also greatly influenced by ministers who sensed the call of God on my life and celebrated that consecration. They encouraged me to follow the voice of God.

INTERVIEWER: What is the greatest single theological theme that seems to come out in your sermons and books?

CHAPLAIN BARRY C. BLACK: The theme that reoccurs in my preaching is: the unstoppable providence of the loving God who seeks to bring us to a desired destination. Trust the process He puts us through.

INTERVIEWER: How have you stayed focused on what God has called you to do? What role have spiritual disciplines, such as Bible study, played in keeping that focus?

CHAPLAIN BARRY C. BLACK: Striving to be a life-long learner has been the most important habit for maintaining a passion for my call. I read voraciously. I keep notes in my journal on the themes I find in my reading. I meditate often on what I am learning. I see learning as a journey rather than a destination.

INTERVIEWER: What makes you laugh?

CHAPLAIN BARRY C. BLACK: I laugh at those who say God can't do something. My life has taught me that God can do anything.

INTERVIEWER: What has been your greatest temptation?

CHAPLAIN BARRY C. BLACK: My greatest temptation has been to choose less than the best. To settle for lower levels than I know God desires. They are not illegal levels, but simply not the best.

INTERVIEWER: What resource (book, ministry, place, etc.) has had the most significant impact on your life?

CHAPLAIN BARRY C. BLACK: The Bible is obviously number one. The Britannic Great Books of the Western World, a sixty-volume set, is the second.

CHAPTER 15

A CONVERSATION WITH

Mark Hall

As lead singer of Casting Crowns, one of the most successful and well-known Christian bands touring today, Mark Hall is a man of dedication. Dedication to his calling, his family, and his local church. Not only does Mark feel called to spread the gospel through music, he also has a strong calling to the local body of Christ. That's why, when he is not busy songwriting or touring, you can find Mark and his family leading a youth group at Eagle's Landing Baptist Church just outside Atlanta, Georgia.

INTERVIEWER: Describe the experience or moment when your calling became evident to you.

MARK HALL: I was raised in church and got saved when I was nine, but no one ever really discipled me. Our church had seven youth pastors in six years, and so a leader was never around long enough to build a relationship and pour into me. As a result, church was nothing more than listening to guys talk and then chasing girls . . . My spiritual life was very shallow. Church was life enhancement rather than community. The leaders of our student ministry became the senior guys, so the idea of chasing girls was really just following the leaders. Then I got a girlfriend and basically built my whole life around her. Then when I went to college she broke up with me and because she was my life, I totally hit rock bottom. It was the lowest I had been up to that point and I even contemplated suicide. During this time period I took a road trip up to Birmingham, Alabama, to stay with a friend named Jimmy for a couple of days. I had never been away from home very much, and one night I was sitting alone in Jimmy's house and had this thought: *There's got to be more to God and church and all of this than what I've got.*

When I came home, I began to read the Bible for myself for the first time in my life. I'm dyslexic and ADD so I chose to read the book of James first, thinking, *I can handle this; it's only two and a half pages.* As I started reading I felt that for the first time in my life God was talking to me. It wasn't someone teaching or preaching or singing to me; I was hearing from God and it was like a friendship was evolving. All of this happened over the course of about three months. Shortly thereafter I started dating a girl who had been best friends with me for ten years. She was in my youth group, worked with me at the mall, and basically we had grown up together. But for some reason I now saw her differently than I ever had before . . . it was as if God was taking off blinders. Also during this time period I started feeling like God wanted me to do something, but I had no concept of calling. All I knew was that God had a different idea for my life than I did. So I thought that maybe God wants me to be in ministry, and since I had sung in church with my dad earlier in life, I thought I would be a music minister. So there was this whirlwind of activity surrounding the moment I knew I was called: I start walking with Jesus; Melanie and I started dating and got married after four months; and I had all these songs in my head and I felt God leading me into ministry. It was like God had all these plans and all this stuff in store and He was just waiting on me to be ready. And He, in the state that I was in, if He had given me any of those things earlier, I would have run straight in the ground and destroyed myself. So that is how God called me to ministry. The mistake that I made was thinking, *It must be music*, which is what I studied when I went off to college. While in college God started showing me that I have a love for teenagers, which was something I had never realized. One day I had a guy ask me if I wanted to be a youth pastor and I quickly responded no. I wasn't qualified to lead students because I had a quick temper and didn't have a good experience with youth pastors in my church growing up. But I started praying about it and the next thing you know, I'm in this little church in Bethlehem, Florida, with eight kids and loving it. So I stumbled into the ministry that God had for me almost by running past it. But now I have been in student ministry for seventeen years. I love what I do. Our band Casting Crowns travels Thursday, Friday, and Saturday, and we're home Sunday through Wednesday. So, basically, I lead the worship at the eleven o'clock service and it's office every day and being involved on school campuses and Wednesday night services. But at 8:15 on Wednesday night after service we go home, pack up a bus, and Casting Crowns heads out and then rolls back in Sunday morning right before church begins. My wife is our road manager and my kids also travel with me. The reason my wife is our manager is that it allows me to focus on my responsibilities at the church and keep my head in the game.

INTERVIEWER: What has been the biggest shift as you look back on the landscape of your journey? How has your calling matured or evolved?

MARK HALL: The biggest shift would certainly be the evolution from building a youth group, and by that I mean heavy on the programs and big crowds, to making disciples. I never ask someone how many people is their ministry running, because at the end of the day building a crowd is so unimpressive. What I want to ask so many times is, how many disciples are you making? I started seeing the extraordinary value in one-on-one relationship. You see, I can teach to a crowd, sing to a crowd, but I cannot stand on a stage and disciple a crowd . . . that requires a relationship. To my knowledge right now I know of about sixty students who are on staff at churches doing ministry work, and every one of those students has three things in common: *they all had one-on-one discipleship with me or my wife or a godly adult; they all had family members who supported their faith; and they had a ministry of their own they were in charge of when they were in our student ministry.* So I try to see myself as partnering with mom and dad as they raise spiritual champions. I used to stand in our youth room and think, *I have to fill these chairs!* But my calling is so much more than building an audience. An audience is known for doing nothing . . . an audience killed Jesus. So now my thought is not to fill chairs but to get students out of these chairs and actively engaged in living out their faith before they graduate. They need to know what their gifting is and begin using that to serve God's Kingdom. And by the way, that doesn't always mean standing and talking or singing; their gifting may be completely different.

INTERVIEWER: Who have been the most influential people (*that you know personally*) in your journey? How did they influence or impact you?

MARK HALL: My dad would be number one. He gave his life to Christ when I was eight and he was thirty-two, so he was growing in his walk with Jesus as I was growing up. I remember having a bad attitude and getting into arguments with him . . . yet I never wondered where Dad was. He would go to work every day and come home and we would go out in the yard and throw the football . . . he was always there. Today he is a minister in a church, but the biggest impact he has had on me was that he was present. I am surrounded by boys whose dads are not around or they are there without being *there*.

INTERVIEWER: What is the greatest single theological theme that seems to come out in your sermons and songs?

MARK HALL: I would say that there are a couple of themes that always come through in our music and when I speak. First a one-on-one relationship with God. To understand that God actually wants to know and pursue a relationship with us. Secondly, that God wants you to grow deeper in your friendship with Him by conforming us into the image of His Son. I'm not here to be a youth pastor or a husband or a college student or anything. That's the journey I may go on, but the only reason I'm breathing right now is He's turning me into Jesus. He loves His Son so much that He's going to fill heaven with people just like Him. That's why we're all still around. The journey that He's going to take me on to get me there is by making me an author and you a teacher and so on.

INTERVIEWER: As you look back over the last seventeen years, how have you stayed focused on what God has called you to do? What role have spiritual disciplines, such as Bible study, played in keeping that focus?

MARK HALL: I think the greatest spiritual discipline is the accountability that comes from spiritually mattering to another person. When you are in a discipleship relationship with somebody and you are pouring into people, you can't coast on yesterday's faith. That is what keeps me focused.

INTERVIEWER: What makes you laugh?

MARK HALL: My kids totally make me laugh.

INTERVIEWER: What has been your greatest temptation?

MARK HALL: Control. That's the thing that I always fight with . . . leaving my hand open. Understanding that God can put something in my hand, He could place a ministry in my hand or a song, but that's not why I'm here. Going back to Romans 8:29, I'm here to know Him. That means my hands must stay open and He can place whatever He so pleases in and take whatever He so pleases out. My struggle or temptation is to not allow God to do what He wants to do in His timing and how He wants to do it in my life.

INTERVIEWER: What resource has had the most significant impact on your life?

MARK HALL: *My Utmost for His Highest* by Oswald Chambers.

INTERVIEWER: If you were on a deserted island and allowed a certain number of books, what would be your top five?

MARK HALL: In addition to *Utmost* . . . *Mere Christianity* by C. S. Lewis, *Just like Jesus* by Max Lucado, and Chuck Swindoll's character study books on Joseph and Paul.

INTERVIEWER: What concerns you most about the church right now?

MARK HALL: What concerns me most is that we have this Christianity culture where believers are leaning more on other people's walk with Jesus instead of growing their own. So, when they go to church, they've got the "worship service Jesus" and the students have the "youth group Jesus," and here's the "Casting Crowns' concert Jesus," and the "conference Jesus," and as long as you are with those people in those places then everything is great. But then you go home and you don't have those people around, it seems like whatever you had has been lost. And if there is no personal growth as a result of a personal relationship with Jesus, then I am just trying to grow off of someone else's relationship and faith. You must have your own relationship with Jesus, because when the storms of life hit me, and they will, I can't lean on someone else's Jesus.

INTERVIEWER: What encourages you most? What is the church doing right?

MARK HALL: I'm seeing more openness about hurt and struggles than I've ever seen before. This seems to be another theme in our songs . . . God has put it on our hearts to talk about what isn't being discussed. Therefore so much of our music is saying, "Hey, this struggle, pain, shame, and the list goes on, is going on. Anybody else want to talk about it?" It also seems that men are more open about what they struggle with and as a result families are talking about more. I think that this honesty and brokenness about all the hurts of life is going to lead to healing.

INTERVIEWER: When I say the word *accountability*, what or who comes to mind? Why?

MARK HALL: Accountability has many different levels and forms. There is friendship accountability where I've got someone who has the right to ask me at anytime the hard questions. If there is not someone in your life who has the right to question you on anything at anytime, then you are living in a very dangerous place. I need someone asking me if I am spending time in the Word, spending time with my kids, what I am looking at on the computer, and the list goes on. Tony Nolan is one of those guys who I have given permission to get up in my business and ask the hard questions. For example, we are accountability partners with all things Internet . . . every week we both receive a list of what the other one has looked at on the Internet. I also have accountability that comes from being in ministry and pouring into other people. There is a sense of responsibility in ministry that keeps you accountable. A little motto I came up with is: *In the war of the mind, I will make my stand. With the battle of the heart, the battle of the hand.* And the battle of the heart is pouring new life stuff into my life, right?

INTERVIEWER: On the following subjects, what nuggets of wisdom come to mind that you would want to pass on to this next generation desiring to serve God . . . beginning with marriage?

MARK HALL: Your spouse is not the well that will feed you. Jesus is the well. And if you are walking into marriage thinking this person is going to complete you . . . there was that line from a movie a number of years ago, "You complete me," and that is just not reality. God is the one that completes me, and because of that I can invest in my wife in a manner that is pleasing to Him. That's why marriages aren't working, because people don't complete people . . . only God can do that.

INTERVIEWER: On raising children?

MARK HALL: They need you in so many ways. They need you to be there. They need Daddy's approval. They need Daddy's acceptance. And if they don't get your approval, they'll go look for it somewhere else and get your attention that way. Sometime back I read *Raising a Modern Day Knight* by Robert Lewis and walked away from it convinced that I want to be a strategic father . . . not just an involved father.

INTERVIEWER: On finances?

MARK HALL: Stay away from credit cards because they will consume you.

INTERVIEWER: On communication?

MARK HALL: In one word: transparency. As someone who preaches and teaches the Word of God, if impressing an audience is all that happens, then nothing has been accomplished. So when I open my mouth to speak, I want to do so in a manner that is honest about my own need for God. Once an audience sees that I am normal, dealing with some of the same issues they are, then they are more willing to listen. In my opinion this is the best approach to communication.

INTERVIEWER: If you permit I would like to ask some light questions that have some pretty short answers . . . beginning with, what is your favorite sports team?

MARK HALL: I honestly don't watch sports. I'm a player fan. For example Shaun Alexander is a good friend of mine, so I am a Shaun fan, but other than that I just don't watch sports on TV.

INTERVIEWER: Favorite movie?

MARK HALL: *Gladiator.*

INTERVIEWER: Greatest band ever?

MARK HALL: One of my favorites of all times has always been Delirious. But I would have to add Third Day and Toby Mac to the list.

INTERVIEWER: Dream vacation?

MARK HALL: Mountains.

INTERVIEWER: Hobby?

MARK HALL: Tennis.

INTERVIEWER: Favorite TV show as a kid?

MARK HALL: *Incredible Hulk.*

INTERVIEWER: If your own child were graduating from high school, what would be the main piece of advice you would offer to them on graduation night?

MARK HALL: I'll tell you this: that won't be the night when he gets the main piece of advice or encouragement, because he's getting it now. We're talking through the elements of manhood: understanding what a godly man looks like and what it means to have honor, to love your family, be loyal, be a servant, walk in humility, and live courageously. So when we get to that night I simply want to be able to say as Paul said, "Live up to what you have already attained." In other words, there's nothing new to tell you because I've been telling you since you were a little guy.

CHAPTER 16

A CONVERSATION WITH

Ed Young

Ed Young is a creative and straightforward communicator who uses unique means to apply God's unchanging truth to today's shifting culture. Ed is the founding and senior pastor of Fellowship Church, which has its main campus just north of the Dallas/Fort Worth airport and operates three satellite campuses in the greater Dallas/Fort Worth area and one in Miami, Florida. He has authored several books and is a frequent conference speaker. He and his wife, Lisa, have been married for twenty-four years and have four children.

———————

INTERVIEWER: Describe the experience or moment when your calling became evident to you.

ED YOUNG: It was during my teenage years that I began to sense God's call on my life. While attending church I took on a leadership role speaking and leading some in the student ministry. The call was crystallized through when I was at Florida State playing basketball. I took my team-mates who had no clue about Christianity to church, and I saw church through their eyes. I knew if the church was going to reach them, it had to change a lot of stuff. God used that experience of being thrust into a very ungodly environment to bring me to the point of calling me into the ministry. There was an official or defining moment when after a Sunday night service I walked forward to the altar and knelt, realizing and surrendering to God calling me into ministry.

INTERVIEWER: After you sensed this calling, what were your first actions? How did your life change immediately after your calling?

ED YOUNG: My first action was to begin volunteering and serving the church. I started as a part-time staff member and then became full-time. After I finished college I went to seminary, so my life really didn't change that much after my "calling."

INTERVIEWER: When did you get a vision to become a pastor and/or author?

ED YOUNG: I worked with students for many, many years, and it was kind of a natural thing. I knew I was supposed to be a senior pastor when I was in my mid twenties. I really felt a prompting to do my own thing, to go and pastor my own church. As far as being an author, I've always written my sermons before I preach them. I've had some people approach me about certain message series and topics, and my books are messages that I've put together in written form.

INTERVIEWER: What has been the biggest shift as you look back on the landscape of your journey? How has your calling matured or evolved?

ED YOUNG: I think the greatest shift would be getting comfortable in my own skin. As a young person you look at this person or that person. You should learn from everyone; however, you need to be the best YOU you can be. That's the thing I would encourage anyone to do. It feels though my calling has evolved, because it's all about the next generation. I really have a heart for pastors and leaders to try to mentor and help them.

INTERVIEWER: Who have been the most influential people in your journey? How did they influence or impact you?

ED YOUNG: Obviously, my father Ed Young Sr., who is one of the most outstanding leaders I have seen. I definitely had an advantage growing up in our home on a steady diet of his leadership. So much of what I learned from him was more caught than taught. I didn't realize how much I knew about leadership until I actually was on my own. Other people that God has used in my life in great ways as far as leadership would be Bill Hybels and Rick Warren.

INTERVIEWER: What is the greatest single theological theme that seems to come out in your sermons and books?

ED YOUNG: I would say it would be the church being unleashed, the church being that Acts 2 body of Christ entity that takes risks and rides on the ragged edge of creativity.

INTERVIEWER: How have you stayed focused on what God has called you to do?

ED YOUNG: We're in a faith fight and the main thing that God has called us to do is to build the church, and to do that you've got to do to keep the fires of evangelism white-hot. This is a battle for people's eternity and we must never forget that. People always say, "Well, we're victors; not victims." They say that but they never talk about the battle. The battle is for people who don't know Christ.

INTERVIEWER: What role have spiritual disciplines, such as Bible study, played in keeping that focus?

ED YOUNG: For me, it would be journaling my prayers. This has played a huge role in my journey. This exercise has allowed me to look back and see how God has answered prayers. It has also been helpful for me to go and look through different journals and reflect on how I've struggled with doubt and dealt with different situations. For these reasons I would have to put journaling at the top of the list.

INTERVIEWER: What makes you laugh?

ED YOUNG: People make me laugh; specifically, crazy people.

INTERVIEWER: What has been your greatest temptation?

ED YOUNG: My greatest temptation would be to tend to relax too much.

It is easy for me to put life on autopilot as opposed to keeping the leader's edge as far as in my marriage, in my family, and also in church.

INTERVIEWER: What resource (book, ministry, place, etc.) has had the most significant impact on your life?

ED YOUNG: I don't really read very many leadership books. I don't really have one book, ministry, or place that has been the most significant. A lot of things are.

INTERVIEWER: What is the single most influential piece of advice someone ever gave you?

ED YOUNG: To walk on your knees in prayer.

INTERVIEWER: Is there one particular quote that has always stuck with you?

ED YOUNG: One life to live soon will pass; what is done for God is the only thing that will last.

INTERVIEWER: What concerns you most about the church right now?

ED YOUNG: The tendency that every church has to turn inward and to become a stained-glass fortress as opposed to really reaching out and thinking about others. In short: *selfishness* versus *selflessness*.

INTERVIEWER: What encourages you most? What is the church doing right?

ED YOUNG: I think a lot of churches are beginning to really understand what it means to be multi-sensory leaders and learners.

INTERVIEWER: When I say the word *accountability*, what or who comes to mind? Why?

ED YOUNG: Accountability is the most misunderstood word in Christianity. Accountability always emerges out of affinity. It is important but has to be practiced in the right context. In other words you are only as accountable as you want to be. Leaders must lead and accountability structures must allow leaders to lead. But at the same time a chosen group of people must be able to always see what's going on. They have to know where everything is going and what everybody is doing. Then again, one can have all the accountability in the world and still fall. The great modern example of this is President Bill Clinton, who had more accountability in his life than any other human being and he was having sex in the Oval Office. The point is, if one is going to have accountability then one must have enough character to desire the reason for accountability.

INTERVIEWER: On the following subjects what nuggets of wisdom come to mind that you would want to pass on to this next generation desiring to serve God, beginning with marriage?

ED YOUNG: It's about the marriage. It's not about the kids. Kids stand for Keeping Intimacy at a Distance Successfully. The marriage is the main thing. So goes the marriage, so goes your family; so goes your family, so goes your community; etc. The greatest sermon that anybody can ever preach is how they treat their spouse, so make sure to have that date night and to realize the marriage is the only relationship that is analogous through God's relationship with His people.

INTERVIEWER: Raising children?

ED YOUNG: I think you have to be yourself. What you are in public is hopefully what you are and who you are in private. Children can smell out fakery so easily. Children want discipline. They want you to draw the lines in the sand. They want there to be consequences when they step over the line. Parenting is not being your child's friend or buddy. Parents must be parents. Spouses stay, kids leave. Parenting is teaching and training your kids to leave.

INTERVIEWER: Finances?

ED YOUNG: Churches need to step up and pay pastors and staff members very well, because we need to bless those who bless others. And as far as finances, make sure that you bring the minimum worship requirement to the church: the first 10 percent of everything you make—and tragically, a lot of people in the ministry don't even do that. That's the first thing. If you want to be blessed, if you want to have a handle on your finances, bring the tithe into the storehouse. Then establish some sort of saving program. Try to save at least 10 percent of what you make and then you can enjoy the rest. Enjoy the 80 percent. Materialism always begins where your income ends. That's something to think about.

INTERVIEWER: Living healthy?

ED YOUNG: You've got to work out. You've got to eat clean for the most part. I try to eat clean about 90 percent of the time and then cheat 10 percent of the time. What's so funny is to hear pastors talk about how they don't drink beer and their potbellies are so big they can't even walk around. We need to be healthy because our bodies are for God.

INTERVIEWER: Communication?

ED YOUNG: Be yourself. I think people understand and connect with stories, but I think you need to be heavy on application. Sixty-nine percent of Christ's words were words of application according to Walk Through the Bible Ministries. And we have to illustrate. We have to say memorable things in memorable ways in order to communicate well. I appreciate the approach of speaking to a crowd instead of preaching at a crowd.

INTERVIEWER: If you could give just one piece of advice to this generation, what would it be?

ED YOUNG: It's time to go to an HNL—a Holy 'Nother Level.

INTERVIEWER: One or two word answers: Favorite sports team?

ED YOUNG: I don't have one.

INTERVIEWER: Favorite movie?

ED YOUNG: Jaws.

INTERVIEWER: Greatest band ever?

ED YOUNG: U2.

INTERVIEWER: Dream vacation?

ED YOUNG: Fly-fishing in the Seychelles Islands.

INTERVIEWER: Favorite hobby?

ED YOUNG: Fly-fishing.

INTERVIEWER: Favorite TV show as a kid?

ED YOUNG: Andy Griffith.

INTERVIEWER: If your own child were graduating from high school, what would be the main piece of advice you would offer to them on graduation night?

ED YOUNG: Follow the Lord tenaciously, passionately, intentionally, and creatively. The time is now to do what He wants you to do. Don't waste your time doing anything else. Do it God's way.

CHAPTER 17

A CONVERSATION WITH

Dr. Warren Wiersbe

Author of over one hundred books, and Distinguished Professor of Preaching at Grand Rapids Baptist Seminary, Dr. Warren Wiersbe has been called by Billy Graham "one of the greatest Bible expositors of our generation." Adding to his list of accomplishments, Dr. Wiersbe has also been senior pastor of Moody Bible Church in Chicago, a teacher at Trinity Evangelical Divinity School, and a producer of the Back to the Bible radio program. Dr. Wiersbe and his wife, Betty, live in Lincoln, Nebraska.

INTERVIEWER: Describe the experience or moment when your calling became evident to you.

DR. WARREN WIERSBE: On a Saturday evening in May of 1945 I was busy ushering for a Youth for Christ rally and helping behind the scenes, so I can't recall what was on the program. What I can tell you is that when Billy Graham began to preach, I was captivated. I stood against the back wall of the auditorium, unable to move and unable to take my eyes off the preacher. I heard every word he spoke and every Bible verse he quoted, and everything he said went right to my heart. Sure, I had heard it all before, but for the first time it came together and made sense. I saw that in spite of my character, my confirmation, my church attendance, and my host of religious relatives, I was a lost sinner who needed to trust Jesus Christ. I didn't wait for the public invitation to be given. Right where I stood, I asked Jesus Christ to come into my heart, *and He did!* I didn't raise my hand for prayer, I didn't fill out a card, I didn't even go forward when the crowd sang "Just As I Am," but I did trust Christ and become a child of God. With my conversion came the conviction that the Lord wanted me to be in ministry. I knew then that I wanted to go to school, get some Bible training, and preach the gospel.

INTERVIEWER: After you sensed this calling, what were your first actions? How did your life change immediately after your calling?

DR. WARREN WIERSBE: I attended the midweek service at the church I grew up in and told the people there I had been saved and called to ministry. They were a great encouragement to me, prayed for me, and in the months ahead, gave me jobs to do in church to help me find my gift(s). It turned out I had a gift for teaching the Word. The most dramatic change in my life was the presence of a great appetite to read and study the Bible. This conviction, that the Lord wanted me in ministry, continued to grow in the months and years following my salvation experience.

INTERVIEWER: When did you get a vision for your present ministry of writing?

DR. WARREN WIERSBE: Since the time I had been in sixth grade, I had been dabbling in writing, and when I moved into middle school my sixth-grade teacher encouraged me to do a lot of reading and writing. During both middle and high school I was on staff of the school paper. I never had a "vision" to be a writer, though; rather it was something that came gradually. As a child and a teenager I practically lived in the library.

INTERVIEWER: What has been the biggest shift as you look back on the landscape of your journey? How has your calling matured or evolved?

DR. WARREN WIERSBE: I don't recall any dramatic "shifts." After graduation from high school, I spent a year at Indiana University and then transferred to Northern Baptist Seminary, then in Chicago. I began to do some preaching at rescue missions, youth meetings, Youth for Christ meetings, banquets, etc. and got my feet wet. I was able to also hear some good preachers at YFC conferences—Billy Graham, Bob Cook, and others. The Lord was molding me in various ways, but there was no dramatic shift.

INTERVIEWER: Who have been some of the most influential people in your journey? How did they influence or impact you?

DR. WARREN WIERSBE: Different people influenced me in different ways at different times, so the list could be long. Our Youth for Christ international leaders—Torrey Johnson and Bob Cook especially—influenced me in the areas of prayer and preaching. Three seminary professors were very kind to me and spent time with me: Dr. Lloyd M. Perry taught preaching; Dr. W. Warren Filkin taught Christian education; and Dr. Stephen Douglas taught Greek and Hebrew. The president of the school, Dr. Charles W. Koller, was also a great example to me.

INTERVIEWER: What is the greatest single theological theme that seems to come out in your sermons and books?

DR. WARREN WIERSBE: My "life message" is probably the Word of God and its importance in the life of the believer.

INTERVIEWER: How have you stayed focused on what God has called you to do? What role have spiritual disciplines, such as Bible study, played in keeping that focus?

DR. WARREN WIERSBE: I am a one-talent person, so it hasn't been difficult to stay on track. God has enabled me to use words—speak them and write them—and that is all I have really done my entire ministry. I am a teacher and a writer, and what I write has grown out of what I've taught. When it comes to administration, I did the best I could and relied on my associates to help me. I've never been afraid to surround myself with people who can do things better than I can. My early morning devotional time in the Word and prayer has been the most important hour of my day. I've avoided running here and there to conferences, looking for shortcuts or the latest fads in ministry, and I haven't been afraid to be a "loner" or a non-conformist. It takes discipline to get up every morning and to spend hours studying and reading, but it can be done, with the Lord's help. I've tried to stay in good fellowship with more mature friends (some of them pastors) who have helped me keep my perspective.
INTERVIEWER: What makes you laugh?

DR. WARREN WIERSBE: Anything that is clean and really funny. I like satire a lot. If ministers can't laugh, they won't make it. We must laugh at ourselves and so many of the situations we constantly meet in ministry, but we must not become shallow and careless. Some things just aren't funny.

INTERVIEWER: What has been your greatest temptation?

DR. WARREN WIERSBE: Being Swedish, I'm pessimistic, and my greatest temptation is to see the problems but not the possibilities. My years in Youth for Christ helped to cure some of this malady, but it still shows up. More than once I've gone to board meetings prepared to quit, but never did. The part of our life that only God sees is the most important part.

INTERVIEWER: If you were on a deserted island and allowed a certain number of books, what would be your top five?

DR. WARREN WIERSBE: I suppose it would be a good book on how to build a boat! My list would change from time to time, depending on what is going on. But I would want a Bible, of course, a complete concordance with Hebrew and Greek dictionaries; a Bible dictionary; a systematic theology (Strong or Culver); and Fowler's *Modern English Usage*.

INTERVIEWER: What is the single most influential piece of advice someone ever gave you (for better or worse)?

DR. WARREN WIERSBE: More than one come to mind, so if it is all right I will share several. Torrey Johnson, the first president for Youth for Christ, told me to "find the one thing you do that God blesses, and stick with it." Bob Cook, the second president of YFC, shared with me, "If you can explain what's going on, God didn't do it." Peter Quist would often say, "Faith is living without scheming." And finally, Andrew Bonar said, "The best part of all Christian work is the part that only God sees."

INTERVIEWER: What concerns you most about the church right now?

DR. WARREN WIERSBE: The church is not practicing incarnation (the Holy Spirit working in and through us) but imitation—acting like the world. We entertain, not edify. We don't depend on prayer. We've gotten so big that it's impossible to know people and meet their needs. We should start smaller churches instead of megachurches.

INTERVIEWER: What encourages you most? What is the church doing right?

DR. WARREN WIERSBE: It is called by different names in different places. Some call it Life Groups, others Home or Small Groups, but really it is the idea of community to give a personal pastoral touch. But most people in larger churches don't seem to attend one. However, when it's done right, it helps a lot of people where they really hurt. I think that ministries away from the church building—coffee shops, etc.—are still available.

INTERVIEWER: When I say the word *accountability*, what or who comes to mind? Why?

DR. WARREN WIERSBE: First, my wife and family, and then a few life-time friends who know me well. One such person was one of my pastors here in Lincoln, who is now in heaven. He was a great help for many years. We'd have lunch together and really get down to business.

INTERVIEWER: On the following subjects what nugget(s) of wisdom comes to mind that you would want to pass on to this next generation desiring to serve God, beginning with marriage?

DR. WARREN WIERSBE: Betty and I have been married for fifty-five years; we have four children and eight grandchildren. A marriage is held together by the kind of love described in 1 Corinthians 13, by growth in the Lord together and in character, and by having the right priorities. Success in marriage requires sacrifice and service, living each for the other and both for the Lord.

INTERVIEWER: Raising children?

DR. WARREN WIERSBE: Find the special things about each child and build on them. In the home, an atmosphere of love, laughter, work to do, and recognition. Teach them early how to have their own devotional time. Never say, "Your father is a preacher, so you have to be good." I know that only a small percentage of your readers will be preachers, but the same applies to every devoted Christian involved in their local church. Our children should never feel like they are obligated to be "good" just because of our positions or roles in our churches.

INTERVIEWER: Finances?

153

DR. WARREN WIERSBE: My wife handled all the finances since the day we were married, and she keeps all the records. She is better at this than I am. A great rule that we have always tried to follow is: *when your outgo exceeds your income, then your upkeep will be your downfall.*

INTERVIEWER: Living healthy?

DR. WARREN WIERSBE: I was supposed to die at age two, but I am now eighty years of age. I took off each Thursday to rest and always took my family on good vacations. My wife also always provided balanced meals, but we were never fanatical about food.

INTERVIEWER: Communication?

DR. WARREN WIERSBE: God called us to express truth, not to impress people. Always speak and write as though you were addressing only one person, a conversational style, not oratorical, not a "preacher tone" or "scholar style." Very early in a message or chapter or paper, state the theme in one propositional sentence, and develop the theme in a logical and interesting manner and don't try to be cute; ministry is serious business.

INTERVIEWER: If you permit I would like to ask some light questions that have some pretty short answers . . . beginning with what is your favorite sports team?

DR. WARREN WIERSBE: I don't have one; I have no interest in professional athletics.

INTERVIEWER: Favorite movie?

DR. WARREN WIERSBE: Moby Dick with Gregory Peck and *Harvey* with James Stewart.

INTERVIEWER: Dream vacation?

DR. WARREN WIERSBE: Several weeks visiting historical places in Great Britain, including famous churches.

INTERVIEWER: Favorite hobby?
DR. WARREN WIERSBE: I really don't have any hobbies, unless you

count building my library to hold all of my eleven thousand books and then reading them.

INTERVIEWER: Favorite TV show as a kid?

DR. WARREN WIERSBE: When I was a kid we didn't have a television! We enjoyed the radio, so I suppose *The Dick Van Dyke Show* was a favorite and also the original *Candid Camera*.

INTERVIEWER: And finally, if you could give just one piece of advice to this generation, what would it be?

DR. WARREN WIERSBE: Know yourself, be yourself, develop yourself—your best self—and fulfill the work God created you to do.

CHAPTER 18

A CONVERSATION WITH

Louie Giglio

Louie Giglio is hands down one of the most influential voices of truth in this generation. A true visionary, his passion for leading others to worship God with authenticity and expression is exhibited in his captivating teaching and leadership. Through the weekly Bible studies Louie has led, Choice and 7:22, and through his unparalleled Passion Movement, literally hundreds of thousands of tomorrow's spiritual leaders have been impacted for the glory of God. As part of the Passion movement, Louie also heads up Sixsteps Records, a record label that develops and promotes Christian worship artists. In what Louie would call his greatest challenge yet, he and his wife, Shelley, have recently surrendered to the call to begin a church in the metro Atlanta area called Passion City Church.

INTERVIEWER: Describe the experience or moment when your calling became evident to you?

LOUIE GIGLIO: Growing up, I felt pretty in tune with God . . . even from an early age. Yet, the passion of my life as I reached my later high school days was tennis. In fact, I was on the tennis court at least four to six hours a day and was on track to play at Georgia State University. At that point, if I were bold enough to say what I really wanted to do with my life it would be "to be a professional tennis player." Looking back, that was a laughable goal, but at the time, it's what I dreamed about—playing professional tennis for the glory of God. I add that last bit because even at this age I had worked out that tennis wasn't worth my whole life, so I was going to sign every autograph with a verse of scripture and make it all count for God. Nice plan, huh?

Well, life rarely works out as scripted, and soon my dream had unraveled before I even reached the first day of class at GSU. An injury knocked me out of fall tryouts, the team passed me by and suddenly my life came to a standstill. Since then, I have learned that these moments are where God often speaks most, but at the time there was a huge void in my world.

Soon, my heart started turning upside down and I was sensing the voice/stirring of God like never before. There was a growing and compelling urge to serve God in a complete way (for lack of a better term). It's as if I was looking through a lens that was just starting to come into focus, and what I was seeing was me in the ministry.

I went to my pastor, and he encouraged me to spend as much time as possible alone with God over the next few weeks and suggested I read Oswald Chambers's *So Send I You*. I hesitate to say that now, thinking someone will read that looking for confirmation of God's will, which I'm not sure I found within its pages. But, the passage from Isaiah was enough for me as His calling grew stronger in me heart.

A few days into this process, once I had crossed the line in my own mind that I was going to "be a preacher" in response to God's calling, I experienced an intense time of spiritual attack. I vividly remember waking up in a cold sweat in the middle of the night feeling a barrage of accusation coming my way. Everything was doubt and fear and the enemy planted questions in my mind about all the negative things that would come with serving God in this capacity. I had seen my own pastor go through difficult and trying circumstances, and the voice I was hearing that night shook me deep inside.

Suddenly, 1 Thessalonians 5:24 came flying out of my mouth (out loud). I'm not sure exactly when that verse went in to my mind, but it powerfully came out in this moment: "Faithful is He who calls you, He also will bring it to pass." As soon as the words passed over my lips the accusation stopped and my room seemed to be blanketed by an even more intense calm. It's two a.m. and I'm sitting straight up in the bed, my heart beating out of my chest, and "faithful is He who calls you" surrounding me on every side. As I lay back down I knew two things beyond any doubt: God has put a stamp on my life and in following Him, everything is going to be all right.

The next Sunday night I went forward and told my pastor I knew God had called me into ministry. For me, this was a step I was sure of, yet one that was not readily affirmed by everyone around me. That Sunday afternoon I shared the decision with my father, and told him I'd be making it public at church later that night. Though I knew I had my dad's love and acceptance in life, he couldn't hide the disappointment in the moment. Not a passionate follower of Jesus, and Baptist by marriage, Catholic by birth, my dad was now saddled with the reality that while all his buddies' sons were going off to be businessmen, football players and the like, his son was going to be a Baptist minister! Oh wow.

My dad didn't make it to church that night. In hindsight I think his choice not to come was more about his own insecurity as opposed to a lack of support, but the sting was there nonetheless. But I knew I wasn't the first person to experience family turbulence in following God's calling and that experience somehow prepared me for all the "what if" moments that come with leadership of any kind, but especially with leadership from a ministry point of view.

Interestingly, later down the road after ten amazing years of collegiate ministry among students at Baylor University, Shelley and I moved back to Atlanta because my dad had become disabled. I was prepared to get a job and help with his care, but he died in this transition process and soon the beginnings of what is now the Passion Movement were taking shape. When we went to the bank to open new business accounts it was suggested we pick a number higher than 0001 for our first checks to begin with (apparently you want people to think you are not a brand new venture!). Without a pause I replied, "1524." "That was quick," she responded, "is that a Birthday or Anniversary?" We were able to share the significance of 1 Thessalonians 5:24 and still cling to it every step of our journey of faith. And, yes, I still have that first check.

INTERVIEWER: After you sensed this calling, what were your first actions?

LOUIE GIGLIO: There's not much you can do differently. I couldn't just wake up the next morning and say "I'm a preacher" and head toward the nearest church and put my name on the sign out front. That's not how following God works, anyway. From the moment of my calling I knew the "what" of my life (in the sense of my function in the Body of Christ) but none of the when or how. For me, following God has been one assignment at a time.

I'm encouraged by God's call to Moses which was basically, "go to Pharaoh and tell him to let my people go." Not, "Go to Pharaoh, endure the plagues, figure out how to lead a million-plus people in the night, provide for them, build a tabernacle, establish worship, receive the Law and so on."

And before I was going to be ready to lead anything I had a lot of growing up to do. In this same time frame I was working as a youth assistant at my church and attending GSU. Thinking that the ministry was totally more important than an education, I was blowing off classes left and right and eventually was asked to not return to GSU for two quarters. That's a kind way of saying I failed out of college. And, to add insult to injury, I failed out of the community college I went to during my "time away" from GSU, as well.

All this time I was busy serving God, totally blind to the reality that I was embarrassing the very Kingdom I sought to advance and excusing immaturity with pseudo-spirituality. My wake up came one day on I-75 as I was driving north of Atlanta having a conversation with the Lord. I sensed Him saying, "So you want to serve Me, speak for Me, give your heart to the ministry?" My response was unequivocal. "Absolutely! More than anything."

What happened next was amazing. And so practical. Without much drama (though I wasn't hearing an audible voice there was tone in what God was speaking to me) God calmly said, "So . . . you know you will want to go seminary and get more training for that." Again, my instant, "Absolutely! Can't wait." He went on, "And you know you'll need a Bachelor's degree for that?" I instantly exited and turned the car around. No kidding. I headed straight for downtown and GSU, parked and went up to my academic advisors office and humbly asked to see him, even if I'd have to wait all day.

In short, he finally did see me, and though classes had been going in the new quarter for several days, he enrolled me and set me on a path towards redemption . . . one that ended with me completing 35 hours in my final summer quarter and making it to seminary in Texas by the fall.

The point for me is that I had to learn that life is not always about the thrill of the call or vision, but learning to be faithful in the little things and the tiny steps. I meet so many young people who want to change the world for God, yet they can't make it to class at 9 AM. Trust me, I understand the challenge, but eventually we have to understand that God's Word teaches us to "dwell in the land and cultivate faithfulness." It's rare that people change the world in giant leaps, rather in small increments of faithfulness that lead them into God's purposes and plans.

INTERVIEWER: Your ministry, the Passion Movement, influences college students all over the United States and around the world. When did you get a vision for this present form of ministry?

LOUIE GIGLIO: After seminary I headed south to Baylor University to work on another Master's degree in Church-State Studies. During my seminary years I had been spending my summers working with college students at two churches in Houston and had fallen in love with leading them in the most critical window of life.

In all honesty, I went to Baylor to be close to Shelley (whom I had met during the summer in Houston). But, just before my first semester there God spoke through another one of the students in our college group and allowed me to see that I was headed to Baylor for a bigger reason.

A few weeks after arriving on the campus, a handful of us (about six students and myself) started meeting to pray and soon a tiny campus Bible study was born. At first, Shelley and I assumed that this would just be a temporary thing until we both finished our programs. Yet, ten years later our ministry was still growing and I had become a campus pastor.

If you'd asked me even a year before I finished seminary if this would be the case I would have said no way. In those days there were only a limited number of "boxes" you could slide into as a minister (pastor, evangelist, missionary, minister of music/youth/education, etc.) and I really didn't see myself fitting into any of them. But in time I figured out that God doesn't put us in boxes after He calls us, rather He builds boxes for us . . . or has assignments for us that match our gifts and His purposes in calling us in the first place. Who better to know where we fit than the One who created us and knows better than we do how we are wired.

If we feel called by God, we have to keep our eyes on the One whose voice we have heard, not the "boxes" and options that are before us. His plans always are so much more amazing than ours, anyway. In most every conversation I have with a university-aged person they ask me how you figure out what God wants you to do with your life. I guess they assume I'll know how to help them discover their five-year plan or life course. Unfortunately, they are usually a little rattled by my reply, when I say, "I don't know. In fact, I don't know where I'll be in five years, either!"

Our Baylor days of ministry morphed into Passion through a brief vision I experienced on a plane in the season following the death of my father, which I mentioned already. I would have never dreamed that our love for the students of one campus would spill over into a moment seeking to inspire the students of the world. Nor would I have known if this interview happened three years ago that I would now be watching God transform the Passion Movement into a global-local church movement of which I am the pastor. So it's imperative for Shelley and me to keep our eyes on the Caller, not the calling, because as it turns out calling is a moment by moment thing and He is leading even in this moment. For me, it's a simple as that.

It's important to mention that the "calling" of God I have sensed for my life has been confirmed each step of the way by the Church. Even in the early days, people were telling me what my life of service was going to look like long before I figured it out. I have always had people around me that have the freedom to speak into the vision or calling I receive. Without that, I am a fool. I often hear people say God has called them to make certain decisions or launch certain causes and I always ask, "What does your pastor think? What do the people in leadership over and around you think?" Some, even without this kind of affirmation run ahead convinced they have heard from God. But when you're getting a lot of "no" from the people who know you best, it's best to slow down and wait. When God speaks, it's always confirmed in the community of faith.

INTERVIEWER: Who has been the most influential person (*that you know personally*) in your journey?

LOUIE GIGLIO: There are so many people that have and continue to shape my person and my journey, but in the formative stages there were three. Charles Stanley, Dan DeHaan, and Ian North. Sadly, two are gone and probably unknown to almost everyone reading these words.

I was in sixth grade when Dr. Stanley came to our church and soon became the pastor. As a result, the church split and there was some unbelievable turmoil in the congregation. The church went from thousands to hundreds on his first Sunday, yet throughout my teenage years I watched first-hand as God grew the church to thousands again. In those days we went to church THREE times a week, and Dr. Stanley taught in all three. His style was short on funny stories and anecdotes and heavy on Scripture, a beautiful foundation that has served me so well over the years.

Ian was a pioneer of the missions organization Ambassadors For Christ International and was the first real global-Christian I knew. He was also the closest thing to a Biblical character I have ever known. Once, while attending a conference of world mission leaders with him outside Toronto, Ian came out of a side room where he was praying with a few of the men prior to the evening session. It may have just been me, but

I could swear his face was literally glowing, something I've never seen before or since. Ian believed in sacrifice for the sake of the Gospel, was counter-culture to the "balanced life movement" and put the unreached of the world ahead of all other possessions. Interestingly, all of his children (those who were away from him for much of his life) are all serving in various parts of the world today. Ian spoke with the blazing fire of the throne of God in his eyes and made me want to be less normal and more "other."

Dan was my hero as a teen and an incredible teacher and follower of Jesus. Dan loved Jesus and wanted to know Him. He was the speaker at our youth camps when Andy Stanley and I were kids, and he spoke for a community Bible study in Atlanta called Metro. When I first started going in the seventies about 300 people were coming every Tuesday night, but that number eventually grew to 3000-4000. Dan died in a small plane crash in 1982, the week his first book was published, *The God You Can Know*. I remember being at Dan's house the night his body was found and the very first copy of the book had just arrived and was on the kitchen counter. My copy is by my desk, the binding long gone and a rubber band faithfully holding its pages together. In time I learned than Dan was channeling A. W. Tozer in a language that I could understand as a teen and still gravitate to today.

INTERVIEWER: What is the greatest single theological them that seems to come out in your sermons and books?

LOUIE GIGLIO: There are three. The Glory of God, Radical Grace and Extravagant Worship. The revelation of God's glory and grace produce worship, which is a response to who He is and encompasses everything in life. If there is a fourth, it would be Intimacy With God.

These themes have come in waves, the first coming as a college student when I really began to understand grace-life . . . not just the grace of forgiveness that gets you to heaven, but the grace I define as "God at work" that powers every moment of life as Christ lives in me.

During my seminary days I was in contexts where freedom in worship was awakened in my life and over time, that sense of personal freedom has become linked with justice and mission, the sacrifices God really desires. Hearing John Piper speak in 1994, I was jolted by the idea of God's passion for His own glory and began to see His glory and fame on every page of Scripture and at every turn in His eternal activity. Grace, Worship, and seeing His Glory as the aim of my existence changed the landscape, not just a seasonal segment of the journey, and are the theological anchors of my life.

INTERVIEWER: How have you stayed focused on what God has called you to do? What role have spiritual disciplines, such as Bible study, played in keeping that focus?

LOUIE GIGLIO: The "major" disciplines, Bible study, prayer, reflection, solitude, fasting and community are givens. No one can effectively lead without them. But in addition, service and humility are the place where true leaders are formed. These are the pathways to true greatness in the Kingdom. We often focus extensively on encouraging younger people to discover their strengths, hone their gifts, attach to a mentor, etc. Yet some of the most powerful formative days of my life were making photocopies (imagine the day) of medical journals for doctors at the Centers For Disease Control library here in Atlanta as a college student, or teaching every Tuesday for teens who were incarcerated at the Lena Pope Home in Fort Worth during seminary.

In both settings there was no glory but God's glory, no stage, just service. In these settings the heart is shaped and prepared to lead. That's not to say the other disciplines are not essential, but rather that there are no shortcuts to favor and influence.

INTERVIEWER: What makes you laugh?

LOUIE GIGLIO: I like to laugh at the little things. I laugh at myself and all my own jokes. Shelley cracks me up. We laugh a lot together. But basically, I'm an introvert. Not so much on the stage in front of people, but I really love quiet space alone.

INTERVIEWER: What resource (book, ministry, place, etc.) has had the most significant impact on your life?

LOUIE GIGLIO: Honestly, I would not categorize myself as a monster reader. I usually read a few books a year, mostly biographies or non-fiction. I don't have a huge appetite for non-fiction (I have a vivid enough imagination already), but would rather read a story about something that really happened. I am currently reading the speeches of Sir Winston Churchill. As far as personal impact, the book I mentioned by Dan DeHaan would be up there, The God You Can Know, and anything by A. W. Tozer, especially, The Knowledge of the Holy, The Pursuit of God, and Whatever Happened To Worship. Currently, our Passion City Church core group is using the 365-day devotional guide that compiles much of Tozer's work.

INTERVIEWER: What is the single most influential piece of advice someone ever gave you, for better or worse?

LOUIE GIGLIO: Probably the best positive advice was from a friend who encouraged us to "never be in a hurry." That's not to imply we are not supposed to live with urgency, rather that we are walking with a God who created time and space and He will cause everything to come together in His plans. On the negative side was the person who told me that when we started that small little Bible study at Baylor I was making the biggest mistake of my life. He said, "Louie, you are a really gifted speaker and you'll be the pastor of a huge church (I think he said First Baptist Church) in ten years. Why would you want to waste that on a handful of college students and a ministry that doesn't even exist?"

I have no doubt this person had my best interest in mind, but in the process his words solidified for me a principle that has remained, namely that God doesn't always work in a linear fashion. He could have led the Israelites directly to the Promised Land on a two-week trek, but He led them straight out into the wilderness. Often God will lead us in what looks from man's point of view like side-ways or even backwards directions. In His economy, A does not always lead to B and on to C. So, there I was, with that huge pronouncement hanging over my head, leading six students in my apartment. But, it turns out God was in it and the path eventually led me to speak at many of the FBCs of the world.

So to reverse that person's advice: don't be afraid to follow what looks like an unconventional path. Just make sure you can see Him up ahead.

INTERVIEWER: Could you discuss a temptation or struggle that you may have presently in ministry, and how you are able to deal with it?

LOUIE GIGLIO: I think anyone in public ministry deals with the flesh and comparison. Jealousy comes when someone else's message is celebrated more than mine. To combat this cancer we must choose the celebration of other's success.

And above all, the main challenge of life is to walk humbly . . . to remember that I am a grain of sand in the Sahara Desert of God's activity on earth. That's why it's important always to find a little quiet (or not so quiet) and darkened corner behind the scenes or stage, get down on my knees, confess my inadequacies and His sufficiency, and humble myself before the God of goodness and grace. It's hard to be jealous or full of yourself when you are on your knees in the presence of the God of gods.

CHAPTER 19

A CONVERSATION WITH

Vonette Bright

Married for fifty-five years, Mr. and Mrs. Bill and Vonette Bright were the founders of Campus Crusade for Christ, one of the world's largest evangelistic organizations. A well-respected leader and accomplished author, Mrs. Bright also served for many years as the chairwoman of the National Day of Prayer Task Force. In the recent past she has launched Women Today International, a ministry to help women grow in their relationships with Christ. Currently Mrs. Bright can be heard on Christian radio stations throughout the country as she shares her heart and challenges women of all ages to take the next step of faith.

INTERVIEWER: Describe how and when your calling became evident to you to join your husband in starting Campus Crusade for Christ; and what were those first actions that followed the realization that God had called you to this?

VONETTE BRIGHT: I came home from teaching school one day and re-member kneeling by our bed and praying, "Lord, if this is what you want us to do, you've got to give me a heart to respond." I was and am con-vinced that prayer could only have come from God. I remember feeling frightened and scared but at the same time drawn to sharing my faith with students. So we moved out to the UCLA campus and I began to experi-ence great joy in studying the Bible, and of course Bill was very happy too. At this point I was also enjoying some success in teaching and I had been able to write a course of study for the Los Angeles city schools that they allowed me to teach. During this same time there arose a need for girls to be serving the ministry Bill was having on campus. Now these girls were going to be working very closely with my husband and they would know more about what he was doing than I would know. It was then that I decided that I wanted to be that influence in my husband's life, and so I stopped teaching to join with Bill full-time. When I led my first person to Christ, a little girl that I hear from every December 2 for now over fifty years, then I felt that God would use me. That was my call. I knew my call was to fit into my husband's plan, but now I felt like I could also handle this ministry. Henrietta Mears always said, "Find the place that's marked X for you," so I felt like I had found that place. I knew I was to be Bill's wife and involved in the ministry. But it was that experience, kneeling at the foot of the bed and then seeing God use me in a signifi-cant way, that helped me understand this calling.

INTERVIEWER: One of the fascinating ideas about Campus Crusade for Christ is that the original vision has never changed. Is that your feeling? That the calling has not in any way changed or shifted?

VONETTE BRIGHT: Absolutely, and the rhetoric has never changed. It has been adapted culturally, but if you were to go back to some of the early writings you would see that our vision hasn't changed one bit, and that has to be credited to Bill.

INTERVIEWER: What has been the biggest shift as you look back on the landscape of your journey? How has your calling matured or evolved?

VONETTE BRIGHT: The ministry had grown and our children were grow-ing and Bill was traveling a great deal. We had four men from Harvard University who came to help us by doing a study of our ministry. It was the worst year that they could have possibly done it because we had mutiny with about six of our men. So, they had left and we thought, *You know, we're going to have to start all over again.* Bill came to me one morning really low and said, "You know, we may have to start this ministry over again." And I said, "Well, we can do that." But the shift in my ministry came when these Harvard men arrived. I was no longer included, and our children were growing and I began thinking, *Where do I fit in here?* There was so much going on I didn't know about and, suddenly, I wasn't consulted. I was feeling a little bit misplaced and I'll never forget one morning while we were getting dressed I said to Bill, "What am I going to do? I don't feel like I'm a part of this ministry anymore." And he said, "Honey, if you will just keep me in clean shirts and take care of these children, that's all I need you to do. Don't worry about trying to be fitting in with some business arrangement or what's happening in the growth of the ministry." And so I was very happy doing that because it's what he wanted me to do. But all along I felt like there was some other ministry I needed to be involved in and was praying, "Lord, show me what You might have me to do." Then in the late fifties and the early sixties there was all of the revolution that was going on morally with the rebellion of the students on the campus. Henrietta Mears always said, "The moral character of a country is determined by the women of the nation. What a woman wants done, gets done." And I realized that women could have a tremendous impact. I had heard about the women of Brazil marching, threatening to flood their runways should the communists try to land their planes and disrupt an election. And in Indiana, a newspaperwoman and a group of women in the Methodist church decided they wanted to do something about the crime rate. So they mobilized and went downtown, talked to the police, and through their involvement saw the crime rate dropped tremendously. Instances like these were bearing in my mind in terms of what women can do, and I was concerned about prayer being removed in our schools. I was concerned about the student revolution, and I felt like that women ought to be able to do something about this. During this time I attended a congress on evangelism Billy Graham was putting on in Minneapolis in 1969. This was the first meeting of its kind and I had been asked to help host a women's luncheon. At the luncheon we trained women in basic evangelism efforts like writing out and sharing their testimony. Afterward, I met with Ruth Graham and some other leaders involved with the luncheon and we all shared some of our concerns in an effort to figure out our involvement. Ruth Graham spoke up and said the answer is prayer and the mobilizing efforts to get people to pray. While I certainly was a believer in prayer, I wanted us to do more than just sit around on our knees; I was thinking action. Over the course of the next few days, I was reading in the Book of Acts where Peter and John had been released from prison and they went to look for the others. And I thought, what could we do if we had wisdom, power, and direction as these characters had? What could we do if we could unite the minds and hearts of the people and particularly women to take action? I realized that this could only be accomplished through prayer. So, we organized prayer groups all over the nation in preparation for the bicentennial year. I believe the actions of Christians began to hold things together and we were able to stop amendments that were inconsistent with what God had called us to be. This calling, which would go on to be named the Great Commission Purpose and would lead to the beginning of the National Prayer Community, was a definite shift in ministry. It was a great support and great complement to Campus Crusade for Christ, and it was definitely a call from God. It was *my* call. And this shift led to another shift when later I discovered the National Day of Prayer was struggling to have any kind of recognition or power. After some research I found out that Eisenhower said that he didn't believe it would ever be significantly served until it became a permanent date and so we got it through legislation. Of course it bothers me greatly when groups try to declare that the National Day of Prayer is unconstitutional. I mean, it's kind of my baby. Anyways, that was the greatest shift and I always wanted to ensure that my actions were the greatest complement to Bill's ministry. I would like to add that I always knew I was a partner with Bill in ministry. I was on the board of directors and included. I didn't feel like I was reading out of a newspaper or sitting in the stands watching my husband be used of God. I felt like together we were being used to be part of something big for His Kingdom.

INTERVIEWER: Who would you say throughout this incredible journey has been the most influential person in your life?

VONETTE BRIGHT: Well, I think my mother who groomed me to be a leader. She taught me I had something to offer the world, and nothing could be more wonderful than being a woman and not always feeling like you are in competition with men. I know this helped me serve Bill and the ministry. Other than my mother I would say Henrietta Mears, even though all her books are out of print now. The last statement she made before she died was, "If I had my life to live over again, I would just believe God." She believed God for the impossible and helped me to do the same. Some of the highlights of what I have learned from her have been statements like, "Don't count criticism; weigh it." She also used to quote 1 Peter 5:6-7 alot: "Humble yourselves under the mighty hand of God, that He may exalt you in due time, casting all your care upon Him, for He cares for you." And in the Amplified Version it says, "Cast all of your hurt, all of your cares, all of your worries, all of your concerns once and for all upon the Lord for He cares and He watches you lovingly." I saw that in action in her life and she taught me to do so in mine.

INTERVIEWER: What would you say is the greatest theological theme that has risen to the surface throughout your ministry?

VONETTE BRIGHT: I would say prayer and evangelism.

INTERVIEWER: What role have spiritual disciplines played in your life?

VONETTE BRIGHT: Well, I think of the contract that Bill and I wrote and signed together to be slaves to Jesus. As I have reread that over the years, it is such an inspiration because Bill gave all he had to the ministry and held nothing back. In my mind he was such a complete leader. He had a great sense of humor. He was well read. He could talk with anybody on any subject. I mean he always found a way to relate to people. He was such a man of God that he spent time in the Word. He spent time on his knees. He constantly prayed and communicated with the Lord all of the time about all his decisions. He certainly was an overwhelming presence when he would walk in a room, and his ability to be such a man of God stemmed out of our commitment and the contract we signed. Paul was Bill's inspiration and where he got the idea to call himself a slave of Jesus. And I have to say to you that even though we called ourselves that I didn't really feel like a slave. I never felt deprived of anything. I found that God called us to a ministry and He provided for us. Now, we have always lived in somebody else's house and have never owned a home. We've always driven a car that's been furnished to us. God has always met our needs. The thing that I would want to communicate is that you cannot out give God. And if you're obedient to what He calls you to do, He's going to provide what you need to get the job done. Now, then, not all of our staff live on the same economic level. They raise their own support, but if they're working in Washington DC, they're going to have to live somewhat like the people they're going to meet. If they're working with people who have been incarcerated, then they're going to need to identify with the people in that area. We're all basically given the same living allowance in terms of what it takes to live where we are.

INTERVIEWER: What makes you laugh?

VONETTE BRIGHT: Bill Bright made me laugh. He had such a great sense of humor. I could never stay mad at him because he wouldn't allow it every time. My father always said two of the most important things you can have are a smile and a firm handshake.

INTERVIEWER: What resource, other than the Bible, has been the most influential resource in your life?

VONETTE BRIGHT: Well, I think, probably Catherine Marshall's book *Beyond Ourselves*, because I was just learning to walk in the Holy Spirit when I read it. The backbone of this ministry is the Holy Spirit, and Bill's making it practical and simple. That has been the reason why I think we've had longevity and retained the caliber of people that have come with us. We have several hundred people that have been with us more than forty years. I would also say any book by Andrew Murray, *My Utmost for His Highest* by Oswald Chambers, along with the Amplified Bible and the New Living Bible.

INTERVIEWER: What concerns you most about the church right now?

VONETTE BRIGHT: It seems there's a lot of entertainment that's going on in the church. In terms of capturing people's imaginations and young people busy just to stay busy. I think in the midst of it all we have failed to really explain who God is and to teach people how to depend upon Him in every situation. And we're not living what we profess.

INTERVIEWER: When I say the word *accountability*, what comes to mind?

VONETTE BRIGHT: Everybody needs it and not a lot people have it. There seems to be a lot of "I" and not a lot of doing life together.

INTERVIEWER: On the following subjects, what nuggets of wisdom come to mind that you would want to pass on to this next generation desiring to serve God, beginning with marriage?

VONETTE BRIGHT: First of all, don't be married until you know that this is the person that you're going to want to spend the rest of your life with. Understand you're making a covenant that is not to ever be broken and the word *divorce* should not be in your vocabulary. Bill used to often say, "You know, we're going to be together all of our lives, we're going to have fun with this." And that's how he got me laughing at him so many times. If an argument or disagreement would arise, that is how we would get through it, with the understanding that this marriage is for life so let's just figure it out. And sometimes, he came over to my thinking or I came over to his thinking. The greatest secret to our marriage was the fact that we prayed together every morning and night. Even when he was overseas, he tried to call home at the time the children would be getting ready for bed so that we would pray together with children on the phone.

INTERVIEWER: Raising children?

VONETTE BRIGHT: Teach them the Word of God. I think Proverbs is extremely important for children to know and to be aware of and of course the teachings of Jesus. Also make sure that you set time aside to discuss and ask questions about the Word and how it applies to their lives. Anything you can do to help children discover God is a good thing.

INTERVIEWER: If you could give this generation one piece of advice, what would it be?

VONETTE BRIGHT: Protect your character. You know, health is important, education is important; but you can have poor health and poor education but if you have a good character, you can be used of God. It's your character that is most important so develop your character. I owe that to my grandfather. I never knew him but he ingrained that into my grandmother and she shared that with me.

CHAPTER 20

A CONVERSATION WITH

Mac Powell

With one of the most recognizable voices in all of Christian music, record sales in the millions, and dozens of Grammy and Dove awards, Mac Powell has managed to stay humbly grounded in the midst of all the recognition and fame. Mac was raised in a small town in Alabama, moved to Georgia in high school, and married his high school sweetheart. He played in garage bands for several years with friend Mark Lee before eventually forming the internationally acclaimed band Third Day. Mac is an artist and songwriter who is well respected by his peers and has written a library of songs that explore everything from the glory and majesty of God to the depth of His love and forgiveness. When not serving as a front man, Mac is also a producer and collaborator on projects such as the critically acclaimed Glory Revealed records. Deeply committed to his family, Mac is the husband of Aimee and the proud father of Scout, Cash, Camie Love, and Emmanuel. The Powells live in Marietta, Georgia.

INTERVIEWER: Describe the experience or moment when your calling became evident to you.

MAC POWELL: A lot of it comes down to your definition of calling, meaning "what I feel like God wants me to do with my life." I in no way want to minimize or belittle that idea, but first there was the original "calling" to spend time and to be with Him. I grew up in Clanton, Alabama, which was a small town where everyone knew each other. My family and I attended a Baptist church and even at a young age of eight or nine years old, I realized I believed in God . . . I believed that He's the Creator . . . I believed in His Son Jesus Christ, that He gave His life for me . . . and I believed I was a sinner that needed to be saved. So at an early age I realized my calling of needing God and that He actually wanted to have a relationship with me. While I didn't understand the depths of what it means to follow Jesus, and am still wrestling with that today, I knew whatever I decided to do, my life was devoted to Him. My senior year in high school was a time when my life was awakened to the grace and love of God in a way that had never happened before. It was then that my "first calling" motivated me to explore my "calling" to make music in a band called Third Day.

INTERVIEWER: After you sensed this calling what were your first actions? How did your life change immediately after your calling?

MAC POWELL: It seemed that God had prepared me throughout my life because I had grown up in a home that placed a high priority on music. We listened to music all the time, both my parents played guitar and sang, and I spent many of my early years singing in the church choir. So I had the opportunity to be in front of audiences, albeit, small audiences, early on. Throughout my life God has prepared me, as well as given me the desire and talent to make music and sing in front of people. The desire to write songs has existed within me from an early age when I would write songs about video games, playing baseball, and things like that. I think for the most part our calling comes from our own desires that God has given us for things we enjoy doing in life. God wired me to do what I do and so His calling on my life is consistent with how He has created me.

INTERVIEWER: As you look back, was there a particular moment or memory that shaped you or changed the trajectory of your life?

MAC POWELL: I remember my junior year in high school getting invited to sing at this outdoor revival-type event. At that point I wasn't completely living for God, even though I was singing in my home church. There was something different about this event and I realized the contradiction between what I was singing and the manner in which I was living. Through that experience I made the decision to never be a hypocrite on stage. My journey really changed after that, and the songs I sang started becoming the testimony of my life. Immediately following that experience I started trying to write songs. I was in a garage band in high school, and realized that I was singing some things I didn't need to sing and hanging out places I didn't need to be. I soon made the decision to quit the band, which was really hard; I'd always wanted to be in a rock band, and now that I finally was in one I felt God was asking me to quit. Even though it was a struggle at first, I realized my love for God was consuming my love for a dream I had for my own life. By making that decision, God replaced my dream with His dream for my life, which was obviously bigger and grander than I could have ever imagined. Right away I started writing songs about my faith, and one of the first songs I ever wrote was entitled: "You're Never Alone in Solitude." I was probably seventeen or eighteen, and even though the song wasn't very good I remember purposely thinking, *This is what I want do with my life.*

INTERVIEWER: When did you get a vision for your present form of ministry, Third Day?

MAC POWELL: About a week after I quit the garage band, my friend Mark Lee suggested we start a Christian band where we share our faith through our songs. Even though I didn't know much about that or what it would exactly look like, I knew it was something I wanted to do. We played together for about a year and then were playing together at a youth group when we met David our drummer, and Tai our bass player, who was in that youth group, and started making music with them. We played our very first show together at a little church outside of my hometown of Clanton, Alabama. That first show there were no more than fifty to sixty people who showed up, but there was just something about it, and that is when I thought, *Okay, now this is for real and we're doing this.* So early on in the life of our band we were playing in front of small crowds and had only recorded a few demos.

INTERVIEWER: What has been the biggest shift as you look back on the landscape of your journey? How has your calling matured or evolved?

MAC POWELL: People always ask if we ever thought we could have the success that we've had. And the answer is both yes and no. After I graduated and moved out of my parents' house to Marietta, Georgia, and the band was together, we had the great dreams of playing outside of the state and even outside of the country. Then our music started getting played and listened to all over the place, and we hadn't even started playing shows outside of the Atlanta area. This was a big sign to us. I remember a DJ called for a radio interview somewhere up in the Northeast and I thought, *How in the world does this guy know about us?* So the big shift for me was when we realized how much bigger this thing could be than we had ever planned. I guess it comes back to the realization of God's dream for your life. Another shift took place with the *Offerings* record. Even though we had great success from the beginning, there was a big jump when we put out that record. It was our first worship album and really was a combination of songs from our previous records that were the more worship-focus songs. We discovered that our audience's favorite part of the show was when we would play worship songs. Prior to *Offerings* there weren't a lot of worship records in the mainstream of Christian music, so it really seemed to be a project that ministered to a lot of people as well as caused our band to evolve in how we minister.

INTERVIEWER: Who have been the most influential people (*that you know personally*) in your journey? How did they influence or impact you?

MAC POWELL: That's a really tough one because there are so many people who have influenced us and have also helped us through the years. Many great artists, like Rich Mullins, Steven Curtis Chapman, and Michael W. Smith, who we were able to spend time with and be encouraged by. So many great artists not only showed us how to be better at what we do, but also demonstrated how to be a person of integrity. But the biggest influence on us has been Nigel James, who is our road pastor and has been with us since '98. He has brought friendship, encouragement, accountability, and spiritual discipline to the band. He not only helps us stay close to God but close as a band. And he truly fulfills the role as pastor because there are times when you feel like there is no one to talk with and yet he has always been both an ear and a voice. It's kind of backwards, but the most influential person in Third Day is also the least known. He is an amazing guy and we are so grateful for him! Tai and I were discussing this the other day. We may go to church ten Sundays out of the year. But we get to have church all the time since church is God's people coming together, sharing the Word, sharing the song, encouraging one another, praying, and helping other people. So on the road, we have our own church and Nigel is the pastor of that church. That's not an excuse to not go to church, but that's what we have.

INTERVIEWER: But you're putting it in the budget, you're making room for him on the bus, you're having him around, which sometimes can be a logistical and financial inconvenience.

MAC POWELL: Very much so . . . it's not always an easy decision to make but we made that decision early on because we know who we are. We know that if we don't have that someone to pastor us, then we set ourselves up for failure. I would also add that part of the reason he is such a great influencer is that he knows he's not the decision maker. He's very good about not telling us what to do, but helping to bring us to a point where we're the ones who make the right decision.

INTERVIEWER: What is the greatest single theological theme that seems to come out in your songs?

MAC POWELL: There are a couple of themes that continually rise to the surface. First would be the abundant life that can only be found through Christ. Sometimes it is hard to express that concept because it can be so misunderstood. For example, some would think it means "I'm going to drive a better car and have a bigger house," and if anything, that gets in the way of having the abundant life. Secondly, the idea of daily surrender, knowing my sins are forgiven and that I have a home in heaven. I don't ever want to miss a daily relationship with Christ experiencing a hope, peace, and joy that can only come from surrendering my life to Him. Obviously these two themes overlap onto each other, which is demonstrated in one of my favorite Scriptures when Jesus said, "I've come to this world to give you life, and to give it to you abundantly in its fullest."

I think too many people in the church are Christians yet are missing out on the abundant life that Christ has. They have eternal life, but they're missing out on the abundant life that we have here on this earth. The desire of my heart is to share that message with people. I feel like my calling is mostly to people in the church. A lot of people question why we make Christian music, saying that we are only preaching to people in the choir. Well, I was in the choir and I can tell you we needed to be preached to. I want to help people avoid merely a cultural Christianity and have a real relationship with God. That is my heart and musically tied in to that has been the message of Third Day. Most of our songs deal with the subject of hope and hopefully we are encouraging people towards a healthy relationship with God.

INTERVIEWER: How have you stayed focused on what God has called you to do? What role have spiritual disciplines, such as Bible study, played in keeping that focus?

MAC POWELL: It is interesting that we are talking about calling because I have had so many people who have come up to us at our concerts and said thank you for being obedient to what God has called you to do. I think a lot of times people can see success and assume they're successful because they are doing what God has called them to do. But there could be times when God is calling me to do something different and I refuse, yet the band still does well. There are many people out there who are successful but they're not doing what they're supposed to be doing. In other words, calling is a matter of the heart. So to stay focused, the message I share has to be the message I live. I can't just share something that I think other people ought to do. I must be daily seeking God in prayer, in His Word, in decision making, and surround myself with other believers. I believe there are three witnesses to God. There's His Spirit, which speaks to us in our hearts, minds, and our spirits. There's the Word of God that we can read and know His explicit moral will for our lives. Finally there is the body of Christ, the church. All three witnesses are the main sources of revelation that keep you in your calling. We should regularly ask ourselves if we are in the place or doing the thing that God has called us to . . . because it could certainly change. But again, the only way to know the answer to that is to focus on the fact that I am first called to Him and what I do with my life is an offshoot of that. Moses is a great example of how our calling can change or evolve. I can tell you I am not going to be seventy-five years old on stage in a rock band . . . but I will be seventy-five and still called to know Jesus every day. I feel like God is preparing me for something else besides Third Day, and it could be bigger, brighter, and better; or it could be the opposite and no one would ever hear from me again . . . and if it is what He has for me then it is ultimately better.

INTERVIEWER: With your permission I would like to ask some light questions that have some pretty short answers . . . beginning with what is your favorite sports team?

MAC POWELL: Alabama Crimson Tide.

INTERVIEWER: Favorite movie?

MAC POWELL: *To Kill a Mockingbird.*

INTERVIEWER: Greatest band ever?

MAC POWELL: Beatles.

INTERVIEWER: Dream vacation?

MAC POWELL: Secluded island in Hawaii.

INTERVIEWER: Favorite hobby?

MAC POWELL: Music.

INTERVIEWER: Favorite TV show as a kid?

MAC POWELL: *Superfriends*.

INTERVIEWER: If you were on a deserted island and allowed a certain number of books, what would be your top five?

MAC POWELL: *How to Build a Life Raft, Living on a Desert Island for Dummies, Celebration of Disciplines* by Richard Foster, and *History of the World*.

INTERVIEWER: If your own child were graduating from high school, what would be the main piece of advice you would offer to them on graduation night?

MAC POWELL: Do what you love and live with Jesus.

CHAPTER 21

A CONVERSATION WITH

Dr. Howard Hendricks

Although a shy, soft-spoken man, Dr. Howard Hendricks is a spiritual giant in the eyes of many. In his fifty-two years as a professor at Dallas Theological Seminary, Dr. Hendricks has had the opportunity to help shape the minds of some of this generation's foremost evangelical icons—Tony Evans, David Jeremiah, Bruce Wilkinson, Erwin Lutzer, and Charles Swindoll, to name a few. Respectfully called "Prof" by most of his current and former students, his life has been one of consistency and integrity and has impacted his students just as much as, if not more than, any words he has ever spoken in the classroom. The influence he has had on so many lives is mainly birthed out of the energy and effort he puts into developing real relationships, and using his time with his students for encouragement, inspiration, and true mentorship.

INTERVIEWER: Describe the experience or moment when your calling became evident to you?

DR. HENDRICKS: As a teenager I recognized that I had natural leadership skills. One example of an early recognition of this gifting occurred while playing with a neighbor girl. She was a child who was a year younger and I was delighted in "teaching her." Then in a church group I recognized that I had motivational abilities, which only helped me gain self-confidence.

INTERVIEWER: After you sensed this calling, what were your first actions? How did your life change immediately after your calling?

DR. HENDRICKS: I had plans to go to med school but could not escape an urge to prepare for ministry. So I set my sights towards preparing for vocational Christian ministry.

INTERVIEWER: When did you get a vision for your present ministry?

DR. HENDRICKS: After college and graduate school I served as pastor of a church and was asked to teach a class two days a week in a nearby city. In the classroom I discovered complete fulfillment. I knew I had to move toward full-time teaching.

INTERVIEWER: What has been the biggest shift as you look back on the landscape of your journey? How has your calling matured or evolved?

DR. HENDRICKS: With a clear goal and conviction that teaching was my "sweet spot," I pursued further graduate work and was soon offered full-time work as an instructor. The positive feedback from students and my own sense of satisfaction confirmed that I had made the right choice.

INTERVIEWER: Who has been the most influential person in your journey? How did they influence or impact you?

DR. HENDRICKS: Out of many mentors, Dr. Merrill Tenney, a professor at Wheaton College, impacted me more deeply with his unmatched scholarship and demonstration of academic discipline. He pushed me hard, but also lavished on me positive affirmation and encouragement.

INTERVIEWER: What is the greatest single theological theme that seems to come out in your sermons and books?

DR. HENDRICKS: The power of the Holy Spirit reproducing change through discipleship.

INTERVIEWER: How have you stayed focused on what God has called you to do? What role have spiritual disciplines, such as Bible study, played in keeping that focus?

DR. HENDRICKS: My focus has been my students; watching change take place in them has invigorated my own desire to study the Word, to read widely in my own field of endeavor, and to spend much time in prayer for my students.

INTERVIEWER: What makes you laugh?

DR. HENDRICKS: Slapstick comedy always amused me as a child, such as the Marx Brothers. I suppose incongruity, which stretches into all of life, makes for good humor, which I have used characteristically in public speaking for years.

INTERVIEWER: What has been your greatest temptation?

DR. HENDRICKS: Born with Type A temperament, I tend toward nonstop activity. I am still trying to learn the value of "Sabbath day rest." Without it, I have learned, orderliness becomes slipshod and overall energy is compromised.

INTERVIEWER: What resource has had the most significant impact on your life?

DR. HENDRICKS: Professors in college and seminary, I could name half a dozen, still speak to my thought processes, but also interaction with non-believers has been a huge stimulus. One example is when I served as chaplain for the Dallas Cowboys for almost a decade. Also, numerous books have influenced me.

INTERVIEWER: If you were on a deserted island and allowed a certain number of books, what would be your top five?

DR. HENDRICKS: Wow, that is a difficult decision, but probably: *He That Is Spiritual* by Louis Sperry Chafer; *The Training of the Twelve* by A. B. Bruce; *The Gospel of John* by Merrill C. Tenney; *The Knowledge of the Holy* by A. W. Tozer; and *How to Read a Book* by Mortimer J. Adler. And if I could add one more to the list it would be *The Daily Drucker* by Peter F. Drucker.

INTERVIEWER: What is the single most influential piece of advice some-one ever gave you?

DR. HENDRICKS: Lie low and exalt Christ.

INTERVIEWER: Is there one particular quote that has always stuck with you?

DR. HENDRICKS: "He is no fool who gives what he cannot keep to gain what he cannot lose" by Jim Elliott.

INTERVIEWER: What concerns you most about the church right now?

DR. HENDRICKS: There seems to be a disappearance of theology from preaching along with a conforming to secular culture. Another concern would be vacuous [meaning empty-headed or unintelligent] worship and a lack of clear-eyed leadership and purpose.

INTERVIEWER: What encourages you most? What is the church doing right?

DR. HENDRICKS: The power of the Holy Spirit present in community and some excellent music.

INTERVIEWER: When I say the word *accountability*, what or who comes to mind? Why?

DR. HENDRICKS: The Lord holds me responsible, not pleasing people, but obeying Him.

INTERVIEWER: On the following subjects, what nuggets of wisdom come to mind that you would want to pass on to this next generation desiring to serve God, beginning with marriage?

DR. HENDRICKS: An earthly picture of Christ and His church. Marriage is the greatest privilege when Christ is central in the relationship.

INTERVIEWER: Raising children?

DR. HENDRICKS: They are a gift from God. Learn to know each one, understand them intelligently, and love them unconditionally.

INTERVIEWER: Finances?

DR. HENDRICKS: I have learned that everything belongs to God and we are simply stewards. Therefore everything we spend is an investment in something . . . always invest in eternity.

INTERVIEWER: Living healthy?

DR. HENDRICKS: We are responsible to care for this temple where the Holy Spirit dwells, which means proper physical food/exercise/rest. For my mind there must be proper mental intake and exercise, as well as for spiritual food from the Word of God, coupled with prayer and well-chosen fellowship with other believers.

INTERVIEWER: Communication?

DR. HENDRICKS: Be aware that everything comes out of my inner passions. God uses what He has gifted me with, but I must think carefully. Every message must be fresh, never stop learning, and always allow yourself to be evaluated for future improvement.

INTERVIEWER: If you could give just one piece of advice to this generation, what would it be?

DR. HENDRICKS: You have only one opportunity to live today. The past is unchangeable and the future is uncertain. Make today count for eternity.

INTERVIEWER: If you would permit me I would like to ask some light questions that have some pretty short answers . . . beginning with, what is your favorite sports team?

DR. HENDRICKS: Dallas Cowboys (as it was under Coach Tom Landry).

INTERVIEWER: Favorite movie?

DR. HENDRICKS: *The Ten Commandments* by Cecil B. DeMille.

INTERVIEWER: Greatest band ever?

DR. HENDRICKS: That would have to be a great drummer from the 1940s named Gene Krupta.

INTERVIEWER: Dream vacation?

DR. HENDRICKS: Hawaii.

INTERVIEWER: Favorite hobby?

DR. HENDRICKS: I played college baseball for Wheaton University when I was in college, so I guess that would have to be my favorite hobby.

INTERVIEWER: Favorite TV show as a kid?

DR. HENDRICKS: We only had radio, but my favorite program was *The Lone Ranger*.

INTERVIEWER: If your own child were graduating from high school, what would be the main piece of advice you would offer to them on graduation night?

DR. HENDRICKS: Take an honest look at yourself and determine your giftedness. Make every effort to attend the best school available to train for your future. Pray consistently that God will develop you and call you where He wants you to be. Discipline yourself to find where you fit best. Choose mentors carefully and know that you always stand on the shoulders of others who have gone before you. Learn to improve your people skills by studying the life of Christ. Note particularly His humility and reliance on history, as well as His sacrificial giving to others. The best things in life are not things, but people. Invest accordingly.

CHAPTER 22

A CONVERSATION WITH

Dr. Charles Ryrie

Born in 1925, Dr. Charles C. Ryrie is an acclaimed theologian and author of many books on theology and Christian living. In addition to this, he is editor of the highly popular Ryrie Study Bible. *For many years he served as professor of theology and dean of doctoral studies at Dallas Theological Seminary and as president and professor at Philadelphia College of Bible, now Philadelphia Biblical University.*

———

INTERVIEWER: Describe the experience or moment when your calling became evident to you.

DR. CHARLES RYRIE: There was a specific time when I became concerned about my future and all the decisions that accompany such thoughts. I sought out a well-known Bible teacher, who was speaking in a nearby city, and he gave me time one night after he was done speaking. We met in his hotel room, and after some discussion I gave my life to the Lord.

I also mark that night as the time I was called to full-time service. So for me it was simultaneous in that I gave my life to Christ and felt called into a lifetime of service.

INTERVIEWER: After this calling became evident to you, what were some of the first actions? How did your life change immediately after this?

DR. CHARLES RYRIE: Nothing spectacular changed about my life because I was in college. I simply applied myself to studying, taking exams, and finishing courses. I soon began to realize that I needed to go to seminary. In the right time and sequence, I made that application to the seminary without knowing what that might lead to. I really never felt at that point that I should or should not be a pastor or evangelist or teacher or whatever. What I did know is that the next step was to get training.

INTERVIEWER: And after you received a theological education, what along your journey helped you get a vision for your present form of ministry?

DR. CHARLES RYRIE: I know this is not the kind of answer you would expect or even want, but I didn't know what I was going to do when I finished seminary. I had several opportunities; one was assistant pastor, one was in youth ministry, and one was to go on with more education. Even though more education sounded like a great idea, at the end of it I still didn't know what kind of ministry I was supposed to be a part of. Then I got an inquiry from a Christian college to teach, but the offer had one stipulation, that for at least the first year I would have to teach mathematics along with Bible courses. I felt this to be an open door of opportunity because I had majored in math in college. That was my first teaching opportunity, and that's where I've been ever since, at schools teaching.

INTERVIEWER: As you look back on the landscape of your journey thus far, how has your calling matured or evolved?

DR. CHARLES RYRIE: Well, there is a very natural evolution or progression because every time you get a new course it requires one to study more, and when you teach courses you have taught before, there is still the responsibility to review and refresh. Even though I am a teacher I have to keep studying. I'm sure that's true for the pastor who has to preach two or three times a week. In other words you cannot ever coast. I look back on some of the courses I've taught or sermons I preach and have thought they weren't very good at times, but I have tried to the best of my ability to continually study the Scriptures. Even now when I have new opportunities to preach, I try to prepare new sermons because I never want to be guilty of just trying to coast.

INTERVIEWER: Who have been the most influential people (*that you know personally*) in your journey? How did they influence or impact you?

DR. CHARLES RYRIE: The founder of the Dallas Seminary, Lewis Sperry Chafer, was teaching when I was a student, and he had a very profound influence on all of us who were students in those days. And there were other teachers throughout my formal education who had differing influences. I also think of a retired, not by choice, missionary named Isaac Page who had to leave China when missionaries were kicked out. He influenced me in a different way because he was a lover of books. He would come often to speak in chapel or he would write letters to me, and in our correspondence and his messages he constantly referenced books. I have to credit him for putting me on to good books that I found to be the beginnings and foundation of my own library.

INTERVIEWER: What is the greatest single theological theme that seems to come out in your sermons and books?

DR. CHARLES RYRIE: While I have not consciously picked this theme, underlying much of my communication efforts would be the inerrancy of the Bible and how it impacts our lives. If you believe in the inerrancy of the Scriptures, then it will impact all you do. I would like to think that inerrancy is the underlying emphasis and foundation for all ministers, but it simply isn't true.

INTERVIEWER: Practically speaking, how have you stayed focused on what God has called you to do? What role have spiritual disciplines played in your life?

DR. CHARLES RYRIE: The usual deadlines that come with, in my case, preparing courses and getting ready to teach next semester. I would add preparing to speak at a conference in the summer or some other opportunity. Practically speaking, it is the external demands of ministry and being willing to do whatever comes down the pike. As far as spiritual disciplines, memorizing Scripture has been very instrumental in helping me stay focused. Unfortunately memorizing Scripture has become kind of a lost cause with some generations. Maybe that is due to the multiplicity of translations or maybe it is due to laziness, but nevertheless it is a discipline that need be resurrected.

INTERVIEWER: What makes you laugh?

DR. CHARLES RYRIE: I like a good joke, bantering with friends, a string of puns, and an old television show entitled *Hogan's Heroes*.

INTERVIEWER: What resource has had the most significant impact on your life?

DR. CHARLES RYRIE: I think in the latter years and in the latter part of my public ministry, I would say regular exercise.

INTERVIEWER: If you were on a deserted island, and you were only allowed five books, what would they be?

DR. CHARLES RYRIE: Well, I'm going to give you kinds of books rather than necessarily specific titles: First would be a good study Bible like *The Ryrie Study Bible*. Grace and humility should forbid my telling you that, but the reason I list it is not to self-promote but it gives you, in one resource, so many other aids. Second, a good theology book. Third, a good Bible commentary. Fourth, a good complete concordance. Fifth, a good Bible dictionary.

INTERVIEWER: What is the single most influential piece of advice someone ever gave you?

DR. CHARLES RYRIE: Well, I don't know the origin of this but: *Be willing to do anything, anytime, anywhere for God*. I found this is advice that we need to take at every stage of life. This idea of "be willing" needs to be the filter for all of life's decisions both big and small. Now there are limitations to this. I can't physically do certain things because of my age. For example, on my first trip to a mission field I had to spend two days on horseback getting to the place where we were going to serve. Obviously, I can't do that now. But I still have decisions to make and I try to keep in mind anything, anytime, anywhere. My observation is, and I know it is risky to say something like this, that we really talk about dedication, and most Christians are using "selective dedication." That is, they select what they want to give to God and they keep the rest; in other words, they'll take care of the rest. I also have observed a lot of "negotiating dedication," which says I'll do this *if* God will do that. Whether it is selecting what you want God to control or negotiating the terms of His control, both are extremely risky. Basically, these two distorted views of dedication reject the *anything, anytime, anywhere* principle.

INTERVIEWER: What concerns you most about the church right now?

DR. CHARLES RYRIE: I believe the greatest need in the church is for dedicated Christians. Individuals who are willing to hold nothing back and are totally committed to following Christ.

INTERVIEWER: Along those same lines, what encourages you about the church right now? What is the church doing right?

DR. CHARLES RYRIE: Well, certainly there is a lot more knowledge or information available. I'm old and from the B.C. era, which stands for "before computers" or "before cell phones." Because of these luxuries there is a whole lot of information a person can get. Even though the Internet has not replaced hard copies of books and good radio and TV programs, it still offers quite a bit of information. Another positive about the church right now is the type of questions that are being asked. When I sit in a Q & A session and field questions, they are much deeper and less simplistic than they used to be. I interpret that to mean that the one asking the question has some deep concerns and is wrestling with deep issues.

INTERVIEWER: When I say the word *accountability*, what or who comes to mind? Why?

DR. CHARLES RYRIE: First John 1:9, the Lord. That is where primary accountability takes place, and in a good sense, it is the most challenging and frightening kind. When I look back there were people who crossed my path who offered serious help at times when I needed it. This was an answer to prayer and I believe it fits into the accountability discussion. People will come into your life for certain seasons and certain reasons. I would also add, and this is pretty hard for this generation because they're so busy, learn what the Scriptures mean when it says to pray without ceasing. There are a number of ways to wrap your mind around this discipline of capturing the moments at hand in prayer. But the idea is that it becomes a habit of looking for those moments. And at that point I believe we will begin to understand praying without ceasing. The way to accomplish this begins with being willing to turn some things off, whether that is a radio or cell phone in the car or whatever, in an effort to search out those times to pray.

INTERVIEWER: On the following subjects, what nuggets of wisdom come to mind that you would want to pass on to this next generation desiring to serve God, beginning with marriage?

DR. CHARLES RYRIE: Don't panic if God keeps you single.

INTERVIEWER: On raising children?

DR. CHARLES RYRIE: Do your best, pray, and you will discover the formulas don't always work.

INTERVIEWER: On finances?

DR. CHARLES RYRIE: Flee and fear debts, both personal and organizational.

INTERVIEWER: On living healthy?

DR. CHARLES RYRIE: Exercise, because being overweight, in most cases, is a sin.

INTERVIEWER: On communication?

DR. CHARLES RYRIE: A well-known writer told me years ago, "Have something to say and say it clearly." And that applies to writing, teaching, preaching, or any type of communication.

INTERVIEWER: With your permission I would like to ask some light questions that have some pretty short answers . . . beginning with what is your favorite sports team?

DR. CHARLES RYRIE: It used to be the Dallas Cowboys.

INTERVIEWER: Favorite movie?

DR. CHARLES RYRIE: It has been a long time since I have been to a movie. I typically don't see them unless I am on a plane traveling. But there was one movie called *Chariots of Fire* that has been my favorite.

INTERVIEWER: Dream vacation?

DR. CHARLES RYRIE: Going on a cruise. One doesn't have to pack and then unpack or wonder where you are going to eat. It is a great way to relax and vacation.

INTERVIEWER: Favorite hobby?

DR. CHARLES RYRIE: Sitting down and reading an old book.

INTERVIEWER: If your own child were graduating from high school, what would be the main piece of advice you would offer to them on graduation night?

DR. CHARLES RYRIE: Be closely connected to the Lord in various ways. That could mean connecting with Christian groups on campus and a good local church. If it were my child graduating I would want them to be connected and to do their own consistent Bible reading.

CHAPTER 23

A CONVERSATION WITH

Scott Dawson

Scott Dawson is committed to sharing the gospel. Through the Scott Dawson Evangelistic Association, hundreds of thousands every year hear the life-changing message of Christ through camps, conferences, and festivals. While an anointed communicator, Scott feels that his calling has developed from being a platform speaker to being the one who facilitates large groups of people being exposed to the message of salvation. His vision is to see crowds of people hear the gospel, receive Christ, and then be assimilated back into the local church for accountability and discipleship. Scott and his wife, Tara, live in Birmingham, Alabama, with their two children, Hunter and Hope.

INTERVIEWER: Describe the experience or moment when your calling became evident to you?

SCOTT DAWSON: My calling was birthed out of a passion to share my faith and a concern for those around me. There wasn't necessarily a "Damascus road light appearing before me," but rather a building burden that life is not about you. When I awakened to the idea that Christianity is not about what you can get but what or who you can give, I started sharing my faith and then the Lord opened up opportunities. And out of that it became obvious to me that He was calling me into vocational ministry. I remember making this public at my church and thinking everyone would come up and pat me on the back and my pastor would take time with me, but none of that happened. I went down during the invitation and told the pastor I felt like the Lord was calling me and he said, "That's great, we'll talk later." And the service closed and he walked out. I tried it again the next Sunday only with the same results. I didn't try that again and instead I called his office and made an appointment. I guess about a month later we met and I said, "Look, the Lord is calling me and I really don't know what I'm doing or where I'm going, but it feels like His hand is upon me and if you don't help me, I will talk to somebody else who will." His response was a great piece of advice: "You know, I have people all the time that think it would be great to go into the ministry, and they get all emotionally worked up, but a calling is something you can't get away from . . . it is something that captures your heart's attention." From that moment on we became dear friends because I understood what he was doing. It turned out to be one of the greatest lessons about calling I ever learned. Calling is not based on the whim or even on a moment; it is a direction.

INTERVIEWER: After you sensed this calling, what were your first actions? How did your life change immediately after your calling?

SCOTT DAWSON: I immediately felt this sense of release because my life now had direction. I now had the foundation upon which I could build a plan for my life. I was very grateful for the leadership books from guys like John Maxwell and Stephen Covey that were coming out dealing with the leadership principle Begin with the end in mind. So I started dreaming the dream of where I wanted to be . . . what would I do if I knew I could not fail? In fact, I had been specifically studying the life of Paul, and his calling was to get to Rome. So through studying his life I found my "Rome." I knew God was calling me to be an evangelist. With calling, the Bible may not always give us a step-by-step process but it will always give direction.

INTERVIEWER: When did you get a vision for Scott Dawson Evangelistic Association, which serves as an umbrella to several great ministry events like Safe at Home, Strength to Stand conferences, and Stadium Fest?

SCOTT DAWSON: The association was birthed out of necessity. I wanted to have integrity and be above reproach with the finances, so by creating an association I wasn't putting the money in my own pocket. We also needed the structure an association provided so we could organize and facilitate conference experiences. But the main vision for our organization came when I was sitting in a hotel on the Gulf Coast after an event being so frustrated that more people weren't coming to Christ. In that moment I had a thought that has determined the direction for our ministry ever since: *Wherever people are, the gospel must be shared.* So if they are online, at a baseball game, in a golf tournament, or wherever . . . the gospel needs to be shared. Acts 2:37 says, "Peter saw the crowd and he addressed them." So many times, we see the crowd and we give an excuse why not to address them.

INTERVIEWER: What has been the biggest shift as you look back on the landscape of your journey? How has your calling matured or evolved?

SCOTT DAWSON: The biggest shift in my ministry is when I realized that my true calling as an evangelist is not to be a platform speaker. My true calling is to get the gospel outside of the local church into the community confronting the church with the claims of Christ and then assimilating the new converts back in the local church. While that strategy does involve a platform, it is more than just showing up and then packing up and going on to the next city.

INTERVIEWER: Who have been the most influential people (*that you know personally*) in your journey? How did they influence or impact you?

SCOTT DAWSON: Dr. Jay Strack and Luis Palau have influenced me greatly through the years as both friends and mentors. Dr. Lewis Drummond, who is now in heaven, because he really drilled into me what is actually the gospel. The gospel is not preaching against sin but is preaching the claims of Christ. He helped to refine and shape my calling. I have discovered that when we're young, we just have a glimpse of what God wants us to do. Mentors are not necessarily to be looked for; rather they are to be birthed in your life. Every time I have tried to find a mentor I have been greatly disappointed. But every time God has birthed a mentor in my life, they have been used to shape my calling.

INTERVIEWER: What is the greatest single theological theme that seems to come out in your sermons and books?

SCOTT DAWSON: John 3:16.

INTERVIEWER: What roles have spiritual disciplines played in helping you stay focused?

SCOTT DAWSON: Daily Scripture reading. Right now in my devotional time I am reading through some classical commentaries written by John Calvin, Martin Luther, John Wesley, and George Whitefield. I am doing this because I've read the Scriptures so many times and I want a fresh approach.

INTERVIEWER: What has been your greatest temptation?

SCOTT DAWSON: My greatest temptation has been to take shortcuts in ministry. For example, early on in my ministry I had the opportunity to take a staff position at a church. I really struggled with the opportunity because it would have offered financial security, but it wasn't consistent with my calling. I ended up turning the opportunity down, and looking back I am so glad I did. Life is too short to take shortcuts, and therefore it is certainly too short just to get a job that has nothing to do with your passion or calling.

INTERVIEWER: What resource has had the most significant impact on your life?

SCOTT DAWSON: The Cove up in the Carolinas, mainly because it is a place to go and see where a hero of the faith, Dr. Billy Graham, walked and was refreshed.

INTERVIEWER: If you were on a deserted island and allowed a certain number of books, what would be your top five?

SCOTT DAWSON: The Bible, a good dictionary, *Born Again* by Chuck Colson, *The Soul Winner* by Charles Spurgeon, and a collection of Spurgeon's sermons.

INTERVIEWER: What is the single most influential piece of advice someone ever gave you?

SCOTT DAWSON: Live your life so that if an investigative reporter called you and said he needed five minutes of your time, you wouldn't be scared to death of what he found out.

INTERVIEWER: Is there one particular quote that has always stuck with you?

SCOTT DAWSON: When Milton Berle, the legendary comedian, was young and just getting started, a friend said to him, "You'll never make it, you might as well give up." Milton Berle later commented on that experience by saying, "I had to do something, I had to find new friends." I have always remembered that because bad company always corrupts good habits. And if you are around people who are always down on you, then you have to make the decision to separate yourselves from them.

INTERVIEWER: What concerns you most about the church right now?

SCOTT DAWSON: We have become lethargically apathetic. The greatest challenge of the church is not the enemy from outside the walls but the indifference within the walls. I am afraid we are praising Jesus with our lips but our hearts are far from Him.

INTERVIEWER: What encourages you most? What is the church doing right?

SCOTT DAWSON: There is a holy desperation that is starting to take place within the church to see a move of God.

INTERVIEWER: When I say the word *accountability*, what or who comes to mind? Why?

SCOTT DAWSON: I think of the Modesto Manifesto, which was when Dr. Billy Graham, Cliff Barrows, George Beverly Shea, and Grady Wilson got together in Modesto, California, and articulated the non-compromising principles by which their ministry would operate. Number one, there would be financial integrity in all aspects of our life both in living and with the ministry. Two, there will be no emotional manipulative tactics given from the platform. Three, there will be sexual purity in their lives, to the extent they're never alone with any woman other than their wife. Fourth is that they would never talk bad about other ministers. When I think about accountability I always think of those four principles. As far as personal accountability, it all comes back to my relationship with Jesus because He is the only one I cannot fool. That doesn't mean that I don't have a group of guys I meet with; rather it means that I am willing to answer the questions they would ask before they would ask them.

INTERVIEWER: On the following subjects what nuggets of wisdom come to mind that you would want to pass on to this next generation desiring to serve God, beginning with marriage?

SCOTT DAWSON: Your wife must be your best friend and you can allow no one to come between you and your spouse. I will literally separate myself from anyone else for my wife. I have always said that it didn't matter where I may be, if I was needed at home I would be there. The past year my wife was diagnosed with a type of glaucoma where she was just hours away from losing her sight. I made the decision to come off the road for two months and just be home for her. Thankfully the Lord spared her sight and she is in great health today, but I wasn't going to allow anything to come between us.

INTERVIEWER: On raising children?

SCOTT DAWSON: Consistency is the hardest battle. This is one of the greatest lessons my kids taught me, and I'm still learning that more every day. I want them to listen to my voice, and not just when I am upset or correcting them, because I don't want them to think they are to only listen to their heavenly Father when they mess up or think He is mad.

INTERVIEWER: On finances?

SCOTT DAWSON: David Ramsey says, "Live like no one else so you can live like no one else." God is faithful to meet your needs. So be a good steward and trust His faithfulness.

INTERVIEWER: On living healthy?

SCOTT DAWSON: Being healthy is more than just physical appearance. While you can see an overweight person coming down the street, you can't see if someone has addictions or a variety of other issues like lust or stress. It is one thing to control your weight but be out of balance emotionally or spiritually. Having said that, I know what it is like to struggle with your weight. My freshman year I was 5'6" but I weighed 270 pounds. I understand that with physical appearance can come a lot of mental baggage of wondering, *Am I really going to be accepted?* You hear the remarks from other kids and the criticism hurts, and the way you try to overcome that is you lash out to those people. The turning point for me came in Louisville, Kentucky, one night when I was having dinner with Dr. Lewis Drummond and a gentleman by the name of Tom Phillips. Dr. Graham was speaking to commemorate the starting of the Billy Graham School for Evangelism at Southern Seminary. I was about to put some mashed potatoes in my mouth when Tom Philips looked across the table and said, "Scott, God wants to use you but He can't." And I was like, "Excuse me?" He said, "God wants to use you but He can't because you're not disciplined." And I looked over to Drummond and he dropped his head and said, "I've been trying to tell you that for three years, just not as boldly." I really studied about how to lose weight, and in four months I lost close to fifty pounds and I've now lost over seventy-five pounds and have kept it off as I try to live a healthy life.

INTERVIEWER: On communication?

SCOTT DAWSON: Right. There's the old phrase, "You can't do what I do, until you do what I did." I tell people I was the original member of the 3H club. Every time I spoke, I got a handshake, a hotdog, and a hundred dollars. I learned more about conferences when I had eighty-nine people there than I do when we have seventy-five hundred. I learned more about preaching when I was out in the middle of nowhere preaching to a small congregation, than I do when I'm speaking in the arena. Everybody wants a big crowd. Everyone wants to have that major instant success, but I would remind us of what Dr. Adrian Rogers said: "There is something called instant success. There is nothing called instant maturity." We're supposed to be Crock-Pots in a microwave society, and that is never more true than with the art of communication. I talk to young pastors in small churches and every one of them can't wait to get somewhere bigger and have a lot of influence. My thought is, *Man, do you know God has given you the best opportunity you'll ever have right now? You can fine-tune your communication skills. You can make mistakes and only have seventeen people hear it.* So when it comes to communication, don't rush it . . . let it simmer.

INTERVIEWER: If you could give just one piece of advice to this generation, what would it be?

SCOTT DAWSON: I would say don't let people just hear you talk about Jesus . . . let them understand you know Jesus. Be real. You may not be the next Billy Graham or Mother Teresa, but you can be a hero to the family of God by just being real.

INTERVIEWER: If you permit I would like to ask some light questions that have some pretty short answers . . . beginning with, what is your favorite sports team?

SCOTT DAWSON: Alabama Crimson Tide.

INTERVIEWER: Favorite movie?

SCOTT DAWSON: *White Christmas*.

INTERVIEWER: Greatest band ever?

SCOTT DAWSON: It is a tie between Lynyrd Skynyrd and Bing Crosby.

INTERVIEWER: Dream vacation?

SCOTT DAWSON: A week in the president's suite on a Disney cruise.

INTERVIEWER: Favorite hobby?

SCOTT DAWSON: Spending time with my kids.

INTERVIEWER: Favorite TV show as a kid?

SCOTT DAWSON: *SWAT*.

INTERVIEWER: If your own child were graduating from high school, what would be the main piece of advice you would offer to them on graduation night?

SCOTT DAWSON: Don't settle for good . . . choose God's best. Just don't settle.

CHAPTER 24

A CONVERSATION WITH

Chris Tomlin

Chris Tomlin of Grand Saline, Texas, has been called everything from a Grammy-nominated songwriter to a modern-day psalmist. TIME magazine even called Chris "arguably the most often sung artist in the world." If you ask Chris if he ever thought someone would one day reference him this way, his answer would be a resounding NO! Chris is the perfect example of how from humble beginnings God can use a servant's heart to do great things in His Kingdom. He wrote his first worship song at age fourteen, and has been writing ever since. He spent his earlier years leading worship at Dawson McAllister Youth Conferences, youth camps, and festivals, and has since been the prominent voice of worship at the Passion Conferences and the One Day World Tour. Drawing from his experience of being the lead worshiper at Woodlands United Methodist Church and Austin Stone, both in Texas, Chris has recently relocated to Atlanta, Georgia, to help lead worship at Passion City Church.

INTERVIEWER: Describe the experience or moment when your calling became evident to you.

CHRIS TOMLIN: I was thirteen years old . . . I can still remember it like it was this morning. Our church had taken some of the youth to a somewhat intensive training and discipleship week called Super Summer in Texas. On a Wednesday night with I guess about two thousand or so gathered in an auditorium singing worship songs to God, I began to sense something powerful. I really didn't know and couldn't explain what was going on inside of me, but for some reason I knew God was speaking to me. It was as if my spirit was on fire. I don't think the gathering had been going long before I couldn't even stay in the building. I ran out the back of the auditorium and hit my knees under a tree on the lawn. I began to pour out my heart to God. I remember telling God in the most honest and pure way I could that He had all of me and that I would follow wherever He sent me. That night was a marker for my life. To fully answer the question, the only thing evident that night for me was that I was answering the voice of God in my life. I had no idea what I would do or how I would do it . . . all I knew was that God was leading me to something much bigger than myself. I never prayed, "God, make me a singer, put me on a stage, let me travel around and make records." None of that was evident to me then. What I did have great clarity on was that I knew God was after my heart and I was awakened.

INTERVIEWER: After you sensed this calling what were your first actions? How did your life change immediately after your calling?

CHRIS TOMLIN: My first action was to tell my church that very next Sunday when I got home. I thought it was important to have accountability and witness to what was happening in my life. And I also knew I needed to have a place of support and guidance for the steps and road ahead now that my life was on a new path. I had a strong desire to make my days count for God and His Kingdom.

INTERVIEWER: When did you get a vision for your present ministry?

CHRIS TOMLIN: There was a man by the name of David Crain in my home church. He recorded albums and traveled around the country singing and speaking in churches, at conferences, etc. By watching him, I could see and begin to dream about someday having a similar ministry. In fact, David took me with him to one of his concerts when I was in high school. I kind of went as the roadie! In the middle of his concert, he stopped and asked me to come on stage and sing a couple of my songs. I was terrified but God used that one opportunity to open the floodgates for what was to come. I will always be so grateful to David for his faithfulness and influence on my life.

INTERVIEWER: When did you get a vision for your present ministry?

CHRIS TOMLIN: Interestingly, before I even knew the term "worship leader" or "worship music," God was uniquely gifting me in that way. When I had the opportunity I would sing, but I was never satisfied with the audience just listening to me. I wanted to somehow cause them to sing and worship God. So early on I began trying to write songs with that in mind; songs that would be singable and say something that helped inspire people to worship God.

INTERVIEWER: How has your calling matured or evolved?

CHRIS TOMLIN: My calling is continually maturing because I continually learn more of what it means to worship God and thus lead His people in that way. For me to truly lead people somewhere I need to know how to get there myself.

INTERVIEWER: Who have been the most influential people (*that you know personally*) in your journey? How did they influence or impact you?

CHRIS TOMLIN: I've been fortunate enough to have many people believe in me along the way. Undoubtedly the biggest influence in my life is my friend and pastor, Louie Giglio. I first met Louie when I was in college, and he was able to see past a guy who wasn't quite sure who he was or where he fit. We became fast friends and from that day on he began to pour his life into me. I've learned most of what I know about leading worship from him. Some of this I learned by listening to him, but mostly by watching him run the race.

INTERVIEWER: What is the greatest single theological theme that seems to come out in your songs?

CHRIS TOMLIN: There are really two themes that find their way into my songs. They are the "greatness" and the "grace" of God. I continue to see that if I can help people set their hearts and mind on these two themes, then consequently lives are reordered and changed. It's so easy for our gaze to fall on ourselves and our world begins to revolve around us. When we worship we are reminded that in truth, God is the creator and center of all things and holds us all together. Hopefully my songs continually point to this.

INTERVIEWER: How have you stayed focused on what God has called you to do? What role have spiritual disciplines, such as Bible study, played in keeping that focus?

CHRIS TOMLIN: From a young age, I grasped the need for a continued living out of my faith. I wholeheartedly agree that personal space and time alone with God is of utmost importance. To create space of solitude, open up the Scriptures, and listen to God . . . And I believe that the Bible teaches that our faith is not only personal but communal. The testimony of my life is the people God has placed in my life along the journey. The church and community of faith is what has kept me focused on what God has called me to do.

INTERVIEWER: What makes you laugh?

CHRIS TOMLIN: I laugh at good humorous stories and good storytellers. The real life stories are more hilarious than anything you could make up on your own. And as far as a movie, the first time I saw *Dumb and Dumber* I didn't think I was going to be able to breathe I was laughing so hard!

INTERVIEWER: What has been your greatest temptation?

CHRIS TOMLIN: If you would have told me I would have gone this far without being married, I would have thought you had lost your mind. I have so wanted to be married and have a family by now, but it hasn't happened yet. And in one sense, it has kept me in a place of humility and dependence on God. So what has been a "thorn in the side" has also been a shaping tool in my life.

INTERVIEWER: What resource (book, ministry, place, etc.) has had the most significant impact on your life?

CHRIS TOMLIN: First, of course, is the Bible. It is the source of my music. Secondly, it would be the Passion movement. Passion was the first platform that launched my songs to world. It is the place that God has done a significant work in my own life.

INTERVIEWER: If you were on a deserted island and allowed a certain number of books, what would be your top five?

CHRIS TOMLIN: My list would be: my grandfather's Bible, *Systematic Theology* by Wayne Grudem, A. W. Tozer on *The Almighty God*, a subscription to *Men's Journal* magazine, and *A Christmas Carol* by Charles Dickens.

INTERVIEWER: What is the single most influential piece of advice someone ever gave you?

CHRIS TOMLIN: It truly is better to give than receive.

INTERVIEWER: Is there one particular quote that has always stuck with you?

CHRIS TOMLIN: Actually there are two quotes: "Nothing ventured . . . nothing gained" (don't know the author) and "It is not the critic who counts: not the man who points out how the strong man stumbled or where the doer of deeds could have done better. The credit belongs to the man who actually is in the arena, whose face is marred by dust and sweat and blood; who strived valiantly; who errs, and comes short again and again and again because there is no effort without error and shortcoming; who does actually try to do the deed; who know the great enthusiasm, the great devotion and spends himself in a worthy cause; who, at the worst, if he fails, at least fails while daring greatly. Far better it is to dare mighty things, to win glorious triumphs even though checkered by failure, than to rank with those poor spirits who neither enjoy nor suffer much because they live in the gray twilight that knows neither victory nor defeat." [from Teddy Roosevelt]

INTERVIEWER: What concerns you most about the church right now?

CHRIS TOMLIN: That we are far more worried whether the people enjoy it or get anything from it than whether God actually enjoys or gets anything from it. When we come together truly to worship God and experience His presence, then the rest takes care of itself. Let us not forget that the church is God's idea and is for His glory.

INTERVIEWER: What encourages you most? What is the church doing right?

CHRIS TOMLIN: I see a renewed spirit in the church to reach and care for the least and last of these in the world.

INTERVIEWER: When I say the word *accountability*, what or who comes to mind? Why?

CHRIS TOMLIN: God is the first that comes to mind . . . At the end of the day we are accountable to God for what we did with the gifts and talents He gave us.

INTERVIEWER: On the following subjects what nuggets of wisdom come to mind that you would want to pass on to this next generation desiring to serve God, beginning with marriage?

CHRIS TOMLIN: I will hopefully let you know in the next book.

INTERVIEWER: On raising children?

CHRIS TOMLIN: Raising children is an opportunity to leave a legacy behind and it ultimately shows how selfish you are.

INTERVIEWER: On finances?

CHRIS TOMLIN: Be generous.

INTERVIEWER: On living healthy?

CHRIS TOMLIN: If you are healthy, you are rich!

INTERVIEWER: On communication?

CHRIS TOMLIN: Be yourself . . . and for me, I want to sing and write what people feel, what they want to say themselves.

INTERVIEWER: If you could give just one piece of advice to this generation, what would it be?

CHRIS TOMLIN: Live life to the full and take big risks for the glory of God.

INTERVIEWER: With your permission I would like to ask some light questions that have some pretty short answers . . . beginning with what is your favorite sports team?

CHRIS TOMLIN: Roger Federer (I know he is not a team, but he does his interviews in five languages . . . Come on . . .)

INTERVIEWER: Favorite movie?

CHRIS TOMLIN: *Seabiscuit.*

INTERVIEWER: Greatest band ever?

CHRIS TOMLIN: U2.

INTERVIEWER: Dream vacation?

CHRIS TOMLIN: The one I take with my future wife!

INTERVIEWER: Favorite hobby?

CHRIS TOMLIN: Tennis.

INTERVIEWER: Favorite TV show as a kid?

CHRIS TOMLIN: *Dukes of Hazzard.*

INTERVIEWER: If your own child were graduating from high school, what would be the main piece of advice you would offer to them on graduation night?

CHRIS TOMLIN: The most important thing is not what you do but it's who you are.

CHAPTER 25

A CONVERSATION WITH

Nick Ayers

What Nick Ayers lacks in age, he makes up for in maturity and ac-complishment. Although only in his twenties, he currently serves as ex-ecutive director of the Republican Governors Association (RGA), which is the premiere national campaign organization dedicated to the election and re-election of Republican governors. In his role as executive director, Ayers manages RGA operations, budget, and strategy, and works day-to-day with the White House, governors, and other key organizations. In addition to this, Ayers also serves on the board of Leading the Way, an international Christian ministry that broadcasts the gospel of Christ to over a hundred countries around the world. Nick is married to Jamie Floyd Ayers, and they reside in Alexandria, Virginia.

INTERVIEWER: Describe the experience or moment when your calling became evident to you.

NICK AYERS: Going back to my earliest memories as a child, I've always enjoyed politics. I was fascinated when my mother's diligence in canvassing our street and getting signatures resulted in a stop sign down the road from us—she did it because she was concerned for our safety. And whether it was being starstruck by our local mayor or state representative, or constantly watching the news as a child and teenager, I've always enjoyed learning, and now partaking in politics. The moment I recognized politics was slightly more than just an earthly fascination was when through a miraculous set of circumstances I met Sonny Perdue, who was considering a run for governor in the state of Georgia. I had worked very hard to pursue a career in banking and was a freshman in college at the time—so giving all that up to begin what seemed like a short-lived career in state politics was nuts by anyone's standard. However, I felt such a peace about the opportunity and the decision I made to dramatically divert the path I was on. Of course I was only resolute about the decision after spending much time in prayer.

INTERVIEWER: After you sensed this calling, what were your first actions? How did your life change immediately after your calling?

NICK AYERS: My life immediately changed afterwards because I moved from home, quit my job where I had been for four years, quit college as a freshman, took a pay cut, and moved in with a guy who I had only spent two or three days with who was also going on the campaign. I found myself a week later calling my mom and sister asking them to meet me at local airports and bring me fresh clothes, because once I joined the campaign we kicked it off—and I mean kicked it off. I would be on the road for weeks at a time with responsibilities I had no experience in dealing with.

INTERVIEWER: When did you get a vision for your present service?

NICK AYERS: I now better understand that politics is my ministry, because a few times I've considered leaving and pursuing what I believed to be some great opportunities. During those periods of time I had begun to believe politics isn't a place where God wants anyone long, or I believed I wasn't serving God well, but each time He made it abundantly clear I'm exactly where he wants me. And frankly, I've been surprised by that.

INTERVIEWER: What has been the biggest shift as you look back on the landscape of your journey? How has your calling matured or evolved?

NICK AYERS: God sincerely has a sense of humor. I've never been given a job in politics that I've been qualified for, and each time I go through the same somewhat silly cycle. I initially feel overwhelmed, anxious, and stressed out, but then learn that He's always equipped me with the skill set I need to get the job done—as long as I depend on Him.

INTERVIEWER: Who have been the most influential people in your journey? How did they influence or impact you?

NICK AYERS: One of the things I try to consistently thank God for is the strong men who have mentored me in my life. The scope is broad and it's hard to pin down just one, because I've been blessed by at least a half dozen who have impacted my faith, my career, and my personal life in such a positive way. Some were only briefly in my life, while others for a few years, and a few for a lifetime. I pray God will continue to bring those kind of men into my life and work through them. After all, iron sharpens iron, as one man sharpens another. Boy, that's been true in my life, thank God.

INTERVIEWER: How have you stayed focused on what God has called you to do? What role have spiritual disciplines, such as Bible study, played in keeping that focus?

NICK AYERS: Daily prayer and understanding my weaknesses helps me stay focused, although I'm terribly inconsistent. God has so much work to do on me. If there is one thing I understand well, it's simply that He can do what He needs or wants to do without Nick Ayers. He's only doing me a favor by letting me play along. When great men and women fall and become less relevant, it's normally when they start believing they're the one behind their success—I try to always keep that in mind.

INTERVIEWER: What makes you laugh?

NICK AYERS: The news media. Too bad for democracy's sake they're necessary.

INTERVIEWER: What has been your greatest temptation?

NICK AYERS: I face, like all Christians, a lot of temptations. But one that's pertinent here is the temptation to believe what God has called you to do in your career is more important than what your responsibilities are to your family. Whether that be your parents and siblings, your spouse, your children, or all of the above. I see so many great public servants and political operatives struggle with this one—including myself. The reality is, nothing is more important to God than serving your family and equipping them for eternity. But that taking the number one spot over what we convince ourselves is saving a state, or a country, through electing the right politicians and passing the right public policy is something we're all guilty of falling for—and wrongly so.

INTERVIEWER: What resource (book, ministry, place, etc.) has had the most significant impact on your life?

NICK AYERS: The Bible. I go there in the darkest, brightest, best, worst, and most mediocre moments of life and am never disappointed with what I find. I also enjoy reading material on our founding fathers and other great political or military leaders who left their fate and success up to the Lord.

INTERVIEWER: If you were on a deserted island and allowed a certain number of books, what would be your top five?

NICK AYERS: *Atlas Shrugged*, *Don Quixote*, the Bible, Merriam Webster dictionary, and a book on island survival.

INTERVIEWER: What is the single most influential piece of advice someone ever gave you?

NICK AYERS: Advice is nice and I, like you, have heard a lot of it. But I've been far more impacted by what I've seen than what I've heard. I've learned that good guys (or gals) do finish first, that God's plan is always greater than our plan, and to be anxious about nothing.

INTERVIEWER: Is there one particular quote that has always stuck with you?

NICK AYERS: "The man who really counts in the world is the doer, not the mere critic—the man who actually does the work, even if roughly and imperfectly, not the man who only talks or writes about how it ought to be done" by Theodore Roosevelt.

INTERVIEWER: What concerns you most about the church right now?

NICK AYERS: That in an attempt to be more fashionable we would water down the gospel. In some ways I believe we're over-complicating the simplicity of it all. You can live a life with peace or chaos, with eternity or mortality, with 100 percent certainty or doubt, and with hope or regret.

INTERVIEWER: What encourages you most? What is the church doing right?

NICK AYERS: I'm easily encouraged because Jamie and I are members of Church of the Apostles where Dr. Youssef is uncompromising in his convictions as well as being quite articulate, academic, and inspiring. People from all over the world watch him through the Internet and satellite, and we're so lucky to be able to sit on the fifth row most Sundays and hear him preach. What his international Christian ministry is doing in the Middle East, northern Africa, Canada, Indonesia, and of course here in the States is so inspiring—especially within the Muslim community.

INTERVIEWER: When I say the word *accountability*, what or who comes to mind? Why?

NICK AYERS: A question comes to mind—to whom, or to what, are you accountable? The answer to that will tell you a lot about your life, and it's worth asking frequently.

INTERVIEWER: On the following subjects what nuggets of wisdom come to mind that you would want to pass on to this next generation desiring to serve God, beginning with marriage?

NICK AYERS: Two ideas: first, spend a lot of time seeking God's guidance. When you're sure He's spoken to you about your potential soul mate, double that amount of time. Secondly, unless you and your future spouse have a higher purpose for your marriage, it will not last. I repeat, it will not last unless you have a higher purpose. Maybe a generation or two ago that wasn't true, but today the temptation to "move on with your life" is too great—or too easy depending on how you look at it. Marriage isn't about anything other than being one with God. When you do that the rewards are incredible, but a lifelong marriage will be very hard. My guess is, though, that when I'm old and decrepit it'll be my greatest accomplishment.

INTERVIEWER: Finances?

NICK AYERS: First and foremost I recommend taking God's only challenge to test Him in the Bible: test Him by tithing. See if you can out-give His grace and graciousness. Second, save more than you spend. It is a simple concept that most people in our generation aren't following.

INTERVIEWER: Living healthy?

NICK AYERS: I won't pretend to know anything about this. I have a terrible diet and even worse sleeping habits (or lack thereof), and my addiction to brownies and whole milk discredit me entirely here. However, I hear people who work out and eat healthy love doing it.

INTERVIEWER: If you could give just one piece of advice to this generation, what would it be?

NICK AYERS: Our Democratic Republic is the greatest in the history of mankind, but merely one generation away from failure. If this generation takes our freedom, liberty, and prosperity for granted, America can and will fail. Our government cannot afford, and should not be, the solution to all society's ills—that's our responsibility as citizens and members of the church.

INTERVIEWER: If you would permit I would like to ask some light questions that will have some pretty short answers . . . starting with your favorite sports team.

NICK AYERS: Georgia Bulldogs.

INTERVIEWER: Favorite movie?

NICK AYERS: *Doctor Zhivago*.

INTERVIEWER: Greatest band ever?

NICK AYERS: Rolling Stones.

INTERVIEWER: Dream vacation?

NICK AYERS: Island hopping in the Caribbean.

INTERVIEWER: Favorite hobby?

NICK AYERS: Hunting birds (pheasant, duck, quail and turkey).

INTERVIEWER: Favorite TV show as a kid?

NICK AYERS: The Weather Channel.

INTERVIEWER: If your own child were graduating from high school, what would be the main piece of advice you would offer to them on graduation night?

NICK AYERS: The degree you received today, while an achievement, makes up very, very little in who you are or what you'll be. The person you are tonight—in how you celebrate and whom you celebrate with—says much more about your wisdom, maturity, and future.

CHAPTER 26

A CONVERSATION WITH

Dr. Johnny Hunt

Pastor Johnny, as he's affectionately known, is a pastor's pastor. As se-nior pastor of First Baptist Church of Woodstock, Georgia, and as current president of the Southern Baptist Convention, Dr. Johnny Hunt has a vi-sion to not only see people commit their lives to Christ but also see them grow and deepen in their walk with God. After seeing the great need for a ministry specifically geared toward struggling and fallen ministers, Pastor Johnny began the City of Refuge. City of Refuge serves ministers in need of emotional and spiritual healing, and offers them a place to live, receive counsel, and eventually be restored. It is the only ministry of its kind run and funded completely by a local church, and has been invaluable in saving the families, marriages, and lives of many ministers all over the country. Pastor Johnny and his wife, Janet, live in Woodstock, Georgia, and have two daughters and four grandchildren.

INTERVIEWER: Describe the experience or moment when your calling became evident to you.

DR. JOHNNY HUNT: I had only been a Christian about a year, and I remember a time period where my life came under deep conviction. I would go to the altar at the end of a worship service, kneel, and pray, "Lord, here I am in full surrender. Show me what You would have me to do with my life." I simply wanted to be full of Jesus, so my wife and I would constantly pray, and it was through this reoccurring struggle that I began to sense the call on my life to the vocation of ministry. At that point I wasn't sure if it was to preach or educate . . . I was sure it wasn't to do anything musically related as I have zero gifting for that. We were so happy and filled with joy over that fact that God would call us to serve Him and His Kingdom. Shortly thereafter we made this public in our home church and God starting connecting the dots of what direction our lives were to take. There were some obstacles because I was a high school dropout and therefore had no education. I wanted to tell the Lord to let me get my GED and get accepted into college before making any of this public, but that was not how He was leading us . . . so we moved forward in obedience. And being obedient seems to have offered us great clarity.

INTERVIEWER: After you sensed this calling, what were your first actions? How did your life change immediately after your calling?

DR. JOHNNY HUNT: The first actions were to answer numerous questions from our family about the calling God had placed on our lives. Questions like "Where are you going to live?" and "How are you going to make a living?" and the list goes on. Looking back I realize those weren't our questions to answer until God showed us. I went to a technical institute at night and started working toward a high school education and taking the GED. After jumping that hurdle, then my pastor helped direct me on some of the next steps such as college and seminary. He played a huge role in my life because there were no believers in my family to speak wise counsel into my life and encourage me. My pastor had attended Gardner-Webb College for a two-year degree. So he took me there to visit the campus, meet with the president, and attend some classes. While there, we sensed a peace from God to attend that college. I was reminded of the words spoken to Isaiah when the Lord said, "This is My way. Walk in it." We had a calm assurance that we had heard from the Lord . . . and that started the journey.

INTERVIEWER: What is the greatest single theological theme that seems to come out in your sermons and books?

DR. JOHNNY HUNT: To answer that question I have to go back to experiences following my conversion. I lived in a small city and everyone knew my lifestyle of hustling at pool. I had a reputation of: winning a lot of money, being the good guy to bet on with pool, racing, fighting, and driving under the influence; and spending my fair share of time in the back seat of a police car. So when my life was radically changed by the grace of God, my actions changed immediately. I was doing evangelism and witnessing before I even knew you were supposed to. People would ask why I wasn't in the pool room or going to the bars and it would give me even more opportunity to share with them why that wasn't a part of my life anymore. Sometimes I think we teach an approach to witnessing before someone has a heart to witness.

After I was saved I would witness and people would ask questions like, "Did you see a light like Paul did?" Well, I had never read about Paul because this life was new to me. I became a prolific witness and then learned theology to support and defend my witness. This is different from today where we learn theology and are reluctant to share our faith. Early on God captured my heart with the message of the cross and learning it from every angle. This shaped my thinking and preaching. For example, the old song says, "When Christ was on the cross, I was on His mind." My understanding is that when Christ was on the cross, first the Father was on His mind and satisfying His justice so He could redeem sinners. Therefore throughout my ministry I have simply focused on the message of the cross. But I would say that I have focused on this in my own personal time with God first because I never want to become the main thing.

INTERVIEWER: What has been the biggest shift as you look back on the landscape of your journey? How has your calling matured or evolved?

DR. JOHNNY HUNT: I heard Adrian Rogers say one time, "I have never doubted my call to preach, but I admit there have been moments I doubted my salvation." And I have felt that way, especially early on in my ministry until I became a little better versed in theology. First John 3:3 speaks to the idea of purification and my call has a purifying effect. It helps me wake up every day to serve God, and I serve Him through my calling. I am oftentimes convicted and aware of the purifying effect my call has, because it affords me the ability to realize God doesn't need me and rather He has chosen to use me. I believe I'm here for a purpose, and I believe that God really called me to be a vocational minister. My calling has matured in the sense that Jesus Christ is my life and I am to live out in obedience to what He has revealed to me about what He wants me to do now that He is my life . . . and that pertains to my calling.

INTERVIEWER: What are a couple of books that come to mind that have greatly impacted you?

DR. JOHNNY HUNT: *How to Build an Evangelistic Church* by John Bisagno and *Talent Is not Enough* by John Maxwell.

INTERVIEWER: If your own child were graduating from high school, what would be the main piece of advice you would offer to them on graduation night?

DR. JOHNNY HUNT: I would share with them that the joy their mother and I have shared is tied to obedience to Christ and being willing to follow Him anywhere, even in the little things. Because it is the little foxes that spoil the vine. John Maxwell recently said, "A high school graduate can make 95 percent of the decisions I make, but the 5 percent is what makes the difference between a leader and a non-leader." So I would tell them to trust Christ in the big and little things.

INTERVIEWER: What concerns you most about the church right now?

DR. JOHNNY HUNT: I was reading through Revelation 2 and 3 this morning about the Seven Churches. Five of the seven churches' only hope was to repent and the only two He commended were the one that was faithful and the other that was persecuted yet persevered. That scenario sounds very applicable today. The only hope for a large percentage of churches is to repent. We're rich in so many areas but yet we have, in many cases, left our first love. One of the questions that I have to constantly ask myself is, *Am I pastoring for the same reason I did ten, twenty, or thirty years ago?* I want to make sure that nothing else – not money, fame, or anything – becomes my motive other than obedience to Christ.

INTERVIEWER: What encourages you? What is the church doing right?

DR. JOHNNY HUNT: What encourages me is there are a lot of young pastors out there that are daring to make a difference. And they want to tackle the most difficult tasks. There is a passion to engage the lost like never before, but we must be careful that we don't become like the ones we are trying to reach in the sense that we are affected by what has a grip on them. But I'm very encouraged because I've never seen such a desire to engage those without Christ. My hope is that a younger generation of leaders would both reach back to engage but also look to those who have gone before them for wise counsel.

INTERVIEWER: What is the purpose of City of Refuge, and when did you get a vision for this ministry?

DR. JOHNNY HUNT: I heard someone whom I admire the other day say that this ministry may be my legacy, and I had never thought of it in those terms. The more I was getting connected with other pastors, the more I started getting calls asking for job recommendations. Sometimes it would be one a week, but there were times it was ten a day. There was one particular phone call where the pastor began to weep as he expressed how his marriage was not healthy, his kids had a bad view of the church because of how some of the leadership had treated him, and it had taken a toll on his life. And he was calling me wondering if I could recommend him somewhere else to pastor.

The bottom line is, if I believed what this pastor just said to me, the worst thing I could do is recommend him somewhere else. God brought me under deep conviction and I told him that I couldn't recommend him because I had to help him first get well. Of course he didn't know how that was going to happen because if churches found out that a pastor needed help then no one would ever ask him to come and lead. I spent the weekend praying about it, and God took me to Joshua and Numbers where I read about the city of refuge. Through reading that account I decided to help in a different way than he anticipated. I called him and asked him to resign his church and move into an empty home that our church used to house missionaries on furlough. I told him we would get him in a counseling ministry and he would be involved in a church that would love and minister to him. I shared with our church why he had come and that I had no money to take care of him, and our church responded by lavishing the love of Jesus on him, providing all his needs. In that environment God made him healthy. Of course he had to humble himself and at one point he worked on our custodial staff and his wife served as an administrative assistant. That was over twelve years ago and today he is a healthy pastor leading a good church.

Dr. James Dobson shared with me that to the best of Focus on the Family's research ability, we are the only church in America that has a ministry like this where it is completely in-house. It costs hundreds of thousands of dollars to fund this ministry, but we so believe in this that seven of the people who have come through it in the last seven years now serve on my staff.

INTERVIEWER: What are some consequences, both temporary and permanent, in the lives of those who have fallen morally?

DR. JOHNNY HUNT: There are a lot of issues that the City of Refuge is prepared to handle. We have pastors who have gotten themselves in financial trouble. Some are so busy in the ministry that their marriage has suffered and they need healing, but certainly a majority of them have had moral failures of some kind. The question we must ask is what is our responsibility? And because there is a call on their life issued by God, I feel it is my responsibility to do what our ministry can to help them get healthy so they can again operate in their call. Here is how we help them: First, we want to help them to be right in their relationship with Jesus. In other words, number one is discipleship. Secondly, we want to help them once again to have a healthy family. Thirdly, we want to help them to walk into the church on the Lord's day holding their head up high, knowing that they're forgiven, and that they have great worth and value; not because of what they do but because of who they are. Fourthly, we want them to serve the Lord again, whether that is working in the parking lot on Sundays or teaching Sunday school.

But the consequences are that some of these guys are never going to pastor again. But I would add that a friend who knows of their moral failure and knows they spent two years at FBC Woodstock with great biblical counselors should feel comfortable using them in a number of ministry roles, even if it is not a senior pastor position. The question is often asked of me, do you believe someone who has had a moral failure can return to that same leadership role? Someone told me one time that we need to learn to ask better questions rather than think we have all the answers. The better question is, if they returned to that former leadership role, would Jesus come with them? Would they be anointed knowing the touch of God and the sweetness of service as they once did?

INTERVIEWER: What advice would you give this generation so that they may guard their hearts and run the race looking unto Jesus?

DR. JOHNNY HUNT: There are several observations that I have made throughout the course of City of Refuge. First, everyone needs a "Paul" in their life who can ask you hard questions and keep you accountable. It doesn't matter how young or old they are; they need someone who knows the Lord on a deeper level. Second, I would say to really maintain your personal devotions. You can only appear to be getting by and making it if you aren't in the Word on a regular basis. Thirdly, stay close to your spouse. Fourth, never, never, never, never forget or allow your Damascus road experience to become commonplace. In other words, never forget where you came from. I still get choked up telling a thirty-six-year-old story of how Jesus rescued me. And finally, I would say live your life for others. If I could choose what I would want to be true of me and put on my tombstone, it would be, "He was always thinking of others."

CHAPTER 27

A CONVERSATION WITH

Rick Stanley

Rick Stanley was born in 1953 in Huntsville, Alabama, to an average military family. Through a series of tragic events, his life became irrevocably intertwined with one of the greatest musical icons of all time—Elvis Presley. In 1960, Rick and his two brothers were taken to live at Graceland when their mother married Elvis's father. Eventually Rick became Elvis's personal assistant and worked with him until Elvis's death in 1977. Two months later, Rick surrendered his life to Christ and went on to graduate from Criswell College and Dallas Theological Seminary, and travel around the world sharing his amazing journey of faith. Rick has also made numerous television and radio appearances and authored three books. Rick and his wife, Robyn, have been married for over three decades and have two beautiful daughters, Brittany and Bethany.

INTERVIEWER: Describe the experience or moment when your calling became evident to you.

RICK STANLEY: I found a job cutting the grass at Silver Beach Cottages in Destin, Florida. The owner, twenty years my elder, came from an entertainment background. His parents had owned several casinos in Las Vegas, Nevada. We had a similar background. One day after working for him as groundskeeper, we had lunch together. I shared my testimony with him and noticed tears filling his eyes. We bowed our heads in the restaurant and I led him to the Lord. This was the moment it became evident to me that God was calling me into the ministry. I do not believe it was something I did; it was something God did to me. I later got certified as a lifeguard in Destin, Florida, put a big picture of Jesus on my lifeguard shack, and lead hundreds of Spring-breakers to the Lord. That was the spring of 1978 and I have never stopped.

INTERVIEWER: After you sensed this calling, what were your first actions? How did your life change immediately after your calling?

RICK STANLEY: My first reaction was realizing I was unequipped, not qualified, and unworthy of the testimony God had given me. I was very reluctant to answer the call to ministry. Nobody in my family was in the ministry. Poring over my Bible and looking at the way Jesus was, immediately supported and affirmed my calling. Pastor Jay Zinn moved me into his home and discipled me for ten months.

INTERVIEWER: What has been the biggest shift as you look back on the landscape of your journey? How has your calling matured or evolved?

RICK STANLEY: The biggest shift has been from being around people with, as T. S. Elliot said, "Men with hollow chests." People in entertainment: Eric Clapton, Elton John, Led Zeppelin and the Playboy bunnies at Hefner's mansion who seemed to have it all but didn't. They were all spiritual flatliners, nothing but emptiness behind their eyes. After entering the ministry I noticed the same look in the eyes of so many people who were not in entertainment. People who might not have had the same worldly opportunities, but who had the same spiritual emptiness. People of all ages and backgrounds became a burden for my soul.

My calling has matured and evolved in many ways. Probably raising two wonderful daughters has matured me most. Becoming a parent enabled me to better comprehend the love of God for everyone. Becoming a father took the angry young man out of my preaching. I started to think of how I would like my daughters preached to. I don't talk down to people anymore. I talk to them on their level, not as if I'm six feet above criticism.

INTERVIEWER: Who have been the most influential people in your journey? How did they influence or impact you?

RICK STANLEY: There are several people who have had a tremendous influence in my life. I can only mention a few.

My wife of thirty-one years has been the biggest influence in my life. She prayed for me over seven years to come to know the Lord. She was at Elvis's funeral to console me. Her family took me in when no one else would. They showed me unconditional love. October 16, 1977 (two months to the day after Elvis's death), I experienced forgiveness and was saved and salvaged. Her prayer support has kept God's anointing on my ministry.

Dr. Jay Strack and I met at a Bible conference in 1979. We became immediate friends. I started sharing my testimony at his crusades. He encouraged me to get my education because I was a high school dropout. Acting on his advice I took my GED test. I was actually with him in a crusade in Mississippi when Robyn called and told me I had passed the test. But that was not enough for Jay. He told me I must attend Criswell Bible Institute, and I did. Through a mutual friend, Dr. Freddie Gage, they put the wheels in motion for me to obtain a full scholarship to Criswell Bible Institute. I then went on to graduate from Southwestern Baptist Theological Seminary in 1986.

W. A. Criswell was my pastor for six years. He always allowed me access to his office when I had some hard questions.

Dr. Paige Patterson taught me personal and church evangelism. One day he was late for class. He looked like he had been working on a car, but he hadn't. He had been witnessing to his neighbor for years but got no response. One morning Dr. Patterson saw the man changing the oil in his car and spoke to him. The man responded by saying, "If you want to talk to me about Jesus then get under this car with me and talk." Dr. Patterson did, and led his neighbor to the Lord. His neighbor got more than an oil change that day; he got a new heart! Dr. Paige Patterson not only taught evangelism, but also backed it up with his life. This incident has forever influenced my ministry.

Dr. Richard Land was the one single man that turned on the light bulb in my brain. Listening to this fifth-generation Texan lecture without notes challenged me to "study to show thyself approved." Listening to his lectures from *Thiessen's Systematic Theology* and *God, Man, and Salvation* stretched me immensely.

And, of course, the professors at SWBTS: Dr. Jack McGorman, Dr. Curtis Vaughn, Dr. Tommy Briscoe, Dr. Bill Tillman, Dr. Bruce Corley, and the giant, Dr. Roy Fish, who had me lecture his class on evangelism.

David Nasser came into my life during a turbulent time in his own. We got to know each other at a church camp in the mid-eighties. He seemed to be more concerned about other people than himself. I had only observed this quality in a handful of people, but I had never seen it in a young man of sixteen or seventeen. David wanted everybody to feel special. G. K. Chesterton said, "Greatness is the ability to make others feel great." David did this at every camp we did together. And we did a lot of camps together!

INTERVIEWER: What is the greatest single theological theme that seems to come out in your sermons and books?

RICK STANLEY: First John 4:8: "God is love." Unfortunately so many people think God is mad at them. They perceive God as a "cosmic sadist." Unfortunately I went through a stage of "decisionism" in my early years. I thought that the only test for whether or not God was moving was by the number of people who responded to the invitation. Then after a lot of prayer and fasting, I realized the Holy Spirit was the master evangelist. I still give public invitations, but they are bathed in compassion. Compassion is the dominant theme of all my sermons now.

INTERVIEWER: How have you stayed focused on what God has called you to do?

RICK STANLEY: W. A. Criswell told me many years ago, "You have a gift for preaching and the favor of God on your life." I have never considered leaving my preaching ministry. There have been times when I did not "feel" like preaching. Any man in the ministry will go through times of difficulty. Whenever you face lulls in your ministry or deal with a prodigal child, you start to question God and immediately the enemy jumps on your back. If you are not careful you will start to believe the father of lies. The way I have stayed focused is seeking the counsel of my friends. The enemy wants us to be idle and isolated. Recognizing his tactics, staying busy, surrounding myself with positive people has done more in keeping me focused than anything else.

INTERVIEWER: What role have spiritual disciplines, such as Bible study, played in keeping that focus?

RICK STANLEY: Spending time with the Lord daily has helped me over the years become more and more biblical in my thinking. I try to marinate my mind in the Word of God. Wallow in the Word. Mere human speculation cannot hold a candle to divine revelation. Time in the Word helps me keep things in perspective. Jesus handled temptation by quoting the book of Deuteronomy three times, and this motivates me. Remember when reading the Bible God shouts the loudest in the hush.

INTERVIEWER: What makes you laugh?

RICK STANLEY: I get tickled when a lot of people respond to a public invitation and the pastor turns into a traffic cop at the altar. Also, feeding off the laughter of middle school students during my school assemblies. And then I enjoy TV shows like *Everybody Loves Raymond, King of Queens,* and *Seinfeld.*

INTERVIEWER: What has been your greatest temptation?

RICK STANLEY: To not spend enough time in prayer. You may have your message ready, but not praying for the anointing means there's no power. Preaching with the prayer for anointing affects the preacher, and the people can sense it.

INTERVIEWER: What books have had the most significant impact on your life?

RICK STANLEY: G. K. Chesterton's *Everlasting Man, Orthodoxy* . . . any of his books or poetry. C. S. Lewis's *Mere Christianity, A Grief Observed* . . . any of his books. John R. W. Stott's *The Cross of Christ,* Peter Kreeft's *Making Choices.* All of Os Guiness's books. All the classics—Dickens, Tolstoy, F. Scott Fitzgerald, Oscar Wilde, Hemingway, etc.

INTERVIEWER: What is the single most influential piece of advice someone ever gave you?

RICK STANLEY: I have heard it before in a different way, but I made it my own: "Stay away from the chicks and the checks."

INTERVIEWER: Is there one particular quote that has always stuck with you?

RICK STANLEY: G. K. Chesterton: "Meaninglessness in life does not come from being weary of pain. Meaninglessness in life comes from being weary of pleasure." That is why we are bankrupt of meaning in a land of so much.

INTERVIEWER: What concerns you most about the church right now?

RICK STANLEY: Loss of focus. We are more concerned about the White House than God's House. The lack of compassion for the unforgiven. And no burden for the unregenerate.

INTERVIEWER: What encourages you most?

RICK STANLEY: Young pastors who come up with innovative ways to ingratiate themselves in their communities. I call it "Mother Teresa-style" evangelism. The church seems to understand you have to earn the right to preach to some people, so you have to meet the needs of people.

INTERVIEWER: When I say the word *accountability*, what or who comes to mind? Why?

RICK STANLEY: A person to keep you in line, a person who will confront you lovingly. You are never NOT in the presence of God. I have never traveled alone. My wife traveled with me for many years, then we had children. Then my father-in-law traveled with me. David Nasser traveled with me, as well as several other men. Even to this day, after thirty-one years of ministry, I keep someone with me. Why? You never want to embarrass the body of Christ or your family. And "the brighter the light, the more the bugs."

In fact, Elvis had a policy when we were touring. He never had his picture taken with a woman without one of his guys in the picture. This stopped any paternity lawsuits. Billy Graham's Modesto Manifesto was an agreement along the same lines to keep each other accountable. You watch each other's back.

INTERVIEWER: On the following subjects what nuggets of wisdom come to mind that you would want to pass on to this next generation desiring to serve God, beginning with marriage?

RICK STANLEY: The first thing the devil tells a wife is that her husband cares more about his profession and other people than her. It is up to the husband to prove the devil a liar. I never answer personal letters from individuals, but only letters from churches concerning preaching engagements. Robyn is more than qualified to answer the more personal letters. She knows me better than anyone. And this is my way of letting her know that she is the love of my life. Any nice or flattering comments in these letters have no appeal to me. She can relay prayer requests and praise reports to me. The only good thing people see in me is Christ, and she is the one responsible for that.

INTERVIEWER: Raising children?

RICK STANLEY: Always work around their schedules. The most spiritual thing you can say when you are in the ministry is, "No, some other time." There will be plenty of time for mission trips once the children are grown.

INTERVIEWER: Finances?

RICK STANLEY: Do not fleece the flock. No matter the amount of the offering, just be thankful. You may not get what you should, but it is better to go without the offering than give someone an opportunity to criticize God's faithfulness.

INTERVIEWER: Living healthy?

RICK STANLEY: Take care of the temple. Walk, play golf, break a sweat daily!

INTERVIEWER: Communication?

RICK STANLEY: Return calls. Listen to your wife. God put her with you for a reason. Wives are very intuitive. Turn off the ministry button when you come home. Read *Men Are from Mars, Women Are from Venus.* Wives do not want things fixed; they want to be listened to.

INTERVIEWER: If you could give just one piece of advice to this generation, what would it be?

RICK STANLEY: Show me your friends, and I'll show you your future.

INTERVIEWER: With your permission, I'd like to ask some light questions that have some pretty short answers . . . what is your favorite sports team?

RICK STANLEY: Georgia Bulldogs.

INTERVIEWER: Favorite movie?

RICK STANLEY: Shadowlands and *Tombstone*.

INTERVIEWER: Greatest band ever?

RICK STANLEY: Led Zeppelin.

INTERVIEWER: Dream vacation?

RICK STANLEY: Revisiting Chesterton's home in England, taking the family to Belfast, and going to Queens College to see C. S. Lewis's home.

INTERVIEWER: Favorite hobby?

RICK STANLEY: Golf, reading.

INTERVIEWER: Favorite TV show as a kid?

RICK STANLEY: Man from U.N.C.L.E.

INTERVIEWER: If your own child were graduating from high school today, what would be the main piece of advice you would offer to her on graduation night?

RICK STANLEY: The closer you get to Jesus, the more clothes you put on, the more modest you become. Because if it takes sex to get a boyfriend, it will take sex to keep him. And finally, no matter what happens, I will *always* love you.

CHAPTER 28

A CONVERSATION WITH

Alex and Brett Harris

Twins Alex and Brett Harris, brothers of famed author Joshua Harris (I Kissed Dating Goodbye), are fast becoming Christian cultural leaders in their own right. In their early twenties, they are the sons of homeschooling pioneers Gregg and Sono Harris. Together, Alex and Brett founded TheRebelution.com, a website calling young people to be men and women of maturity, who follow hard after the heart of God and rise above the myth of adolescence. They are frequent contributors to the webizine Boundless. Alex and Brett organize their own conferences, Rebelution Tour, and have been featured nationally on MSNBC, CNN, NPR, and in the New York Times. They are also authors of the ground-breaking book Do Hard Things. Both live near Portland, Oregon, with their parents and three younger siblings where they attend Household of Faith Community Church.

INTERVIEWER: Describe the experience or moment when your calling became evident to you.

ALEX HARRIS: We started the Rebelution blog in August of 2005. From the beginning the message was that young people are far more capable than our society says they are. Looking at God's Word—the theme verse of the Rebelution is 1 Timothy 4:12—we also believe this has been supported throughout history. It was clear that the modern view of adolescence was flawed. But it wasn't until God miraculously opened the door for us to live out the ideas and to see them lived out in the lives of our fellow teens as interns at the Supreme Court of Alabama. Another experience was when we served as grassroots coordinators to four political races, and these combined experiences helped us realize God was calling us to take the message and run with it. And we had just turned seventeen!

INTERVIEWER: After you sensed this calling, what were your first actions? How did your life change immediately after your calling?

BRETT HARRIS: Psalm 127 says, "Unless the LORD builds the house, those who build it labor in vain" [v. 1]. The implication is that when God *is* in our work, none of our labor is in vain! We both felt like we had stumbled onto something God was doing, not something we had engineered, so we were confident and pretty energetic. The first thing we did was to revamp the website. The Rebelution started as a generic Google-hosted Blogger blog, so we spent that summer working with some other teen guys to build a complete site with a revamped blog, discussion forum, and resource section. We also started planning our first conference tour to spread the message to a wider audience and give "rebelutionaries" a place to gather and meet like-minded teens and families.

INTERVIEWER: What has been the biggest shift as you look back on the landscape of your journey? How has your calling matured or evolved?

ALEX HARRIS: Up until this point, with the publishing of *Do Hard Things*, our focus has been almost exclusively on education. The idea that there is a different and better way to live the teen years than what popular youth culture dictates is a new idea for most young people. But now, as more and more teens are embracing a bigger, more biblical vision—and as Brett and I move out of the teen years ourselves—our goal is to move into the role of facilitators for other young people's holy ambitions. As we step into the season of college, marriage, and family, we want to remain faithful and focused, while at the same time continuing to help change our culture's perception of the teen years.

INTERVIEWER: Who have been the most influential people (*that you know personally*) in your journey? How did they influence or impact you?

BRETT HARRIS: Our parents, hands down. The dedication to our book reads, "To our parents, Gregg and Sono Harris. This book is the message of your lives." It's really true. They didn't use the words "do hard things," and they certainly didn't call it a "rebelution," but they modeled for us what it means to do what is right, even when it hurts. Many of the lessons and ideas that we have used to challenge our generation can be traced back to the philosophy with which our parents raised and taught us along with our siblings.

INTERVIEWER: What is the greatest single theological theme that seems to come out in your talks and books?

ALEX HARRIS: One of the biggest themes is the wisdom, goodness, and sovereignty of God. An unwillingness to trust Him enough to obey Him, even when it's hard, usually finds its source in doubting His wisdom, goodness, or sovereignty in and over our situation.

INTERVIEWER: How have you stayed focused on what God has called you to do? What role have spiritual disciplines, such as Bible study, played in keeping that focus?

BRETT HARRIS: Alex and I have really been given a unique opportunity to minister to and instruct our peers. But we've found that unless we're faithful to refill and replenish our own hearts and minds through Bible study, worship, and fellowship in the local church, we dry up pretty quickly and the work we do becomes just that—work. We want to minister out of abundance, out of overflowing hearts, and that's when we feel God's pleasure in the calling He's given us. That's when it stays fresh and exciting.

INTERVIEWER: What makes you laugh?

ALEX HARRIS: Brian Regan. If you haven't seen him, you're really missing out. He is hilarious!

INTERVIEWER: What has been your greatest temptation?

BRETT HARRIS: I think I can speak for both of us in saying that pride is the most subtle and deadly sin we have to fight against. We've been blessed with family and friends who keep our feet on the ground and point us to the cross, but pride gets at you in so many ways. It can blind you to your very real faults and weaknesses. It makes you rationalize and attempt to justify your sin. It can cause you to mistake personality for sanctification, or get complacent about your walk with God. It's also easy to "be humble" when everything is going the way you want it to. It's when people criticize you or things go wrong that pride really shows itself. Pursuing godliness is a fight, and it takes constant vigilance. You can't sit at one place. You're either going forward or backward.

INTERVIEWER: What resource has had the most significant impact on your life?

ALEX HARRIS: John Piper and Desiring God Ministries. We grew up listening to Piper sermons. His heart for the glory of God in all things inspires us. He will always be one of our heroes.

INTERVIEWER: If you were on a deserted island and allowed a certain number of books, what would be your top five?

BRETT HARRIS: ESV Study Bible, *Systematic Theology* by Wayne Grudem, *The Complete Works of Francis Schaeffer*, *Calvin's Institutes*, and *How to Survive and Get Off a Desert Island for Dummies*.

INTERVIEWER: What is the single most influential piece of advice someone ever gave you?

ALEX HARRIS: As life has gotten a lot busier, something Randy Alcorn told us once stands out. He said, "Sometimes you have to say no to a lot of good things in order to be able to say yes to the one thing that God has especially equipped and called you to do."

INTERVIEWER: Is there one particular quote that has always stuck with you?

BRETT HARRIS: One that has really been meaningful to us is by G. K. Chesterton. He wrote, "The Christian ideal has not been tried and found wanting, it has been found difficult and left untried." Our dream for several years now is that our generation of Christian young people would be a generation that finds it difficult and yet still tries.

INTERVIEWER: What encourages and concerns you most about the church right now?

ALEX HARRIS: Looking specifically at our generation, we're greatly encouraged to see a lot of young people embracing timeless truth, and speaking and living it with love and humility. When they are presented with a decision between sound doctrine and biblical orthodoxy on the one side, and *really* living out the life and teachings of Jesus on the other, they say, "Why do I have to choose?" These are young people, fourteen, fifteen, sixteen years old, who are reading *Do Hard Things* and Grudem's *Systematic Theology*—all 1,295 pages of it. These are young people who are passionate about learning more about this God who is worthy of their lives, and who are already making plans with friends to raise money to fight the global slave trade, dig wells in Sudan, and bring hope to the homeless in downtown Portland. But we're also concerned to see a lot of young people embracing a social, feel-good gospel, and denying the truth and power of Christ's death and resurrection. God is not glorified by belief without action or action without right belief.

INTERVIEWER: When I say the word *accountability*, what or who comes to mind? Why?

BRETT HARRIS: Iron sharpening iron. Alex and I have been blessed to be brothers and partners in the work God has given us. The protection of working with someone who can remind you of what is truly important, who can get you on your feet when you're feeling lazy, and who can provide extra strength when you're weak, is an inestimable gift. It doesn't have to be a biological brother, but accountability is vital for all of us.

INTERVIEWER: With both of your permission I would like to ask some light questions that have some pretty short answers . . . beginning with what is your favorite sports team?

ALEX & BRETT HARRIS: Portland Trail Blazers.

INTERVIEWER: Favorite movie?

ALEX & BRETT HARRIS: *Amazing Grace*.

INTERVIEWER: Greatest band ever?

ALEX & BRETT HARRIS: U2.

INTERVIEWER: Dream vacation?

ALEX & BRETT HARRIS: Traveling through Europe.

INTERVIEWER: Favorite hobby?

ALEX & BRETT HARRIS: Reading great books.

INTERVIEWER: Favorite TV show as a kid?

ALEX & BRETT HARRIS: We actually didn't really watch TV as kids.

INTERVIEWER: If you could give just one piece of advice to this generation, what would it be?

ALEX & BRETT HARRIS: Do hard things.

CHAPTER 29

A CONVERSATION WITH

Dr. Jack Graham

As pastor of the twenty-eight-thousand-member Prestonwood Baptist Church in Dallas, Texas, former president of the Southern Baptist Convention, and president of the Southern Baptist Convention Pastor's Conference, Dr. Jack Graham has a lot on his plate. Despite the demands placed on him by his calling, Dr. Graham remains a down-to-earth man who accompanies the teenagers at his church to youth camp every summer. He is highly respected as a teacher by fellow pastors of all denominations, and a compelling voice in church leadership today. Dr. Graham and his family live in the Plano, Texas area.

———————————

INTERVIEWER: Describe the experience or moment when your calling became evident to you.

DR. JACK GRAHAM: I think God put it in my heart early in life to pursue Him and have spiritual goals. This was clarified for me in my high school experience and teenage years when I was attending a student camp and just sensed this extreme, compelling desire to do what God wanted me to do. I remember even before this camp on a Sunday evening in our church talking to my youth pastor and saying, "I think God is calling me and I'm willing." And our student minister said to me, "Go, live for Jesus, work on your character, do the right things, share Christ with your friends, and then when God does call and it is clear, you'll be ready." That was great advice because the call, first and foremost, is an inward call and the character of the one who is called is essential. I followed his advice and began leading my friends to Christ; developing my own character in terms of life decisions, purity decisions; and moral choices and having a mentality that life matters. As a result, within that year it became clear to me that God was indeed calling me to preach. I went forward in my church and made it public, which is something that I don't think we see as much today. There was a phrase years ago that preachers used—"calling out the called"—which was a real emphasis given to call young men and women to consider God's call for full-time ministry, whether it be serving as a pastor, missionary, or whatever. Even though you don't hear a lot about "calling out the called" and public response, we try to set time aside at our church to discuss it and have seen a number of young people respond to the Lord. But, having said all that, I went forward, made a commitment, and began preaching as a fifteen- or sixteen-year-old kid. For me the early evolution of my calling was first, "Lord I'll do what You want me to do"; second, "I think You want me to preach and in full-time ministry"; and third, "I got to the place where I thought Lord if You're not calling me please show me because I'm going forward." I never had this sense of struggle that some people have or resistance. The Scriptures say, "If anyone *desires* the office of the bishop" [see 1 Tim. 3:1], and I think God gives you the desire of your heart. God actually gave me the desire to pursue His will in this way, and so when it got right down to it, I said, "Lord, if You're not calling me, You better show me right now because I sure don't want to make a mistake, but I do want to be in the middle of Your will."

INTERVIEWER: When did you get a vision for your present form of ministry where you serve as a senior pastor?

DR. JACK GRAHAM: There is no doubt that comes from the fact that the local church was so strategic in my family's life and mine. We had a great model in our pastor, Dr. Fred Swank, who served at Sagamore Hill Baptist Church in Fort Worth, Texas, for forty-three years. We had a great pastor and grew up in a great church that during the sixties was one of the most effective and fruitful churches around, so I naturally developed a love for the church. I was so impacted by the local church during my teenage years and believed then as I do now that the church is where the action is. The church is the voice and vehicle of God in the world, and while para-church organizations are helpful and they're arms of the church, the church is always going to be the front lines. I knew that I was called to preach the Word of God and the testimony of Christ, and then I began to wrestle with the forum through which that would be accomplished. The idea of standing week after week preaching to a congregation that was there for the purpose of spiritual growth and nurture and then to be a huge catalyst of the community for evangelism always inspired me. The call to preach also includes the call to do the work of an evangelist, which is clear in Paul's writings to Timothy. I believe the local church functioning the right way is the most effective tool for evangelism in the world. While I affirm other callings and ministries, for me, I know I am called to be a local church pastor preaching week by week to the same people, knowing their hurts, their problems, their struggles, and to be involved and engaged in their lives. To this day that still excites me and I would rather preach in our pulpit than any place on earth. That is the great thing about your calling: it clarifies and simplifies your life, allowing one to know they are in the good place that God has for them to serve. And by the way, that is regardless of what you are doing, whether that means preaching or working construction.

INTERVIEWER: What has been the biggest shift as you look back on the landscape of your journey? How has your calling matured or evolved?

DR. JACK GRAHAM: I could have never imagined when I was a young preacher just starting out serving churches in Oklahoma that I would eventually be in West Palm Beach. When I was there in the eighties, it was a very secular place that had a non-Bible belt, non-traditional culture. By moving me there, the Lord moved me out of my comfort zone, which turned out to be a really eye-opening and stretching experience in terms of our focus on evangelism. Upon studying that culture, we discovered that basically everybody there needed Christ, because out of nine hundred thousand people in the county, less than fifty thousand people attended church or synagogue. Our time in South Florida was a very missional experience. Another shift came when we moved to Dallas in 1989 to pastor Prestonwood Baptist Church, where we have now served for twenty years. I was never prepared for the explosive growth we would experience. In the 1960s a church of two thousand or three thousand people was a mammoth, and now there are churches with fifteen thousand to twenty thousand–plus attendants. Ours is one of those churches, and I could never prepare for something like that. So God has to teach me along the way and give me grace and favor to adjust to these massive shifts in church life. When people ask me if it was my dream to pastor this huge church, I always respond, "Absolutely not. It was a dream of reaching a lot of people for Christ." I would have never conceived of this . . . what has happened here in Dallas is exceeding, abundantly above all that we asked.

INTERVIEWER: Who have been the most influential people (*that you know personally*) in your journey? How did they influence or impact you?

DR. JACK GRAHAM: Early in ministry, of course, my pastor Dr. Fred Swank. He was my father in the ministry and a mentor, long before the concept of having a mentor was ever popularized. Then in my twenties Dr. Adrian Rogers influenced my preaching style and even content as much or more than anyone. I would credit those two men for impacting me greatly, but also in terms of evangelism I, like so many others, was influenced by the ministry of Dr. Billy Graham. In my twenties I would listen to him on the radio every Sunday and just loved hearing him preach.

INTERVIEWER: What is the greatest single theological theme that seems to come out in your sermons and books?

DR. JACK GRAHAM: That would be the message of redemption through Jesus first and the lordship of Christ, which is the message of the Bible. I follow Spurgeon's rule when he said, "I take my message from any text and make a beeline to the cross." The gospel saturates my sermons, which for me is a no-brainer but seems to have been taken from center stage in so much preaching today. While there are many topics and themes we preach about, we must never advance beyond the person and work of Christ and His lordship in our lives.

INTERVIEWER: How have you stayed focused on what God has called you to do? What role have spiritual disciplines, such as Bible study, played in keeping that focus?

DR. JACK GRAHAM: I would start with an extreme sense of gratitude that God would call me to do what He has enabled me to do. And by that I don't mean the size of the church but rather He would take a guy from east Forth Worth, born in a little town in Arkansas, and allow me to be a voice and to be someone that He could use. I mean . . . I have never gotten over the fact that He called and commissioned me. It is liberating to know I am allowed to serve in the manner I do, that I am not driven to get up by the alarm clock but because of the call of God on my life. Years ago I read a book called *Trumpets in the Morning* by Harper Shannon. In it he tells a story of a man who had to leave the ministry, and years later someone asked him this important question: "Is there anything you miss about being in the ministry?" The guy responded, "Well, there are a lot of things I don't miss . . ." but then he said, "I do miss the trumpets in the morning." In other words, that sense of high calling that every day I get to tell someone the good news. That is what keeps me focused.

INTERVIEWER: What makes you laugh?

DR. JACK GRAHAM: A good sense of humor helps keep life in balance. Everyone needs good friends that you can laugh with so you don't get isolated. I have friends and we keep each other from taking ourselves too seriously, which I think helps one to be an authentic follower of Jesus.

INTERVIEWER: What has been your greatest temptation in ministry?

DR. JACK GRAHAM: My greatest temptation has been: When God gives success and everything seems to be flowing well and ministry is exciting and fulfilling, then to assume that it's always going to be this way. If I am not careful I can take for granted what God has done. In a large church, one has to be careful not to become a CEO because we are not running a business. I have to keep my attitude in check making sure I walk in humility. If I don't, then there certainly can be consequences like snapping at the staff and those kinds of things. So my greatest temptation would be, as much as I said I'm grateful and humbled to do this every day, to think it's always going to be this successful. Doing that or thinking that way unplugs you from your power source. I try to keep myself on my knees so I don't become self-dependent and stay dependent upon God.

INTERVIEWER: What resource has had the most significant impact on your life?

DR. JACK GRAHAM: The first thing that comes to my mind is my family, starting with Deb and our children who are now adults but have always been such an impactful part of my life. We call ourselves Team Graham, and we now have a little grandson; he's on the team. Having the resource of a great and godly wife who shares the heart of the ministry and who loves me and loves our kids has always been the greatest resource that God gave me.

INTERVIEWER: If you were on a deserted island and allowed a certain number of books, what would be your top five?

DR. JACK GRAHAM: I would start with *The Saving Life of Christ* by Ian Thomas because it taught me the principles of the Spirit-filled life. Another book at the same genre and era would be *The Key to Triumph at Living* by Jack Taylor. *Ordering Your Private World* by Gordon MacDonald. *On Being a Servant* by Warren Wiersbe. In terms of theology I would want *Why I Preach That the Bible Is Literally True* by W. A. Criswell.

INTERVIEWER: What is the single most influential piece of advice someone ever gave you?

DR. JACK GRAHAM: "Be authentic, be real. Don't put on airs and don't be an actor on a stage; be a proclaimer of the gospel." My pastor Fred Swank shared that with me both in his words and the manner in which he lived his life.

INTERVIEWER: What concerns you most about the church right now?

DR. JACK GRAHAM: The need for spiritual power. There's a lot of "how to" and "get it done" and less and less conversations about the work and the ministry and the Holy Spirit. I just sense that there needs to be a spiritual renewal, much like the Spiritual Life Movement we had in the late sixties and early seventies. It came along with the ministries of Ian Thomas and Jack Taylor. My greatest concern is that while we're better prepared, more equipped, have bigger buildings, and more technology than any other time in history, we haven't left any room for the ministry of the Holy Spirit. Another influential book in my life was *Why Revival Tarries* by Leonard Ravenhill. There's a cartoon in that book of a minister standing in clerical robes, and he looks majestic and powerful when he's standing among the big Corinthian columns of the church and the subtitle is "Everything but one thing." So my greatest concern is that we have everything but the one thing that we must have, and that is the power of God.

INTERVIEWER: What encourages you most? What is the church doing right?

DR. JACK GRAHAM: I am encouraged most by the opportunity we have. There's never been a better day to proclaim Christ. There are bigger churches today than ever before, better technologies, better ability to travel and engage people in evangelism all over the world. I am also very encouraged by the younger pastor's commitment to the Bible, evangelism, and spiritual growth. Older ministers think it their responsibility to be concerned about the next generation, but I've always believed God has His people, and His Word is going to go forward and He is going to always raise up the next generation of committed, biblically devoted, Christ-centered, people-loving pastors and church leaders. There is much to be encouraged about.

INTERVIEWER: When I say the word *accountability*, what or who comes to your mind and why?

DR. JACK GRAHAM: Accountability is critical, but I've always questioned a little bit of the whole idea of how it is portrayed. Sometimes it seems like nothing more than managed sins, because accountability, ultimately, is a matter of the heart. I do think it's important to have friends that keep you honest and accountable, but trust levels or the transparency level have to be developed overtime. And so while accountability is important for the most part, it can be a bit overrated because at the end of the day it is a matter of the heart between you and God.

INTERVIEWER: On the following subjects what nuggets of wisdom come to mind that you would want to pass on to this next generation desiring to serve God, beginning with the subject of marriage?

DR. JACK GRAHAM: Marry your best friend.

INTERVIEWER: On raising children?

DR. JACK GRAHAM: Be real.

INTERVIEWER: On finances?

DR. JACK GRAHAM: Never make money the primary motivation in your life or ministry, and make sure that you always have integrity in terms of what you make and what you could give.

INTERVIEWER: Living healthy?

DR. JACK GRAHAM: Stay active all your life, because the benefits of physical fitness are critical. I don't believe you can be used effectively if you have a worn-out body because of neglect or lack of exercise.

INTERVIEWER: On communication?

DR. JACK GRAHAM: Some people are natural communicators, while others have to work at those skills and develop them. But no matter if you're a natural or if you have to really work at this, you must prepare yourself. You must get ready to bring it and to have passion about what you're saying. One's delivery has to be interesting and inspiring and not just informative. So to me, the greatest communicators have the ability to connect with the congregation or an audience by expressing passion. This is all assuming that you know what you're talking about.

INTERVIEWER: With your permission I would like to ask some light questions that have some pretty short answers . . . beginning with what is your favorite sports team?

DR. JACK GRAHAM: Texas Rangers.

INTERVIEWER: Favorite movie?

DR. JACK GRAHAM: *Forrest Gump.*

INTERVIEWER: Greatest band ever?

DR. JACK GRAHAM: Beatles.

INTERVIEWER: Dream vacation?

DR. JACK GRAHAM: It's probably San Diego, Southern California.

INTERVIEWER: Favorite hobby?

DR. JACK GRAHAM: Golf.

INTERVIEWER: Favorite TV show as a kid?

DR. JACK GRAHAM: *Leave It to Beaver* or *Andy Griffith.*

INTERVIEWER: If you could give just one piece of advice to this generation, what would it be?

DR. JACK GRAHAM: Discover God's plan and purpose for your life and do it. Ride the wave of God's will for your life with the wind at your back and know that sense of hitting your sweat, to use one more sports analogy. Life is too short to do something outside your gifting or calling. And so, discover God's desire, God's dream for your life, and do it with all your heart as long as there is breath in your lungs.

CHAPTER 30

A CONVERSATION WITH

Darren Whitehead

Originally from Australia, Darren Whitehead serves as a teaching pastor, regularly speaking to over twenty thousand people at Willow Creek Community Church. He also leads the Next Gen Ministries and the Creative Arts Departments. Willow Creek's innovative, multi-site ministries have made it one of the most attended churches in North America. Prior to Willow Creek, Darren served as teaching pastor and director of student ministries at The People's Church in Franklin, Tennessee. Darren lives with his wife, Brandy, and their two half-Aussie, half-American daughters just outside of Chicago, Illinois.

INTERVIEWER: Describe the experience or moment when your calling became evident to you.

DARREN WHITEHEAD: When I was thirteen, a volunteer youth worker spoke to me at a camp and he told me that he felt like God was calling me to be a leader, and I had never seen myself in that light before. In my early twenties I moved to America from Australia, and I felt I was supposed to work in the media, so I began working at a radio station, and shortly thereafter I started volunteering part-time in the youth ministry at my church. And the interaction with the young people was so real and so authentic that it just awoke something within me and I felt that this was something I was supposed to do with my life. So, I started to pursue serving student ministry, and the more I started to pursue it, the more authentic it felt and the more that it was being confirmed in me. Several people thought that I was supposed to join the staff at our church and I really didn't think I was supposed to, and that went on for about a year. In the meantime I tried to get a volunteer work permit, and I submitted a bunch of documents to the government and what they ended up giving me was a minister's, or religious worker's, permit to work here. Now, this was not the permit I wanted or applied for but I had a reference letter from the church and I had a reference letter from a Christian radio station. So it was somewhat of an epiphany in my life that I had tried not to do ministry even though I felt like God was pursuing me in it. As I said I really wanted to go into media and I started a Dot-Com that I ended up selling to a public trading company, and all the while I felt God pursuing me on working within the church. And I didn't really catch a vision for the church for quite sometime, but in the end I look back and I think . . . I tried to do other things, and God was pursuing me on this one thing.

INTERVIEWER: After you sensed this calling, what were your first actions? How did your life change immediately after your calling?

DARREN WHITEHEAD: Well, I was working or involved in the church as a volunteer and I started to get more and more involved, and this ministry started to occupy more and more of my thought, time, and my passion. Building the church and the youth ministry began to be the drive of my life. I started to infuse and invest my creativity, energy, new ideas, and basically all of myself. Then I started to try and get a lot of other people a part of it as well and essentially what happened is the ministry just started getting traction. It just started growing and we were starting to see people give their lives to Christ . . . It was pretty exciting stuff.

INTERVIEWER: You have gone from the high school pastor to the teaching pastor at one of the most influential churches in evangelical life. So how or when did you get a vision to serve in this role of executive, communicator, author, and the list goes on?

DARREN WHITEHEAD: I'd say one of the major values that I have tried to live my life by is trying to be diligent and faithful with opportunity that gets presented to me. That has often involved getting out of my comfort zone. I've tried to be faithful in whatever God has entrusted to me. I grew up in a small town, and when I moved to the city when I was seventeen it was a big jump for me 'cause I was out from my comfort zone. Then when I was twenty-three, I moved to America and that was another big jump for me. I had to start my whole life all of over again with new bank accounts; I had to sit for a driver's license test again; and get a new social security number. It was way out of my comfort zone. Then again I had this opportunity to join the staff at Willow Creek Community Church, which is a larger church than the entire city I grew up in. So I have constantly found myself stepping through doors of opportunity even though they may be out of my comfort zone. And now when the opportunity was presented for me to be a teaching pastor and oversee several departments of the church, again, it was pushing me out of my comfort zone. But I find that my growth curve of development is the most aggressive when I'm in a brand-new environment and so I'm just trying to be faithful. I feel like I haven't lobbied or pushed through these different things. I just feel like God has opened these doors and I have tried to be faithful and serve passionately and diligently wherever I've been. I think sometimes when God blesses, we wrap our arms around what He has given and we just want to hold on to it. But we must be careful that in holding on to our present opportunities that we potentially forfeit some future opportunities. The mantra that I've used several times in my life is that I will not sacrifice calling at the price of comfort. And so, that's what pushes me because I only have this one life. And what God has called me to do, I want to be obedient. I don't want to live a comfortable life. America is a very dangerous place to live spirituality because it's very comfortable. The American dream, which says get wealthy, get comfortable, and enjoy the illusion of control in your life, is very prevalent in the church. I must never lose sight of the fact that I am not in control of my life. And at this stage in the journey I'm so aware of that because the health of my wife and my two daughters is only hanging in the balance through the grace of God. And that could change at any moment.

INTERVIEWER: Do you struggle with that? Do you struggle with the contagious, magnetic nature of the American dream?

DARREN WHITEHEAD: Absolutely, and I have people in my life that can challenge me on that very point. Like everyone else there are certain times that I need to reboot my brain and my heart and go, "This is not what I want to give my life towards."

INTERVIEWER: How do you "reboot" your brain and heart and essentially stay focused?

DARREN WHITEHEAD: Well, I think the Scriptures echo with high-definition clarity the call to lay down your life and take up the cross. Even though that's something that is not easy to do it is something I need to be called back to every day. I think the Scriptures do that. Outside of my personal Bible study I am constantly listening to sermons all the time, just to hear people teach the Word of God. It is an ongoing feed of content that helps program my life.

INTERVIEWER: Who have been the most influential people in your journey? How did they influence or impact you?

DARREN WHITEHEAD: The volunteer youth worker named Graham Smith who spoke to me the idea that God was calling me to leadership would certainly have to be at the top of that list. He has continued to speak into my life at very strategic intersections throughout the course of my life. I credit a lot of being in the ministry today to some twenty-one-year-old volunteer that has never been in full-time vocational ministry. Secondly, I would say my best friend, John Tyson, who is a fellow Aussie that is also a church planter in Manhattan, New York. He and I talk at least once a week, sometimes several times a week, and have been very close for sixteen years. Finally, a mentor that I work very closely with is Bill Hybels, and he has had a tremendous influence on my life in the way I think, preach the Scriptures, approach leadership, and even in the way I love the church.

INTERVIEWER: What is the greatest single theological theme that seems to come out in your sermons?

DARREN WHITEHEAD: I love and I believe in the church. There are a lot of people that, especially today, that just want to criticize the church. And I just want to be a voice that is calling the church to greatness. I want to help people realize they're not serving in isolation or autonomously, but rather they are part of a movement that God has orchestrated and that we're in this together. I love talking about the history of the church, especially over the last couple of thousand years and highlighting people who have died for the church . . . people who have given the best hours of their life to the church, that have given money to the church, and who served faithfully in the church. I think the church is so beautiful. The bride of Christ is such a beautiful thing and I want the world to be struck by her beauty.

INTERVIEWER: What makes you laugh?

DARREN WHITEHEAD: Being an Australian, our humor is very satirical, and so satire makes me laugh. I don't take myself very seriously and so I laugh at myself a lot. My wife and I laugh at ourselves a lot. And, of course, my daughters have caused me to have fresh eyes on the world and I have so much delight in watching them. Some of the things they say cause me to laugh a lot. It's just one of the most pure, most beautiful things I have ever seen.

INTERVIEWER: What resource, whether it is a book, ministry, place, or activity, has had the most significant impact on your life?

DARREN WHITEHEAD: About three years ago, I started running the Chicago marathon every year, and that requires of me four or five months of training and a lot of being alone running on a road. While I do long runs with other people, I would do the five- to ten-mile runs by myself. And so during those runs I would listen to lots and lots of sermons and sometimes just find myself weeping while exercising. It is quite an interesting dynamic to have my body exhausted and my spirit is soaring because of what I've been listening to. That has been a wonderful discipline because there are no distractions and it's interesting . . . there's some kind of correlation between physical health and spiritual health. While I don't fully understand it, I certainly appreciate it. When I am healthy and exercising, my relationship with Christ thrives. I would add that three or four times a year, I go to a little beach house that my wife's parents have in Destin, Florida, and I take a bunch of books, and I just read, and I just meditate on the things of God and this has also been extremely refreshing to my life.

INTERVIEWER: What is the single most influential piece of advice someone ever gave you?

DARREN WHITEHEAD: I once asked a friend what's the key to time management. He said it's very simple; it's one thing: "Get up early." And I found that to be so true.

INTERVIEWER: What concerns you most about the church right now?

DARREN WHITEHEAD: What concerns me the most is that throughout history, the church seems to swing towards extremes. Right now, there seems to be a reaction towards the evangelism movement that places a huge emphasis on compassion and social justice and it's a wonderful thing. But my concern is that the gospel is about vertical reconciliation and a horizontal reconciliation, and I don't want us to abandon the vertical reconciliation at the expense of pursuing horizontal reconciliation.

INTERVIEWER: What encourages you most? What is the church doing right?

DARREN WHITEHEAD: I think that the church is waking up to the opportunity to serve and love their neighbors. Efforts of serving for the common good are more visible than ever before. And there are entire communities that are observing the church's efforts.

INTERVIEWER: On the following subjects what nuggets of wisdom come to mind that you would want to pass on to this next generation desiring to serve God . . . beginning with marriage?

DARREN WHITEHEAD: The challenge is to pursue your marriage in the same way that you pursue your ministry or your career. The question we must ask of ourselves is, do we gain the same level of fulfillment from having a wonderful, prospering, and growing marriage, as you do from achieving ministry goals or career goals? Marriage takes creativity and energy and leadership, and the danger is once you get married to say, "All right. That's done and I'm going to pursue other areas in my life now." That is an erroneous idea! I need to be pursuing my marriage with the same level of intensity that I pursue my ministry. I like to think of my wife as being . . . something that is very precious like a flower or a jewel that I want to cultivate so that my wife is thriving.

INTERVIEWER: On raising children?

DARREN WHITEHEAD: It's probably the chief calling of my life. My church will have another pastor, but my daughters will never have another dad, and the true legacy of my life will be the character of my daughters.

INTERVIEWER: On finances?

DARREN WHITEHEAD: The most insightful thing I've ever heard on money is this idea: Luke 16:11—"So if you have not been trustworthy in handling worldly wealth, who will trust you with true riches?" If God can't trust you with earthly riches, how can He trust you with eternal riches or true riches? It's so interesting that God is actually waiting to see how faithful we're going to be with our money and that He's intentionally holding a category of blessing back until He first sees our stewardship. Therefore if you are faithful with your money, He actually wants to entrust you with eternal riches, with true riches. The other side of that coin is that we will never actually experience some of these specific true riches if we are not faithful with our money.

INTERVIEWER: With your permission I would like to ask some light questions that have some pretty short answers . . . beginning with what is your favorite sports team?

DARREN WHITEHEAD: The Adelaide Crows, which is an Australian football team.

INTERVIEWER: Favorite movie?

DARREN WHITEHEAD: *Ferris Bueller's Day Off*.

INTERVIEWER: Greatest band ever?

DARREN WHITEHEAD: The Police.

INTERVIEWER: Dream vacation?

DARREN WHITEHEAD: I go to the beach in Destin, Florida, three or four times a year. It is a good beach with good weather and waves and I look forward to it with all my heart.

INTERVIEWER: Favorite hobby?

DARREN WHITEHEAD: Running.

INTERVIEWER: Favorite TV show as a kid?

DARREN WHITEHEAD: *The Paul Hogan Show*.

INTERVIEWER: If your own child were graduating from high school, what would be the main piece of advice you would offer to them on graduation night?

DARREN WHITEHEAD: I certainly don't think I could get it down to just one piece of advice, but the chief theme that I would want to teach her would be Matthew 6:33, to seek first the Kingdom and His righteousness and to trust God, to care what God cares about. Very pragmatically I would be desperate for her to find a church to use her gifts in. The other night I was putting my daughter to bed and I asked her, "Where was Daddy today?" And she said, "At work." And I said, "Where does Daddy work?" And she said, "Church." I said, "Do you like the church?" And she said, "Yes!" I want my daughter to love the church. I don't want my daughter to think the church is what takes Daddy away. I want her to think the church is beautiful. It is the redemptive community in the world and I want her to discover her own gifts and to deploy them in the church, to use them, to grow them, to nurture them, to bless other people with her gifts. I am hungry for her to discover that. After doing youth ministry for more than ten years, I can pick the girls out whose dads have been absent in their lives, both physically absent and emotionally absent, and one thing I know is that my daughter is going to know how a man should treat her based on her relationship with me. This past Valentine's Day, I bought both my daughters flowers and my wife flowers because I don't want my daughter's self-esteem when she is a fifteen-year-old to be vulnerable to the attention some fifteen-year-old boy can give her. I want her to know that the way he treats or the way he interacts with her would be incomparable to the way her father treats her and the way her father treats her mother. I desire that she would want nothing less than a man of God in her life.

CHAPTER 31

A CONVERSATION WITH

Ron Luce

Ron Luce is the co-founder and president of Teen Mania Ministries located in Garden Valley, Texas. The ministry has expanded greatly and has become very influential within today's Christian youth culture, training thousands of young people to travel around the world to spread the gospel of Jesus Christ. Ron also hosts weekend Acquire the Fire youth rallies and ministry clinics in stadiums and arenas all around the nation. He also hosts a weekly TV show, Acquire the Fire, and provides training for young adults wanting to enter into ministry through his Honor Academy. Recently Ron expanded his ministries by starting the Battle Cry Campaign, which fights to save America's youth from the deadly influence of popular culture. Ron and his family live in Texas.

INTERVIEWER: Describe the experience or moment when your calling became evident to you.

RON LUCE: I was having one of those throw-down times with God where I was praying through all the ministry and job opportunities and wrestling with my future. I found myself with opportunities to do certain things, and yet burning inside me was the idea of young people and missions. So there was this desire to see young people engaged in missions but I had no idea how to start a ministry. I remember praying to God that I would not move forward on a pretty good idea and I must hear from Him. I made the decision not to move forward until He made it clear I was to do so. All of this is taking place in a little condo where my wife and I lived when we first got married. And it was in that time that the Lord just spoke to my heart. It wasn't audible, but it was clear. And the message was to build an army of young people who would go and make His Kingdom known. It was a moment of great clarity . . . everything that I wanted started making sense, and my focus became to present students with a real picture of Christianity, invite them to be a apart of it, and ask them to change their world. One month later we birthed Teen Mania. I had recently graduated from school and finished my master's, and I was ready to go and do something. Even prior to this we had been putting on some teen rallies and calling them Teen Mania, so we already had the name and therefore decided just to continue using it. We would call churches up and ask them if we can do a youth rally and most of them would hang up on me. But a few let me come in 1989 when all this started and we would have ten to twenty students per rally. The crowds are awesome and we were packing out living rooms across the country and preaching to them like there were ten thousand in the room! The numbers didn't upset me at all, because if you are doing what you were born to do, you love it; whether you're flying at thirty thousand feet or ten feet, you're still flying. After we would do a rally, many of those students would go on a mission trip with us, and that was the conception and birth of Teen Mania ministries.

INTERVIEWER: What has been the biggest shift as you look back on the landscape of your journey? How has your calling matured or evolved?

RON LUCE: I would say that I think more deeply about process, that is, what am I leading students to do? What do I want them to do afterwards? The process of the event and what the youth pastor should do beforehand? What should the youth pastor do afterwards and how can we serve the process? These types of questions I have wrestled with greatly in recent years. But a major shift or evolution in my calling has been to think more deeply in terms of what is happening in America and the world and looking at the macro picture asking, "Is there a possible way of making a dent?" We have also tried to look more deeply at systemic issues. For example, if we really want the revival of young people around the country, what's it going to take? Well, senior pastors are going to have to get engaged. Their parents are going to have to get engaged discipling their own children, and things like this. We are looking at the whole system and attempting to work both harder and smarter.

INTERVIEWER: Who have been the most influential people (*that you know personally*) in your journey? How did they influence or impact you?

RON LUCE: The first one is the pastor who preached the gospel in a way that finally made sense to me. I was a sixteen-year-old party animal when a friend of mine took me to church and I heard this guy preach in a manner that I could wrap my mind around. And then three weeks after I got saved, my dad kicked me out of my house because I was a Jesus freak, and I was in high school. I ended up living most of my senior year with my pastor. This pastor invited me to live with them, which was a big miracle because this guy had three very beautiful teenage daughters. But he was a man of great faith. It was an amazing thing to finally feel what it was like to live in a healthy family. I still have a great relationship with him today, and his daughters are like my sisters.

INTERVIEWER: What is the greatest single theological theme that seems to come out in your sermons and books?

RON LUCE: My messages revolve around provoking people to passionately pursue Christ, not just praying a little prayer but really pursuing Him. And then confront them, challenge them, stir them to think, "OK, now what am I going to do with this message?"

INTERVIEWER: How have you stayed focused on what God has called you to do? What role have spiritual disciplines, such as Bible study, played in keeping that focus?

RON LUCE: There is a lot that one may not be good at. For example, one may not be the best preacher or businessman. But anyone can be good at prayer. I refuse in my life to be one of those people who think every time they see an altar call, *Oh yeah, I should be having a quiet time*. There may only be a few things I can do well, but rest assured I will do them. Regularly for years I have fasted two days a week or even longer, and for over fifteen years I have fasted at least one day a week. And there are times I will do a longer fast, for a week or more. I also have a regular everyday appointment with God. I've been doing this since I was in college, where I just decided, *I don't care if I get an F in my class, I'm not going to get an F with God.* I just kind of made some of those fundamental decisions when I was young.

INTERVIEWER: What makes you laugh?

RON LUCE: My kids. My nineteen-year-old daughter came the other day to where I was speaking at one of our events. I was at a breakout session and I didn't know where she was in the room, and all of a sudden she jumps on my back, just like a piggy back ride. She's laughing and it gave me the biggest, best laugh I have had in a month.

INTERVIEWER: What has been your biggest temptation in ministry?

RON LUCE: Busyness. I am constantly studying the news, whether it's on TV, radio, or newspapers; and there are times I just have to shut down all media and not listen. During those times I will barely take any phone calls or look at the e-mail, or anything as a way to keep myself in check.

INTERVIEWER: What resource (book, ministry, place, etc.) has had the most significant impact on your life?

RON LUCE: A book entitled *The Pursuit of God* by A. W. Tozer. I've read that book more than any other . . . Only one I've read more is the Bible.

INTERVIEWER: What is the single most influential piece of advice someone ever gave you?

RON LUCE: A former board member of mine who is also a mentor to me said, "Now is not the time to retreat. You guys can push the gas pedal to the metal, and I know it's hard, and I know you're tired, but this is your moment." This was shared at a board meeting over fifteen years ago during a pivotal time in our ministry and I have never forgotten it.

INTERVIEWER: What concerns you most about the church right now?

RON LUCE: What concerns me most is the lack of focus from the church on the youth. And not just on the youth, but on passing the baton to the next generation. Oftentimes parents and church leaders have subcontracted their love out to their youth pastor. My prayer is that a lot of senior pastors would become burdened about student ministry. I am also concerned about the type of gospel that's being preached to America for the last fifty years. Think about it: how can you have all these ministries, television ministries, radio ministries, megachurches, all of it, yet get more pornography, more divorces, more issues than ever before taking place inside the church. There was a time hundreds of years ago when people sacrificed for their faith and had to endure all kinds of hardships. But they were willing to follow Jesus no matter what. I don't know if that is what is being currently preached in our churches. I am concerned that we have missed the very essence of the gospel message.

INTERVIEWER: What encourages you most? What is the church doing right?

RON LUCE: I think there are some signs of hope among young people who are willing to throw all of themselves into the movement of Christianity. They don't want a watered-down gospel and recognize the demands of the gospel, knowing it is worth it. When presented with a biblical picture of what it means to follow Him, they are saying, "OK, I will give everything for it." They just simply want the real thing.

INTERVIEWER: When I say the word *accountability*, what or who comes to mind? Why?

RON LUCE: I think of my wife.

INTERVIEWER: What is your view of accountability? How would you define it?

RON LUCE: First, if people were accountable to the Holy Spirit, when He's convicting their heart, you'd have a lot less charades going on in the church. Unfortunately a lot of accountability turns into an empty exercise that yields no power or fruit. I have met Christian bands who say they have a pastor who goes on the road with them for the purposes of accountability, yet they are all drinking and smoking. Often people may be leading an organization and never listen to their board of directors. Just because you have a board doesn't mean you are heeding their wise counsel; again, it is empty and powerless. So we must guard ourselves against this outward form of accountability that, once you pull the layers back, yeilds no substance. Now there are some great resources that help one stay accountable, like protection on your computer. But it is easy to do the form without the function. That is why I say that we must first be accountable to the Holy Spirit.

INTERVIEWER: On the following subjects, what nuggets of wisdom come to mind that you would want to pass on to this next generation desiring to serve God . . . beginning with marriage?

RON LUCE: One needs to prepare deeply for marriage.

INTERVIEWER: On raising children?

RON LUCE: Don't have them unless you're prepared to sacrifice for them. As a parent you must sacrifice your time, your heart, your hobbies, your past times. People ask, "What are your hobbies?" Well, my kids are my hobbies.

INTERVIEWER: On finances?

RON LUCE: Be very conservative. Don't live above your means.

INTERVIEWER: On communication?

RON LUCE: If that's your calling, study it and become great at it.

INTERVIEWER: If your own child were graduating from high school, what would be the main piece of advice you would offer to them on graduation night?

RON LUCE: If it is my personal kid, I would want to say to them, "Hey, you're ready. We trust you. We're glad. You're prepared." But to others I would say, "Don't stumble into your life. Find out the reason you were born and go after it with all heart."

CHAPTER 32

A CONVERSATION WITH

Leeland Mooring

It is rare to find a man so young who has such insight into the heart of God. Leeland Mooring is one of those young men. Now in his early twenties, Leeland has been leading worship since the age of eleven. As lead singer and songwriter of the band Leeland, which has been nominated for several Grammy and Dove awards, Leeland Mooring has also co-written six songs, and entirely written one song, on Michael W. Smith's 2007 release, Stand. *Originally from Baytown, Texas, Leeland grew up in a close Christian family who traveled on the road together for a few years doing ministry. He formed his own band by the age of fifteen and has been performing at conferences, festivals, and camps all across the United States. In 2008 Leeland married the love of his life, Amanda.*

INTERVIEWER: Describe the experience or moment when your calling became evident to you.

LEELAND MOORING: I was eleven years old leading worship with my family in Illinois. My mom asked me to just worship and sing this chorus that I'd just written called "Shine." So I started to worship the Lord, and after a while I looked up and most of the church was at the altar worshiping with me. It was a pretty cool moment and I had never felt the presence of God overwhelm me like that before.

INTERVIEWER: After you sensed this calling, what were your first actions? How did your life change immediately after your calling?

LEELAND MOORING: I started to cry a lot, because God's love is pretty awesome! A couple years later my parents started Celebration of Life Church in Baytown, Texas. Everyone in the family had a job. Ha ha! So mine was leading worship for our youth group. That's when I really started to grow and understand music ministry.

INTERVIEWER: When did you get a vision for your present ministry?

LEELAND MOORING: I was fifteen years old, and it was over the course of a few months. At that time our band was pretty much together, and every once in a while we'd play at other churches. I remembered knowing in my spirit that this is what the Lord wanted me to do . . . that we were onto something big.

INTERVIEWER: What has been the biggest shift as you look back on the landscape of your journey? How has your calling matured or evolved?

LEELAND MOORING: Well, when our band first started we played every Thursday night at youth group and then I lead worship every Sunday. I was really involved in my church. Looking back on the past three years, the biggest change for me has been being away from our church. A lot of the songs that are on the album *Sound of Melodies* were really inspired out of experiences I had with God while leading in my home church. But instead of this experience drawing me further from God, it has actually caused a sense of desperation in me to be closer to Him. Being out of the comfort of home I constantly had to remind myself to be poor in spirit. I could never allow myself to think I had it all together. But instead, recognize my weakness and surrender myself completely to Him so that He can be free to move through me in whatever way He wants.

INTERVIEWER: Who have been the most influential people in your journey? How did they influence or impact you?

LEELAND MOORING: Well, that would definitely have to be my parents. Every day I get a call from my mom encouraging me to get in the presence of God and draw closer to Him. And my dad is a consistent example of a man in love with God that I aspire to become one day. The opportunities in ministry I enjoy today are because I have praying parents and a great God that responded to them.

INTERVIEWER: What is the greatest single theological theme that seems to come out in your sermons and books?

LEELAND MOORING: For me it would be from what Brother Lawrence has said in his book *Practicing the Presence Of God*, "That you can be connected to Jesus and His Kingdom every day through intimacy with Him and making Him the meditation of your heart."

INTERVIEWER: How have you stayed focused on what God has called you to do? What role have spiritual disciplines, such as Bible study, played in keeping that focus?

LEELAND MOORING: Meditation on God's Word—not just reading it but asking Jesus to give me a revelation about it. Just because I've memorized a verse of Scripture about the love of God doesn't mean I fully understand it. But when I feel the love of God pour over my heart like a river, then I begin to understand and experience His love. Also, reminding myself to not just have personal times with Him but to make my mind and heart a habitation for the glory of God all throughout the day. Like the psalmist said, "The Lord inhabits the praises of His people." In other words, He dwells wherever He's honored and glorified.

INTERVIEWER: What makes you laugh?

LEELAND MOORING: Physical humor. Ha ha!! I'm a total kid in that regard!

INTERVIEWER: What has been your greatest temptation?

LEELAND MOORING: For me it would be getting too comfortable and kind of coasting. Being complacent. I never want to be so used to where I'm at that I miss out on the new things Jesus has for me.

INTERVIEWER: What resource (book, ministry, place, etc.) has had the most significant impact on your life?

LEELAND MOORING: I would have to say there are three ministries that have significantly impacted my life: Nigel and Cathy McNiel with Revival Fire Ministries; Dale and Jean Gentry with Breakout Prayer Ministries; and of course my home church, Celebration of Life!

INTERVIEWER: If you were on a deserted island and allowed a certain number of books, what would be your top five?

LEELAND MOORING: The Bible, *Practicing the Presence of God*, *Dreaming with God*, *Heavenly Man*, and *Where the Wild Things Are*!!

INTERVIEWER: What is the single most influential piece of advice someone ever gave you?

LEELAND MOORING: One day I came home pretty discouraged from a show. It seemed like no one cared about the Lord, and it just felt like I was working to get everyone to that place of worship with me. When I shared this with my mom, her response was, "From now on I just want you to sing to Jesus. Just sing to Him." I've carried that thought with me everywhere. Not pleasing people but pleasing Jesus!

INTERVIEWER: Is there one particular quote that has always stuck with you?

LEELAND MOORING: Brother Lawrence in *Practicing the Presence of God* said, "It doesn't matter the size of work, just the amount of love you put into it."

INTERVIEWER: What concerns you most about the church right now?

LEELAND MOORING: That sometimes we try to control everything. I've been in some services where every minute is planned out with videos, media, games, music, and a message, that had no challenge or conviction. We need to be open for God to mess up our plans a little bit. "So as the Heavens are higher than the earth so are God's ways higher than our ways and His thoughts higher than our thoughts" [Isa. 55:9 paraphrased]. It's great to plan and be prepared, but we need to be willing to surrender our plans to the will of God so that if He chooses to move anywhere He is given first place! Our hearts should be soft towards Him and our ears listening for Him.

INTERVIEWER: What encourages you most? What do you think the church is doing right?

LEELAND MOORING: There is a big revival springing up in the church to do something about the needs in our world like clean water, the AIDS pandemic, slavery, and hunger! I think that we're stepping into the revelation that worship without justice is empty, and faith without works is dead.

INTERVIEWER: When I say the word *accountability*, what or who comes to mind? Why?

LEELAND MOORING: Surrounding myself with people like my family and the band. People not afraid to call me out when I do something stupid. Ha ha!

INTERVIEWER: On the following subjects, what nuggets of wisdom come to mind that you would want to pass on to this next generation desiring to serve God, beginning with marriage?

LEELAND MOORING: Keep Jesus the focus of your marriage and have fun following Him!!

INTERVIEWER: On raising children?

LEELAND MOORING: Well, I don't have any yet. But one thing I thank God for is that my parents kept us in environments where we actually experienced the presence of God.

INTERVIEWER: On finances?

LEELAND MOORING: Be faithful with your tithe and offering to the house of God. It is the only principle that God challenges us to prove Him on [Mal. 3:10].

INTERVIEWER: On living healthy?

LEELAND MOORING: Well, our bodies are considered temples of the living God. So even the way we eat, exercise, and treat our bodies should be honoring to God.

INTERVIEWER: On communication?

271

LEELAND MOORING: Some of the best songs I've ever written have been out of a tangible experience with Him.

INTERVIEWER: If you could give just one piece of advice to this generation, what would it be?

LEELAND MOORING: Pray and seek the Lord; stretch out your faith with actions of love (faith without works is dead); don't be afraid to dream big, because all things are possible; and finally, you are a citizen of heaven, so get rid of everything in your life that is taking the place of God.

INTERVIEWER: With your permission I would like to ask some light questions that have some pretty short answers . . . beginning with what is your favorite sports team?

LEELAND MOORING: Liverpool [English Premier League Soccer].

INTERVIEWER: Favorite movie?

LEELAND MOORING: *Wall-E.*

INTERVIEWER: Greatest band ever?

LEELAND MOORING: U2.

INTERVIEWER: Dream vacation?

LEELAND MOORING: Italy, Spain, and Israel.

INTERVIEWER: Favorite hobby?

LEELAND MOORING: Soccer (FUTBOL!!).

INTERVIEWER: Favorite T.V. show as a kid?

LEELAND MOORING: *G.I. Joe.*

INTERVIEWER: If your own child were graduating from high school, what would be the main piece of advice you would offer to them on graduation night?

LEELAND MOORING: You can do anything that's in your heart to do! All things are possible through Jesus! Not through your strength but through your weakness God is made strong!!

CHAPTER 33

A CONVERSATION WITH

Pat Williams

Pat Williams is the senior vice president of the NBA's Orlando Magic. As one of America's top motivational, inspirational, and humorous speakers, he has addressed thousands of executives in organizations ranging from Fortune 500 companies and national associations to universities and nonprofits. Pat is also the author of over fifty books and hosts three weekly radio shows. In addition to these responsibilities, Pat is the proud father of nineteen children, included fourteen who were adopted from four nations, ranging in age from twenty-three to thirty-six. For one year, sixteen of his children were all teenagers at the same time. Pat and his amazing wife, Ruth, are members at First Baptist Church of Orlando, where Pat teaches an adult Sunday school class.

INTERVIEWER: When did it become evident to you that you could be used in the world of professional sports . . . that this could in fact be the calling God has placed on your life?

PAT WILLIAMS: Well, I think it's when I came to the Lord in 1968. I had grown up in a sports environment. I played sports through high school and college and started a career in the Phillies organization as a player and then moved into the front office. I was spending eighteen hours a day involved in a game no more complicated than a ball and a bat and a glove, and trying to put people in the ballpark, and I remember wrestling with the big questions like, "Why am I doing this?" and "Is this really a worthwhile way to spend my life?" And it was right in that period, at the age of twenty-seven, that I was presented with the claims of Christ and I responded by committing my life to Him . . . it truly was life changing. It was as if the scales fell off my eyes and I realized that all of my background up to that point was actually preparation to have a career in sports, but this time with the understanding that it was God's plan and purpose. And sports has been where He kept me all these years and it's a ministry no question about it. Now my pulpit is different, but there's a sense of worthwhileness that what I am doing is really making a difference through this field of sports. It has given a sense of significance to my life.

INTERVIEWER: Tell us a little bit about that . . . I have heard you speak on occasion about your first job and almost the insanity that you were given this big responsibility at such a young age.

PAT WILLIAMS: Well, I think that we do need to get prepared and start to work for Him and dismiss the age game on both the young and the old side. I think there are many who have a mind-set that says, "I'm just too young to do that." And there are those who are older who say, "My time has come and gone and I'm just too old." I think we would be a whole lot more effective if we didn't have to keep track of birthdays and keep score on age. And in my case the Phillies sent me to Spartanburg, South Carolina, to be the general manager of their farm club. I was twenty-four and two years out of college and if not the youngest, one of the youngest general managers in the history of professional sports. Fortunately, I didn't know that and so I just plowed into my work acting as if I knew what I was doing with as much confidence as I could muster up. But I got a very, very early start in my career, and I can look back now and see what an advantage that was. By the age of twenty-nine, I was the general manager of the Chicago Bulls. So five years after I arrived in Spartanburg, South Carolina, I found myself in Chicago running the Bulls. Reflecting on those experiences, I would say to young people, get yourself prepared! Get your formal education done as fast as you can and as completely as you can. I had my degree from Wake Forest University and a master's degree from Indiana University by twenty-three and a half, and so because my formal education was done I didn't have to worry about it and I was ready to hit the ground running. In this competitive society, just an undergrad degree is insufficient, go on and get your master's. So I encourage young people to get their education and then hit the ground running, getting to work in their chosen field so they can start making a difference.

INTERVIEWER: As you look back on landscape of your life thus far, who would you say has been the most influential person, that you have known personally, and how have they influenced or impacted you?

PAT WILLIAMS: Well, I had two very important people in my life early. One was Bill Veeck, the great baseball promoter and Hall of Fame executive. I met him in September of 1962 right after my first summer in baseball. I was twenty-two and sought him out through a mutual friend. And for twenty-five years Bill Veeck was a mentor, influencer, encourager, and a door opener for me and had a profound effect on my life. To this day, I carry many lessons that he built into my mind-set. And the other key person was Mr. R. E. Littlejohn, who was the owner of the Spartanburg club while I was there. He was a businessman who really became a surrogate father to me and invested in my life by pouring himself into me. He just absolutely laid a foundation for my life that carries on to this day. In fact he so impacted me that I've written two books about him and one about Bill Veeck. I met Bill Veeck when I was twenty-two and Mr. Littlejohn when I was twenty-four, and they were both enormous influencers early in my life.

INTERVIEWER: Because of your profession you're in the whirlwind of temptation. How have you stayed focused on what God has called you to do?

PAT WILLIAMS: As I study athletes and their success, the common thread with all of them is the ability to stay focused, which is the ability to black out distractions and hone in on that which is important. I've noticed with these athletes, they literally go through life with blinders on, zoning dead on that which is important, that which has to be dealt with right now. They don't get off on the rabbit trails. They stay focused on the main highway whether it be Tiger Woods, Michael Jordan, Larry Bird, and the list goes on and on. So, I think you've got to get intentional with your life and establish what's important to you. You've got to have your values enumerated. List those values out so you can constantly stay honed in on them. And I think the most important thing I've learned is focus on your strengths. You know, it's an ongoing debate. *Should I work on my weaknesses or should I work on my strengths?* Well, I would really encourage people to spend most of their time taking what they do well up to higher levels. I always try to focus on today and improving on my strengths. So often we get caught up in the past and trying to redo the past and change yesterday, which is impossible. We can also get so caught up with our future that we neglect exactly what's going on today. Coach Wooden, who also had a huge influence on my life, said, "Make each day your masterpiece."

INTERVIEWER: What has been your greatest temptation?

PAT WILLIAMS: Well, I would have to say the temptation of fame, ego, and taking far too seriously your stature or your role . . . my role in life. The sports world is a very glamorous, prestigious world, so I constantly try to take my work and what I am doing seriously without taking myself too seriously. The other thing I try to remember is that there's an adversary in our life as believers who is relentless, very smart, persistent, never lets up, and knows our weaknesses, and he's going to keep getting at us as long as we're breathing. That is why it's important to know yourself and know where you're weak. If you're weak in the area of gambling, I would suggest you better not vacation in Vegas, or if you've got a real problem in the area of gluttony, I would say do not stand outside of a doughnut shop inhaling fumes. I'd go out to the celery farm, you know, or maybe to the carrot plantation. If you are weak in the area of alcohol, I would not hang in the neighborhood tavern watching the ballgame with everyone. I know where I am weak and therefore I never want to position my life so I could potentially fall.

INTERVIEWER: What resource, whether it be a book, ministry, or place, has had the most significant impact on your life?

PAT WILLIAMS: It's a gym that I built at home with my wife's help. We bought equipment to stock the gym and I work out every day, both on the stationary bike and outside on the jogging trail as well as on an elliptical machine and weight machines. I've got a whole gym at home, and without that workout every day I don't function very well. It's a daily discipline that I really need. And if I miss a day, I feel that day doesn't function very well for me or as well as it should.

INTERVIEWER: If you're on a deserted island and you can only have five books, what would they be?

PAT WILLIAMS: First, of course, would be the Bible. But, I tell you I would not take books that I haven't read. So here's my dilemma: I am 375 books behind in my reading right now! There are about 375 books in my office at home on shelves, all by category and sitting there waiting patiently. Some of them have been waiting longer than others and they're getting very restless. Some of them are very unhappy, particularly when new books come and I jump to read the new books and the older ones stay sitting there feeling neglected. So, if I'm heading to a desert island, I'm going to find, out of those 375, the five with the most pages in them. But I think the book that most impacted me was Bill Veeck's autobiography that came out in the summer of 1962. I was in my first summer of baseball in the Phillies organization when that book came out. The book, amazingly enough, forty-seven years later, is still in print. The book is simply entitled *Veeck*, and in it he shares his life story as well as his philosophy of running baseball teams. It had an enormous impact on me. That book, at the age of twenty-two, really established my whole philosophy of sports management, which carries over to this day.

INTERVIEWER: What is the single most influential piece of advice that someone ever gave you?

PAT WILLIAMS: That would have come from Warren Wiersbe, who was my pastor at Moody Church when I lived in Chicago. I called him up one day at the start of my fourth year with the Bulls. Things were in turmoil. I had a wonderful run there, but suddenly there were some real issues and I was just struggling terribly, and I asked him to come over for lunch. I needed to talk to him, so he agreed and we sat over lunch and I gave him a whole rundown of what was going on, and he looked at me and he said, "Don't waste your sufferings." That's what he said. And that's not what I wanted to hear. I mean, my thought was, *Gosh! He's a pastor. I mean, where's the hug? Where is the box of tissue? Where's the Bible verse? Where's the cushy shoulder?* But as I looked back, thirty-eight years later, that may be the single best piece of advice I've ever received . . . *don't waste your suffering*. He was saying that we all go through tough times, and in the middle of the storm, always be learning and growing because the storm is going to end. And on the other side of the storm, are you better, stronger, more capable, more sympathetic?

INTERVIEWER: When I say the word *accountability*, what or who comes to mind and why?

PAT WILLIAMS: The first person that comes to mind is my wife, Ruth Williams. I feel that I am accountable to her, nineteen children, and seven grandchildren. Secondly, I would say Rich Devos, who is the owner of the Orlando Magic.

INTERVIEWER: On the following subjects, what nugget(s) of wisdom come to mind that you would want to pass on to this next generation desiring to serve God, beginning with marriage?

PAT WILLIAMS: Pick the right mate and take your time. The most important question is, does he or she make me a better person and do I make him or her a better person?

INTERVIEWER: Now this next one is . . . you have written a book on, and you could write many more on since you have nineteen children, but what wise counsel would you give on raising children?

PAT WILLIAMS: If you're going to create them, you have got to take an interest in their life. They need quantity time. There's no such thing as quality time. It should be a no-brainer that they need your time. They also need your attention, and you've got to establish the balance of love and discipline as soon as you can, because children must have both. They have to know that there's discipline in their life, that they do not go any which way they want, that they will pay a price if they step over that line, but they always have to know that there is unconditional love raining down on them. And that's the key to parenting in my opinion.

INTERVIEWER: On finances?

PAT WILLIAMS: Save your money. I can still hear the voice of my mother from years ago saying, "We can't afford that." She also told me to "live within your means, pay your bills, and don't do anything to ruin your credit." I can still hear her voice. And I think if we had all followed the advice of my mother, this country would be in a whole lot better shape financially, and I know millions of families would.

INTERVIEWER: On leaving healthy?

PAT WILLIAMS: If you don't feel good physically, then life is hard and you won't be able to function. Therefore, the most important things I can tell any young people are to eat the right food—fruits and vegetables are the key—and get a good workout every day. The body was made for action, not lounging. I would also add: get enough sleep; never touch tobacco, alcohol, or drugs because those three ultimately will destroy your health.

INTERVIEWER: On communication?

PAT WILLIAMS: Join the debate club, take a speech course, join Toast-masters, join the National Speakers Association, study the great communicators of the ages, read the book that Ruth and I wrote entitled *Turn Boring Orations into Standing Ovations*, and study, practice, and work at expressing yourself verbally. I can tell a whole lot about any young person after about twenty seconds of listening to them talk. I would also add to care greatly about your appearance, because people will start forming opinions about you even before you open your mouth.

INTERVIEWER: With your permission I would like to ask some light questions that have some pretty short answers . . . beginning with, what is your favorite sports team?

PAT WILLIAMS: Are you kidding!?! The Orlando Magic.

INTERVIEWER: Favorite movie?

PAT WILLIAMS: *Dances with Wolves*.

INTERVIEWER: Greatest band ever?

PAT WILLIAMS: Glenn Miller

INTERVIEWER: Dream vacation?

PAT WILLIAMS: I'm the worst vacationer in the world. A dream vacation would be visiting Civil War battle sites in the South.

INTERVIEWER: Favorite hobby?

PAT WILLIAMS: Reading.

INTERVIEWER: Favorite TV show as a kid?

PAT WILLIAMS: *The Mary Tyler Moore Show* or *Bonanza*.

INTERVIEWER: If your child were graduating from high school tonight, what would be the main piece of advice that you would offer?

PAT WILLIAMS: Figure out what you love to do more than anything in the world, and then come up with a way to get paid for it every two weeks for the rest of your life, and you will have life by that throat.

CHAPTER 34

A CONVERSATION WITH

Dr. Hank Hanegraaff

A prolific author and president of the Christian Research Institute, Dr. Hank Hanegraaff is otherwise known as the "Bible Answer Man." He has written several books, including The Complete Bible Answer Book, The Face That Demonstrated the Farce of Evolution, *and* Christianity in Crisis, *which has sold over a million copies. Part apologist, part preacher, part teacher, but all minister, Dr. Hanegraaff has made tremendous impact in the lives of millions. Dr. Hanegraaff and his wife, Kathy, live in the Charlotte, North Carolina, area and are proud parents to twelve children.*

INTERVIEWER: Describe the experience or moment when your calling became evident to you.

DR. HANK HANEGRAAFF: It wasn't so much a moment as it was a series of experiences as a new believer where I would share my faith with people and they would ask me questions I didn't have an answer to. As a result of that, I had to say, "That's a good question. I don't know the answer, but I will research and get back to you." Through those experiences I discovered that if you're on the cutting edge of evangelism, you're driven into education. One ends up learning and becoming an ever more effective tool in the hands of the Holy Spirit in the process of reaching people with the message of the gospel. And that was instrumental in my calling because I recognized then that apologetics was a handmaiden to evangelism. So, God could use your well-reasoned answer as a springboard or an opportunity for sharing the goodness of the gospel.

INTERVIEWER: After you sensed this calling what were your first actions? How did your life change immediately after your calling?

DR. HANK HANEGRAAFF: Well, one of the things I did was seek out people who were very accomplished in the field of apologetics, both cult apologetics and apologetics in general. As a result of that I began spending time with accomplished individuals like Dr. Walter Martin. In some sense, that opened the door for me to be involved in doing cult apologetics with Walter Martin, who eventually helped me become president of the Christian Research Institute.

INTERVIEWER: When did you get a vision for your radio program and for being an author?

DR. HANK HANEGRAAFF: I became heavily involved in evangelism and memorizing Scripture, and as a result of that I kind of got pushed forward in ministry. It wasn't as though I had a vision for this as a ministry, but people would be somewhat amazed at what I had memorized, which was a lifestyle very early on as a young Christian with respect to biblical passages or sermons or particular quotations. As a result of that, I was asked to do all kinds of different speaking engagements and asked to preach and that led me towards doing what I'm doing now because I obviously couldn't do the Bible instrument broadcast if I haven't memorized a whole lot of Scripture. I would have to recognize that it was other people who realized my calling long before I ever did.

INTERVIEWER: What has been the biggest shift as you look back on the landscape of your journey? How has your calling matured or evolved?

DR. HANK HANEGRAAFF: I have become increasingly convinced of this idea: *that the real issue is not teaching people all the deviations of all the various cults or world religions but rather becoming so familiar with truth that when a counterfeit looms on the horizon, people will recognize the counterfeit instantaneously.* So, in cult apologetics in particular, there can be an inordinate emphasis on people knowing the cults and all their deviations, and I think the real emphasis needs to be on the truth, and the counterfeit then becomes apparent in light of the truth.

INTERVIEWER: Who have been the most influential people (*that you know personally*) in your journey? How did they influence or impact you?

DR. HANK HANEGRAAFF: In my case there were many people but none more important than my dad. If I look back at his life in retrospect with 20/20 vision, I didn't appreciate him oftentimes as a young person growing up at home. But he influenced me perhaps the most by a life of complete discipline and dedication, such that I learned a lot about the spiritual disciplines through my father. If you look at the embryonic stages of my Christian development, particularly as a Christian leader, it would have been people like Jim Kennedy because through him I learned the principle of spiritual multiplication, which is not just trying to win people to faith in Christ but trying to equip people for evangelism. R. C. Sproul was another influence in the sense of knowing Scripture, which is to say a commitment to learning to read the Bible for all it's worth. Walter Martin in the area of apologetics and reaching the cults for Christ. Jerry Lucas in terms of committing myself to understanding and becoming very conversant with the principles of memorization both with respect to my vocation and my avocation.

INTERVIEWER: What is the greatest single theological theme that seems to come out in your sermons and books and radio programs?

DR. HANK HANEGRAAFF: This may be somewhat counterintuitive but I would say that is the theme of living with eternity in mind. Recognizing that life is a vapor, here today gone tomorrow, and understanding your own mortality as therefore living life in light of forever. I want those I am privileged to influence to raise the gaze from mean earthly vanities to eternal verities so that instead of looking at the temporary, you focus on the eternal.

INTERVIEWER: How do you stay focused on your calling with all the demands that you are under?

DR. HANK HANEGRAAFF: I would say that the primary impetus for focus is involving myself in spiritual disciplines and discipleship. In other words, I think that if you focus on the main and the plain things, everything else falls into place. But if you don't you can easily get distracted by all kinds of peripheral speaking engagements, activities, writing projects, etc. So, you have to focus on the main and the plain things and it starts with your relationship with God then your relationship to your spouse, your relationship to your family members and friends and then to the broader Christian community. *If first things aren't the first things, then everything else devolves.* In other words, if you don't have a relationship with God that's rich and satisfying, then it's going to be difficult to have a rich and satisfying relationship with your spouse.

INTERVIEWER: What makes you laugh?

DR. HANK HANEGRAAFF: In terms of my ministry, I have become sensitized to sensationalism and sophistry. I see so much sophistry, like a pun meister like Bill Maher will say something like, "The Bible was written to be parabolic. It's the idiots who take it literally." And when I hear something like that, which is sensationalism and sophistry mixed together, it makes me laugh because I think, *My goodness, here we are living in an age of scientific enlightenment and here you have a guy who supposedly is sophisticated and smart suggesting that the entire Bible is parabolic when in reality it is a rich reservoir of all kinds of literary genres. And to read the Bible literally doesn't mean to press it into a wooden literal labyrinth but rather to read it in a sense of which it's intended.* And you get these kinds of things from the popular media all the time and I suppose from time to time I'm watching this in amazement and sometimes, I must confess, laugh out loud.

INTERVIEWER: What has been your greatest temptation?

DR. HANK HANEGRAAFF: Well, let me answer that in somewhat of a circuitous fashion. I've often said that if I had known when I wrote *Christianity in Crisis*, which has sold well over a million copies, what I would face as a result of writing it, I probably wouldn't have written it. At first blush that might sound like an expression of cowardice, but what it is in essence, is to say that God gives us the grace we need when we need it. And oftentimes not a moment before and because the grace God gives is moment by moment, oftentimes, there is a temptation to become politically correct as opposed to being biblically correct and being true to the commission that God has given to you in terms of not only a lifestyle but a life calling. I think that temptation always seeps in around the edges because we live in a politically correct society that seeks to shape us in its mold.

INTERVIEWER: What resource has had the most significant impact on your life?

DR. HANK HANEGRAAFF: In my case, as the father of now twelve children, I would have to say the resource that has influenced me the most is actually my children, because my children are consistently giving me insight into life and into living life effectively and into becoming an ever more significant role model. They give me more insights through interaction and through affection and through deep personal relationships than I suppose anybody else. I mean I remember, for example, being with my son David in China just recently and I was asking him, why is it that our children not only loved one another but really loved us as parents? I said to him, "You know, sometimes, I feel like I failed as a father because I'm not a strict disciplinarian. I gave you guys a lot of latitude," And David said to me, "You know, that's just the point." He said, "I don't think on the one hand you tried to micromanage us. On the other hand you have set some boundaries for us." But I think it is when parents try to micromanage their children that their children may end up hating them, whereas on the other hand, if there are no boundaries they may end up not respecting them. So, that to me was a profound insight. It was an insight after the fact to what makes for effective parenting, and that insight came not from a book but came from one of my own kids.

INTERVIEWER: If you were on a deserted island and allowed a certain number of books, what would be your top five?

DR. HANK HANEGRAAFF: Wow! That is difficult for me. You know, I have often said that you have to read the Christian classics. Books like *City of God* by Saint Augustine, and really reading some of the great Puritan writers. So, I think in terms of the genre, Christian classics are significant. In terms of contemporary books, I still remember being deeply impacted by Joni Eareckson Tada's works *When God Weeps* or *Heaven: Your Real Home*, and the reason I think those books were particularly poignant is that they weren't written from the perspective of an ivory tower. They were written from the perspective of a person who had lived what she was writing. Being a quadriplegic in a wheelchair, she's in a very significant place to write about how you can trust God in every single detail of your life whether good or bad, whether difficult or a mountaintop experience. I also think of Os Guinness who has written a lot of books that I think are poignant, profound, and oftentimes very, very short. There's not a lot of fluff involved in his books. And one of the monographs that I'm thinking of as I speak is a book entitled *Fit Body, Fat Minds*. I thought that it was so poignant and profound and the content of it has stuck with me ever since. One of the contemporary writers that I'm reading right now is Rodney Stark I very much appreciate his encyclopedic knowledge of world history.

INTERVIEWER: What is the single most influential piece of advice some-one ever gave you?

DR. HANK HANEGRAAFF: A very significant piece of advice that I got as a new believer was to *memorize Scripture*. In fact, I was told that all Christians memorize Scripture and by the time I found out that that wasn't true, it already become a lifestyle. And I suppose that has impacted my life in ministry as much as anything else. Another very significant piece of advice or information that really impacted my life in a positive manner was hearing early on in my marriage that love was not a feeling . . . that love was a commitment and that feelings ebb and flow but commitments never change. And out of commitments come genuine feeling, but if feeling becomes the bedrock as opposed to commitment, then you have a marriage that is doomed to failure.

INTERVIEWER: What concerns you most about the church right now?

DR. HANK HANEGRAAFF: The number one issue is biblical literacy. I say that's not a problem rather it's *the* problem within the modern Christian church.

INTERVIEWER: What encourages you right now?

DR. HANK HANEGRAAFF: What encourages me the most is my three trips to China where I met with the director of the China Christian Council. They control the registered church in China; CASS, which is a Chinese Academy of Social Sciences that is sort of the Chinese government think tank; and then the director of SARA, the State Administration for Religious Affairs. And being in China, I have seen that even though some of the Chinese policies with respect to Christianity are draconian, in the midst of persecution, in the midst of hardship, I've seen an authentic expression of New Testament Christianity which has been extraordinarily encouraging on the one hand and convicting on the other. To see Christians who, very much like the first-century church, are willing to face whatever indignities they have to face in this life because they recognize the reality of the gospel and are now living with eternity in mind. I often say when people ask me to pray for the persecuted church that I would much rather focus on the fact, or pray for the reality, that the persecuted church is praying for us.

INTERVIEWER: When I say the word *accountability*, what or who comes to mind? Why?

DR. HANK HANEGRAAFF: The first reality that comes to mind is God because I know that while I'm saved by God's grace through faith in Jesus Christ alone, I'm going to give an account for everything I have done in this life. And as Paul says in his letters to the Corinthians, I'm either going to build on the foundation of Jesus Christ using gold, silver, and costly stones or wood, hay, and straw. So, the first accountability I think that every Christian feels is the accountability to God knowing that I cannot live by the dictates of my own will. God has set parameters around my life so that my joy might be complete. In that accountability to Him, if I treat someone in an unkind fashion or if I do anything that is less than consistent with the biblical ethic or worldview, there's a God in heaven that sees and notes how I live my life. And I think that gives me a genuine godly respect and fear in the relationships I have with human beings. I think beyond that all of us as Christian leaders are accountable to our board of directors. Today, because of the landscape within American society, we also are accountable to outside groups like the Evangelical Council for financial accountability. I think though our accountability structures can be manmade they can still have a very significant impact on the way we think.

INTERVIEWER: On the following subjects what nuggets of wisdom come to mind that you would want to pass on to this next generation desiring to serve God, beginning with marriage?

DR. HANK HANEGRAAFF: The one thing that I would harp on, underscore in red, and put explanation points behind is the notion of what love is. I think that all too often, in the modern church, pop culture beckons and postmodern Christians take the bait. And therefore because of watching movies or television, because of the impact of the culture, they come to think that love is a feeling. And therefore, if they don't have the feeling that they must not be in love and then they look for the grass that's greener on the other side of the fence and begin to weave a tangled web. Before long they are getting a divorce and estranged from their children, and then they find out that the grass that they thought was greener was in actuality dead or an illusion. So, I think that the thing that comes to mind with marriage is to recognize that love is not a feeling. Love is a commitment and as a result of the commitment, you'll have feelings. And those feelings will both be negative and positive. In other words, there are times in which you don't feel like you're in love and you think, *How did I ever get myself into this mess?* There are times in which you feel euphoric. But feelings ebb and flow. A commitment should never change.

INTERVIEWER: You have already spoken a great word on raising children . . . would you like to add anything to that?

DR. HANK HANEGRAAFF: The one thing that's critical is unconditional love. That being . . . not just saying to yourself, "I love my kids unconditionally" or "I love my wife unconditionally" but saying it to them often and not with mere words. Only use words when they're necessary and demonstrate your love for your kids with the time you invest in their life.

INTERVIEWER: On finances?

DR. HANK HANEGRAAFF: The greatest thing to know with respect to finances is that I'm a steward not an owner. Romans 12 teaches you to hold everything you have with open hands so that God can take out and put in what He sees fit, and that includes your time, your talents, and your treasure.

INTERVIEWER: On living healthy?

DR. HANK HANEGRAAFF: My thoughts as it pertains to health are words like moderation and balance. One thing I've learned, and this applies not only to living healthy but I think it applies in a much broader sense, is that the Christian life is a life of balance and I think oftentimes we are swept away by faddish formulas where we would be better served to find that happy medium, that balance.

INTERVIEWER: On communication?

DR. HANK HANEGRAAFF: There is no question in my mind that the thing I would want people to know with certainty is that they should be consistent to their gifting. Which is to say, that you have gifts that I don't have. Now, if I try to exercise your gifts, I'm not going to do well and I have gifts that you don't have and if you try to exercise my gifts, you're not going to do so well. So, you need to be consistent with your gifting and I think in a practical sense, evaluate how you speak. There are speakers that I see that I just salivate over because they are so gifted and they are so good at what they do, but they have a completely different style than what I'm comfortable with. If I try to do it their way, I may have a hard time. For example, I can't be inordinately bound by notes and I have to draw from a deep well by being so prepared on a subject. But notes for me are a straightjacket that inhibits my gifting as opposed to displaying my gifting. So, I think in general, the important thing is to be consistent with your gifting and to stand your own style and proclivities and use that rather than trying to use that of someone who is very, very different from you.

INTERVIEWER: If you could give just one piece of advice to this generation, what would it be?

DR. HANK HANEGRAAFF: If I could give one piece of advice it would be to learn to read the Bible for all its worth. What I mean by that is we say that God has spoken and the Bible is the infallible repository for redemptive revelation. If that's true, it seems to me that we would spend an adequate amount of time to understand what God has said. So, if God has spoken, the intended question is "What has God said?" I think that entails learning to read the Bible for all its worth. That is both a science and a skill. It's a science in that certain rules apply. It's a skill in that the more you apply those rules, the better you get at it. The art and science of biblical interpretation is also known as hermeneutics. That the Bible is the infallible repository redemptive revelation is not a narrow-minded perspective but rather an enlightened one. I think that you can build a cumulative case for making that statement and for substantiating that statement. But if indeed we believe that as we should believe that, then I think that we should also learn to read the Bible for all its worth, which is to say that reading the Bible for all its worth is learning to recognize that the Bible is literature. And therefore, we have to understand relationships of words. We have to understand how the Bible uses various genres, how the Bible uses metaphors and prophetic hyperbole and similes such as extended similes like parables. And therefore, if we do, then we're going to read the Bible in the sense in which it's intended, as opposed to reading the Bible in a way that makes God's gift to us less than what it actually is.

INTERVIEWER: If you permit I would like to ask some light questions that have some pretty short answers . . . beginning with what is your favorite sports team?

DR. HANK HANEGRAAFF: The Detroit Lions. Every single year when football season comes around I start thinking about the possibility that they might finally break through and do something significant and actually get into the playoffs. And as long as it is still a mathematical possibility, I watch them and I root for them and I hope. And as soon as the mathematical possibility is over, then I start thinking about the following year.

INTERVIEWER: Favorite movie?

DR. HANK HANEGRAAFF: Well, I'll give you two, the first being *Dirty Rotten Scoundrels*, which is a movie that I remember belly laughing during such that my kids actually moved away from me because they were embarrassed. In terms of a movie that's always impacted me on some sort of a visceral level, *Chariots of Fire*, mainly because of Eric Liddell's statement, "When I run, I sense His pleasure." That has always had such an impact on me because it is an indication that God made Eric Liddell to be fast and he honed the gift that God had given him, and honing that gift opened all kinds of doors for him to be a witness on a broad and national scale. Yet he decided ultimately to shirk the spotlight and to be faithful to a calling that he felt God had on his life with respect to missions.

INTERVIEWER: Greatest band ever?

DR. HANK HANEGRAAFF: Kansas . . . Phil Ehart, the drummer for Kansas, is a good friend of mine.

INTERVIEWER: Dream vacation?

DR. HANK HANEGRAAFF: Anywhere with my wife and kids.

INTERVIEWER: Favorite hobby?

DR. HANK HANEGRAAFF: Golf.

INTERVIEWER: Favorite TV show as a kid?

DR. HANK HANEGRAAFF: *Bonanza*.

INTERVIEWER: If you could give just one piece of advice to this generation, what would it be?

DR. HANK HANEGRAAFF: Seek first the Kingdom of God and His righteousness and all these things will be added to you as well.

CHAPTER 35

A CONVERSATION WITH

Rebecca St. James

Very early on, the spotlight was on Rebecca St. James. She has been an example and inspiration for young women worldwide since her career in Christian music began at age sixteen. Through the years, Rebecca has been a consistent and competent voice in the area of purity, and has refused to compromise on the idea of biblical womanhood. Born in Australia, but now residing in Nashville, Tennessee, Rebecca has received multiple Grammy and Dove awards, record sales reaching into the multi-millions, and international acclaim. She is a spokesperson for the relief agency Compassion International and has recently branched out into the film industry, acting in several national film productions. When not writing, singing, or acting, Rebecca can often be found hanging out with her parents and six siblings and feeding animals on the family farm.

INTERVIEWER: Describe the experience or moment when your calling became evident to you.

REBECCA ST. JAMES: I was twelve years old when I gave my "gifts and talents" to God at my Christian school in Brisbane, Australia. I remember feeling a real passion for God to use my life to impact the world. I wasn't sure what I had to give or how He could use me, but I wanted Him to know that I was available. It is still the passion of my heart to be used by Him . . . to be on His adventure for my life. And I don't want to assume that just because God has used me in a certain way in the past that this is the way it must continue. I want to be open to the new paths He may want to lead me in. It might not be broke, but He may want to fix it in a different way!

INTERVIEWER: After you sensed this calling, what were your first actions? How did your life change immediately after your calling?

REBECCA ST. JAMES: Opportunities to be involved in music started being presented to me very soon after I surrendered what I had to God. He opened a door for me to be involved in a Christian rock band at school and a recording group as well, and that's where and how my music calling really began.

INTERVIEWER: When did you get a vision for your present ministry?

REBECCA ST. JAMES: Along with music, these days I am acting a lot in faith and family films. I love it! It's an art form that I began to have a passion for when I saw *The Sound of Music* in Sydney while growing up there! In watching cultural trends, I have seen that there is a real need for believers to be involved in the very powerful medium of film. We need to be creating content that is God-honoring, excellent, and trendsetting, not trend following. So for the last few years I've had a growing passion to be in the mix here in L.A., partnering with other believers to be a light in a creatively dark world.

INTERVIEWER: What has been the biggest shift as you look back on the landscape of your journey? How has your calling matured or evolved?

REBECCA ST. JAMES: The biggest shift I've seen in me is how I respond now to the pain and challenges of ministry. Burnout has been something that I've struggled with on and off and is more painful than what those who have not experienced it can imagine. Initially I denied that I was running on empty, but then I started diminishing spiritually and emotionally. I would take sabbaticals to help drive off the worst of it, and for a long time I even resented the pain. Now I see that though burnout is not what God wanted for me [Matt. 11:28], He has used it for good in my life. Pain can create greater compassion and empathy for those who are hurting. I was even able to use the experiences I've had to assist the development of my character Sarah in the last film I acted in.

INTERVIEWER: Who have been the most influential people (*that you know personally*) in your journey? How did they influence or impact you?

REBECCA ST. JAMES: I would say my parents. My dad has been my manager for the last fifteen years of ministry and has been the one to steer my focus and largely orchestrate the opportunities I've had. He has also encouraged me not to buy into the traps of the limelight. My mum is a rock that helps bring me balance in the crazy touring-recording-writing-interviewing-acting world that I now find myself.

INTERVIEWER: What is the greatest single theological theme that seems to come out in your ministry, whether it be songs, books, or speaking?

REBECCA ST. JAMES: Probably the two vying themes have been purity and the love of God. I believe that for purity to truly (long-term) play out in our lives, there must be a deep understanding of the fact that God *extravagantly* loves us and that His way is best.

INTERVIEWER: How have you stayed focused on what God has called you to do? What role have spiritual disciplines, such as Bible study, played in keeping that focus?

REBECCA ST. JAMES: Having major accountability, a wonderful mentor, being plugged into my church, having great Christian friends have all played a really important role. Reading the Bible and devotional books, praying before events and other ministry opportunities, reading substantive books and Christian fiction, guarding myself from watching or listening to damaging movies and music . . . Yeah, I would say these have all been very key.

INTERVIEWER: What makes you laugh?

REBECCA ST. JAMES: I LOVE a great romantic comedy. And goofy friends make me laugh. I would also have to say *The Office*.

INTERVIEWER: What has been your greatest temptation?

REBECCA ST. JAMES: Faking it. When I hurt, I want to hide. When you're in platform ministry, you can't hide. So sometimes the way of coping is to go through the motions somewhat. But it kills you. It's slow heart suicide. The way of healthy ministry is for what's happening on the inside to be the same as what's occurring on the outside. Though I have always believed in what I have said and done from the stage, I know that I have resorted to "going through the motions" to survive at times. I'm more committed today to congruency than I have ever been.

INTERVIEWER: What resource (book, ministry, place, etc.) has had the most significant impact on your life?

REBECCA ST. JAMES: Life-coaching has been a massive vehicle of God's love and grace to me. My life coach has been a spiritual advisor, mentor, decision coach, and counselor. God has used this ministry to bring new life to me both personally and vocationally.

INTERVIEWER: If you were on a deserted island and allowed a certain number of books, what would be your top five?

REBECCA ST. JAMES: Let Go by Fenelon. A Voice in the Wind by Francine Rivers. My Utmost for His Highest by Oswald Chambers. The Inner Voice of Love by Henri Nouwen. The Bible.

INTERVIEWER: What is the single most influential piece of advice someone ever gave you (for better or worse)?

REBECCA ST. JAMES: "Don't believe your own publicity." Followed closely by, "Pain can give you the energy you need to propel you into positive change in your life, so don't resist/resent it."

INTERVIEWER: Is there one particular quote that has always stuck with you?

REBECCA ST. JAMES: "A life lived in fear is a life half lived" from Strictly Ballroom.

INTERVIEWER: What concerns you most about the church right now?

REBECCA ST. JAMES: My concern is that the liberalism of the world is infiltrating the church to the point where we aren't any different, and Jesus' love and holiness is not being seen.

INTERVIEWER: What encourages you most? What is the church doing right?

REBECCA ST. JAMES: The church's recent recommitment to social justice is very encouraging.

INTERVIEWER: When I say the word *accountability*, what or who comes to mind? Why?

REBECCA ST. JAMES: My best friend Karleen, my dear friend Vicky, my mentor Evie, my family, my pastor, and the Bible all immediately come to mind when I think of the word *accountability*. I think it's really important to invite people into our lives to challenge us, not just to say things that are easy to hear . . . and I love that these people do that in my life.

INTERVIEWER: On the following subjects, what nuggets of wisdom come to mind that you would want to pass on to this next generation desiring to serve God, beginning with marriage?

REBECCA ST. JAMES: Love unconditionally. Watching my parents' marriage has been the best marriage education ever.

INTERVIEWER: Raising children?

REBECCA ST. JAMES: Promote a "no secrets" policy. It was one of the best things my parents ever did.

INTERVIEWER: Finances?

REBECCA ST. JAMES: Protect ministry life from becoming about the paycheck or materialism. I think it's a ministry/heart killer.

INTERVIEWER: Living healthy?

REBECCA ST. JAMES: Prioritize eating healthy and staying active—it helps work out the stress of leadership.

INTERVIEWER: Communication?

REBECCA ST. JAMES: Be authentic. People want to see your heart and hear your story. Always communicate humanity mixed with hope and stay connected to Jesus.

INTERVIEWER: If you could give just one piece of advice to this generation, what would it be?

REBECCA ST. JAMES: Understand the love of Jesus personally and live out of that LOVED place.

INTERVIEWER: If you would permit, I would like to ask some light questions that will have some pretty short answers . . . starting with your favorite sports team.

REBECCA ST. JAMES: All Australian ones.

INTERVIEWER: Favorite movie?

REBECCA ST. JAMES: *The Wedding Planner*.

INTERVIEWER: Greatest band ever?

REBECCA ST. JAMES: U2.

INTERVIEWER: Dream vacation?

REBECCA ST. JAMES: Rome, Italy.

INTERVIEWER: Favorite hobby?

REBECCA ST. JAMES: Swing dancing, followed closely by roller-blading.

INTERVIEWER: Favorite TV show as a kid?

REBECCA ST. JAMES: *Smurfs*.

INTERVIEWER: If your own child were graduating from high school, what would be the main piece of advice you would offer to them on graduation night?

REBECCA ST. JAMES: Stick close to God and His people and let Him guide you into the adventure of a lifetime.

CHAPTER 36

A CONVERSATION WITH

Tony Nolan

Tony Nolan loves to tell others about Jesus. Nothing lights his fire like seeing others come to a saving faith in Jesus Christ. As an itinerant evangelist, Tony uses his wacky sense of humor and intense speaking style to help people connect with God in a life-changing way. Tony recently served as tour pastor and gospel communicator for Casting Crowns' Lifesong Tour and Winter Jam, the largest Christian concert tour in America. Not only does Tony speak at many conferences, festivals, concerts, and churches, he has also written devotional books and produced several popular DVD and CD teaching resources. Tony lives with his bride, Tammy, and their four children, Christy, Will, Bradly, and Joy, in Woodstock, Georgia.

INTERVIEWER: Describe the experience or moment when your calling became evident to you.

TONY NOLAN: About eighteen years ago I was reading in John 21 for my daily Bible reading where Jesus told Peter to feed His sheep. I can't explain what happened other than to say it felt like God had just sent me a text message. There was a heavy impression and restlessness in my heart to pursue what was meant in that text . . . What was Jesus saying to Peter? And there were individuals in my life who were praying for me and knew that God was calling me, but they wanted me to come to that understanding on my own. After praying through and studying that text, I came to the conclusion that God was calling me to let go of my past jobs, like Peter had to do with his fishing nets, and also let go of my past failures. What I learned is that failures have a way of crippling you from being able to venture out into the unknown with God. So even though Peter had denied Christ, and even though I had a checkered past, God was still going to use me for His purposes. I spent about a month in that segment towards the end of John 21 and realizing that God was calling me.

INTERVIEWER: After you sensed this calling, what were your first actions? How did your life change immediately after your calling?

TONY NOLAN: Practically speaking there were two experiences. I experienced a lot of excitement and then even more tension. I was excited that I was invited by the Lord to join Him on this extraordinary expedition of faith to service. But I was absolutely overwhelmed by the tensions and the unknowns of the journey. Even though I had never been where I felt He was calling me, I really was invigorated by the profound reality that God had an eternal purpose for my existence on this earth. While I can't say there were particular action steps I took towards having an official ministry role, I can say that I was involved in the activity of my life operating in such a way that there was an invitation from God. I just tried to serve Him wherever I might be. At that particular time in life, I cleaned toilets, roofed houses, and mowed yards, but now I was doing it for God.

INTERVIEWER: How did you get a vision for being an evangelist?

TONY NOLAN: I was taught to define vision as a preferred future where God wants me to be. Therefore I had a vision for what I am presently doing from the moment of my calling. The foundation of my calling comes out of Ephesians 2:10, which says, "We are His workmanship, created in Christ Jesus for good works, which God prepared in advance for us to do." So, my calling was simply to be God's. In the beginning it wasn't to be a preacher or an evangelist; it was just to be God's. I was pursuing

"His-ness" where my major focus is that I am His. By focusing on His-ness it kept God unrivaled in my heart, making me aware of the prepared future and good works He has for me. Because of all this, my heart was tender and open to the doors of opportunity God ordained and enabled me to step through.

INTERVIEWER: What has been the biggest shift as you look back on the landscape of your journey? How has your calling matured or evolved?

TONY NOLAN: I was running the race content with being His whether that meant serving in the nursery at church, driving widows to church events, lining up the chairs, opening up the doors at the church, or whatever. Then there was an opportunity that came out of nowhere. People started asking me to come share my story. Then I was invited to do an event with Third Day at First Baptist Church Orlando. It was the Florida State Youth Evangelism Conference, and so that night I preached and over nine hundred students responded during the invitation. After that moment, we started getting invitations to come and preach and draw the net. I was just trying to help people see and seize the love of God and what He did on the cross. So that was the biggest shift in my ministry.

INTERVIEWER: Who have been the most influential people (*that you know personally*) in your journey? How did they influence or impact you?

TONY NOLAN: No one is going to know this person, but it is a guy by the name of Tony Hamet. If there's one person that has influenced me the most to do what I'm doing, it is he. He's not even an evangelist or pastor; as a matter of fact, he was a pot-smoking gambler. Early in my relationship with Jesus, I didn't really know how to share Christ because I had just been converted. But there was an outward manifestation of this inward transformation that happened in my life. So one day I was at the mall looking for a job and I ran across Tony, and God impressed upon my heart to share Jesus with him . . . and I didn't. I was scared and I broke under the pressure. I made small talk and then walked away from this opportunity. As we went two different directions, my heart broke because I had been disobedient to the leading of the Holy Spirit. About a month later, I was working with a friend of mine mowing yards and I was planting flowers in a flower bed for this guy and he said, "Hey, did you hear what happened to Tony Hamlet?" Right then I knew something terrible had happened. He explained to me that Tony had been murdered. And he got murdered by a friend of mine named Kenny who actually came to my house after my conversion and asked me for some pot. I only responded to him that I didn't do that anymore, as if he would put it all together that I followed Jesus now because I don't smoke pot. Within a two-week period of time after seeing Kenny, he had shot and killed Tony. So Tony is the most influential person in my life, because in the back of my mind and heart I never want the Tonys of this world to run past me having not met Jesus. Another very influential person in my life would be Dr. Johnny Hunt—he's my pastor—because the bottom line is his passion for the lost is as contagious as the common cold. I would also say the evangelist Junior Hill has made a great impression on my life because he encouraged me to preach the gospel. I would also add David Nasser, because every time I have connected with him I felt like I have been mentored. The last guy I would mention is Louie Giglio, because he has taught me so much about the greatness and glory of God.

INTERVIEWER: What is the greatest single theological theme that seems to come out in your sermons and books?

TONY NOLAN: Life is so short that we must be prepared for eternity. Now that may mean standing on a platform and sharing a message or paying somebody's rent and telling them about Jesus.

INTERVIEWER: How have you stayed focused on what God has called you to do? What role have spiritual disciplines, such as Bible study, played in keeping that focus?

TONY NOLAN: Pastor Johnny said the other day that the longer one is in the faith the more they forget about what it is like to not have Jesus. So I try to position myself to stay in contact with people who are still outside the Christian faith. I hang out with them whether in the virtual world or face-to-face. Also, I daily get in the Word of God. I also try to make sure I have time when I am alone singing spiritual songs to Him and reflecting upon His goodness in my life. All of this helps me place my ear against His chest and hear His heartbeat for those who don't know Him yet. There is one last thing I do that is going to sound a little crazy. When I am on the road, I will look for a cemetery that is close to the hotel where I am staying. So I will go park my car, get out, and slowly walk through the cemetery stopping at times to read the headstones. I do this because it reminds me of the brevity of life and the finality of death. I always leave that experience focused on my calling.

INTERVIEWER: What makes you laugh?

TONY NOLAN: It seems like in this sin-cursed world life has a way of making us endure Jesus instead of enjoying Him. I think laughter is a great thing and we should enjoy life. Everyone needs to pray for me because I laugh at other people's misfortune. For example, a lady tripped and fell in front of me the other day and it just cracked me up. Don't get me wrong—I helped her up—but something about that whole thing just cracked me up because she didn't just fall . . . she tripped over a cord, took out a rack of clothes, and lost her glasses.

INTERVIEWER: What has been your greatest temptation?

TONY NOLAN: Temptation is that thing that is luring you like the sirens singing their intoxicating song to you. So, it would be clearly the porn on the Internet. When I was a little kid growing up in a home that didn't know God, it was everywhere. And now just knowing the accessibility of it can be tempting. I have places on the backside of my heart that are dark, ugly, and lustful . . . therefore I must never give the devil a foothold in my life and always strive for His-ness. I have an accountability relationship with several guys through a ministry called Covenant Eyes, and it keeps me from letting the beast within be in control and destroy my life. Mark Hall is going to get a copy of every Web site that I go to from my laptop or any computer I have. So when I think of accountability I break it down—account-ability, which means *knowing that I'm going to be given an account for my actions today gives me the ability to give a good account tomorrow.* I enjoy having victory as a result of being in Christ and having a partnership with God.

INTERVIEWER: What resource has had the most significant impact on your life?

TONY NOLAN: Certainly the Bible is number one, because in reading it I am hearing the mind and heart of God. So many times as a result of spending time in the Bible I recall certain verses at important times in my life. It's not like I pushed a button; rather His Word was in my mind and my thoughts were marinating on the Scriptures and they were accessible.

INTERVIEWER: If you were on a deserted island and allowed a certain number of books, what would be your top five?

TONY NOLAN: The Bible; *How to Start a Fire* by Bill Stewart; *How to Eat the Things you Never Thought You Would Eat* by Jim Clifton; *Sending*

Out an SOS That Works by Living with Yourself by Keith Hazel. Dude, if I'm on a desert island, those are the books I want! But some of the books that have most impacted my life are as follows: The Bible . . . hey it made both lists; *The Best Question Ever* by Andy Stanley; *Christian Theology* by Millard Erickson; *I Am Not, but I Know I Am* by Louie Giglio. Actually I want to have two copies of Louie's book just in case I use the first one to start a fire.

INTERVIEWER: What is the single most influential piece of advice some-one ever gave you?

TONY NOLAN: "If you're going to go and preach about faith, you prob-ably ought to have some." My pastor Johnny Hunt shared that with me when I was freaking out about leaving a full-time paycheck as a college pastor to surrender to this call to be an evangelist.

INTERVIEWER: Is there one particular quote that has always stuck with you?

TONY NOLAN: I recently heard Stephen Furtick from Elevation Church say, "When you want what God wants, for the reasons He wants it, you are unstoppable."

INTERVIEWER: What concerns you most about the church right now?

TONY NOLAN: Man, you can put this in all caps if you want—what con-cerns me most is *THE LACK OF CONFIDENCE IN THE POWER OF THE GOSPEL TO REALLY TRANSFORM SINNERS*. Here is how that is mani-fested. I just got this while preaching on this last tour where we saw over 69,000 people respond to the gospel. You would think that people in the church would celebrate that God is mighty to save! Right? Yet I have hundreds of letters from people that are critical and very cynical, saying things like, "Well, I wonder if they really meant it?" or "I bet it was just an emotional decision." And the one that gets to me the most, "I wonder if there will be any fruit that remains?" I read these letters and think where is this coming from? And I think the reason is that our first inclination is to doubt the validity of these decisions instead of rejoice over the fact that the gospel is powerful enough to transform.

INTERVIEWER: What encourages you most? What is the church doing right?

TONY NOLAN: That the gospel is still the power of God to salvation. Recently I was in Columbus, Ohio, and a lady comes up to me and said, "I've been looking for you for two years." She said, "I was a stripper. I went to church and tried it. I heard the whispers from the people and I saw the judgmental looks on their faces." Now she was a very pretty girl, but you could tell that the world had worn her down. Then she said, "I was invited by a friend and attended Winter Jam Tour here two years ago. I heard the music and I heard the gospel and I gave my life to Jesus Christ." So of course I asked, "How are you doing now?" She said, "I haven't given up on the church yet because we are all a bunch of converts anyways, so God help us." She goes on to tell me how she started this ministry to strippers where she goes in and befriends them, lets them live in her home, teaches them life skills, and hopefully leads them to Jesus. She went on to tell me how they become citizens who are now working jobs for the glory of God. Now that is the power of God to salvation. Go God!!! God has allowed me to hear several testimonies like that recently that have been such a phenomenal source of encouragement. So I am encouraged because I am celebrating Jesus and what He is doing in this world.

INTERVIEWER: What do you look for in an accountability partner?

TONY NOLAN: Well, don't just look for a friend, because friends have a tendency to be weak. Many times you can tell a friend your struggles and they will just look back at you and say, "Oh, yeah? I've been struggling with that too. Let's pray together." Then before long you fall victim to what I call the "buddy syndrome." So I would encourage people to have accountability in their life that they are, in one sense, afraid of because they are spiritual heros to you and you don't want to let them down.

INTERVIEWER: On the following subjects what nuggets of wisdom come to mind that you would want to pass on to this next generation desiring to serve God, starting with marriage?

TONY NOLAN: I've not always practiced this, but I think I have broken the code on what it takes to have a good one. It is what I call "The P2:3 Factor." The P2:3 Factor is from Philippians 2:3, which says, "Let nothing be done through establish ambition or conceit, but in lowliness of mind let each esteem others as better than himself." This is the guiding idea in how my wife and I grow our relationship.

INTERVIEWER: On raising children?

TONY NOLAN: When you're home . . . be home. I spend time with each one of my children every day when I'm home. That has been key, and once a month I do something special with each of my kids individually where I may take them somewhere. Also I date my wife regularly. Every Tuesday night I am home I take my wife out, and that provides my kids with a sense of security, knowing that Daddy's still crazy about Mommy. This has proven to be a strong ingredient for us in raising our kids and, obviously, it's going to help out with our marriage.

INTERVIEWER: On finances?

TONY NOLAN: Tithe and don't even debate it. Be crazy giver. Act your wage and never have debt.

INTERVIEWER: On living healthy?

TONY NOLAN: I try to eat lots of protein, drink lots of water, go to bed early when I can, and exercise every day.

INTERVIEWER: On communication?

TONY NOLAN: I write two words at the top of every message I preach, "So what?" I believe everyone is asking that question when they hear anyone communicate: "So what is this going to do for me?" Never apologize for feeling strongly about what you are saying. We live in a pluralistic culture, which causes everyone to feel double-minded. Don't allow pluralism to dumb you down . . . share the message loud and often.

INTERVIEWER: If you could give just one piece of advice to this generation, what would it be?

TONY NOLAN: Don't just talk about community . . . deliver it. Let God love through you and love even those who hurt you, for that very well may lead to forgiveness.

INTERVIEWER: If you permit I would like to ask some light questions that have some pretty short answers . . . beginning with, what is your favorite sports team?

TONY NOLAN: Atlanta Braves and the St. Louis Cardinals.

INTERVIEWER: Favorite movie?

TONY NOLAN: *The Count of Monte Cristo.*

INTERVIEWER: Greatest band ever?

TONY NOLAN: Casting Crowns.

INTERVIEWER: Dream vacation?

TONY NOLAN: Anywhere with my family.

INTERVIEWER: Favorite hobby?

TONY NOLAN: Playing with my kids, surfing, and diving for lobsters.

INTERVIEWER: Favorite TV show as a kid?

TONY NOLAN: *Little House on the Prairie.*

INTERVIEWER: If your own child were graduating from high school, what would be the main piece of advice you would offer to them on graduation night?

TONY NOLAN: Follow God and cash in on Proverbs 3:5-6: "Trust in the LORD with all your heart, and lean not on your own understanding; in all your ways acknowledge Him, and He shall direct your paths."

CHAPTER 37

A CONVERSATION WITH

Dr. Ergun Caner

Ergun Caner is president of the Liberty Theological Seminary at the Liberty University in Lynchburg, Virginia. Raised as the son of a Muslim leader in Turkey, Caner became a Christian shortly before entering college. Under his chancellor and president, Jerry Falwell Jr., Caner has led the seminary to triple in growth since his installation in 2005. A public speaker and apologist, Caner has debated Buddhists, Muslims, Hindus, and other religious leaders in thirteen countries and thirty-five states. The author of seventeen books, Caner lives in Lynchburg with his wife, Jill, and two sons, Braxton and Drake.

———

INTERVIEWER: Describe the experience or moment when your calling became evident to you.

DR. ERGUN CANER: I had been saved eight months, and in my church (Free Church, Anabaptist) there is no difference between the called and the laity. We are *all* called to ministry. So it was a no-brainer. I knew I was called to service. I just did not know where.

INTERVIEWER: After you sensed this calling what were your first actions? How did your life change immediately after your calling?

DR. ERGUN CANER: I told my church immediately in a public invitation. That was Sunday morning. My *first* sermon was *that* Sunday night!

INTERVIEWER: When did you get a vision for your present ministry?

DR. ERGUN CANER: After seventeen years of getting it wrong! I thought I was supposed to pastor, because I thought that was all there was, but I do not have the mercy gift of the shepherd. I was a grumpy pastor, and a poor one at that. By 1999, I knew I was called to teach.

INTERVIEWER: What has been the biggest shift as you look back on the landscape of your journey? How has your calling matured or evolved?

DR. ERGUN CANER: That the call is so much more vast than the role of pastor. There are so many vocational jobs out there! And *now*, we rarely see speakers calling out the called. Most sermons are to the lost or the backslidden.

INTERVIEWER: Who have been the most influential people (*that you know personally*) in your journey? How did they influence or impact you?

DR. ERGUN CANER: Dr. Paige Patterson and Dr. Jerry Falwell. Men of unbridled vision, and without fear of critics who taught me to stand firm, regardless of those who stand against you—even friends.

INTERVIEWER: What is the greatest single theological theme that seems to come out in your sermons and books?

DR. ERGUN CANER: Christ died for the world, and every single beating heart is someone that God wants a relationship with.

INTERVIEWER: How have you stayed focused on what God has called you to do? What role have spiritual disciplines, such as Bible study, played in keeping that focus?

DR. ERGUN CANER: I fast the distractions—Internet, e-mail, Twitter, Facebook. I purposefully limit my own use of them, or otherwise they become time vampires, sucking away from my devotional life.

INTERVIEWER: What makes you laugh?

DR. ERGUN CANER: Well-spoken sarcasm.

INTERVIEWER: What has been your greatest temptation?

DR. ERGUN CANER: Responding to critics. Bill Graham said that the devil would want nothing more than to see us waste time responding to critics, instead of preaching the gospel. I get attacked on all sides—Muslims, Buddhists, activists, vegans. I ignore them all.

INTERVIEWER: What resource (book, ministry, place, etc.) has had the most significant impact on your life?

DR. ERGUN CANER: The *Criswell Guidebook for Pastors* has had an amazing impact on my preaching. *Saving Life of Christ* by Major Ian Thomas drove me to my knees, impacting me greatly.

INTERVIEWER: If you were on a deserted island and allowed a certain number of books, what would be your top five?

DR. ERGUN CANER: Norman Geisler, *Chosen But Free*; *If I Perish, I Perish*, Major Ian Thomas; *Willmington's Guidebook of the Bible*; *Summa Theologica* by Thomas Aquinas; and *Sacred Books of the East*.

INTERVIEWER: What is the single most influential piece of advice someone ever gave you (for better or worse)?

DR. ERGUN CANER: "Never ask the size of the church, or the size of the check"—Dr. Paige Patterson. This wisdom has kept me from becoming greedy.

INTERVIEWER: Is there one particular quote that has always stuck with you?

DR. ERGUN CANER: When I was trying to quote Greek and Hebrew to the people all the time, a lady told me, "Leave the cooking in the kitchen, just bring out the meal." That was in 1986 and I have never forgotten it.

INTERVIEWER: What concerns you most about the church right now?

DR. ERGUN CANER: Young leaders who don't listen to the elders, like Reheboam, and elders who fight to keep their position, like Saul.

INTERVIEWER: What encourages you most? What is the church doing right?

DR. ERGUN CANER: A generation of youth that is fearless.

INTERVIEWER: When I say the word *accountability*, what or who comes to mind? Why?

DR. ERGUN CANER: Local church. Plain and simple—accountability comes through the local fellowship.

INTERVIEWER: On the following subjects what nuggets of wisdom come to mind that you would want to pass on to this next generation desiring to serve God, beginning with marriage?

DR. ERGUN CANER: Never settle and never rush. God will bring the person who lifts you up in His time, not when you are desperate.

INTERVIEWER: Raising children?

DR. ERGUN CANER: They are your first, second, and last priority. Take them with you everywhere, and make the experience a shared one.

INTERVIEWER: Finances?

DR. ERGUN CANER: Never work for a paycheck or you become a slave. Never let anyone or any job own you.

INTERVIEWER: Living healthy?

DR. ERGUN CANER: You can rest when you are dead.

INTERVIEWER: Communication?

DR. ERGUN CANER: Writing, more than anything, is the legacy that lives beyond you. Never take a publisher's "No" as final. If you are called to write, you will keep at it until someone listens.

INTERVIEWER: If you could give just one piece of advice to this generation, what would it be?

DR. ERGUN CANER: Preach, teach, reach, or shut up and get out of the way! The world is dying for the Truth—so share it passionately. It is a sin to be boring.

INTERVIEWER: If you would permit me I would like to ask some light questions that have some pretty short answers . . . beginning with, what is your favorite sports team?

DR. ERGUN CANER: Pittsburgh Steelers.

INTERVIEWER: Favorite movie?

DR. ERGUN CANER: *Monty Python and the Holy Grail.*

INTERVIEWER: Greatest band ever?

DR. ERGUN CANER: Led Zeppelin.

INTERVIEWER: Dream vacation?

DR. ERGUN CANER: European cruise.

INTERVIEWER: Favorite hobby?

DR. ERGUN CANER: Books.

INTERVIEWER: Favorite TV show as a kid?

DR. ERGUN CANER: *Dukes of Hazzard.*

INTERVIEWER: If your own child were graduating from high school, what would be the main piece of advice you would offer to them on graduation night?

DR. ERGUN CANER: No one calls you except God, not even me. Listen to Him alone, and stand strong. The test of your faith will be: can you praise God at midnight? Anyone can praise Him when everything is fine. True faith trusts in Him, not circumstance.

CHAPTER 38

A CONVERSATION WITH

Kevin Huguley

From an early age, Kevin Huguley has dreamed of being in ministry. Now he's getting to see his dreams come true. As vocalist, guitarist, and keyboard player for the groundbreaking band Rush of Fools, Kevin now loads the bus with the rest of his Birmingham, Alabama-based bandmates, touring nationally, as well as performing at many camps, conferences, and festivals. Kevin shares life with his bride Malerie.

INTERVIEWER: Describe the experience or moment when your calling became evident to you.

KEVIN HUGULEY: The Lord used my college years to truly shape *everything* about my life. Having been a follower of Jesus almost ten years at that point, I could sense God really moving me to seek wise counsel in the areas I would need to focus on for my developing passions. I remember a large amount of growth in my life was not just musically, but spiritually and theologically as well. I think the moments or experience to identify *my* calling became most evident to me simply through older godly men pouring into my life, sacrificing their time and energy to let me be their "Timothy." These men ranged from pastors, elders, and campus ministers that woke up early on certain days to grab a bagel and talk Jesus with me. There were a few years towards the conclusion of my collegiate life at Auburn University that I served in a leadership role at a couple of campus ministries leading worship and Bible studies. One of the earliest and most influential times realizing my calling was through being a part of a church plant in the city before my wife and I moved back to Birmingham. That plant, still going on today, and its precious people are one of the absolute highlights of my college days. The callings that God places on our lives seem to become *really* clear once we get our feet wet a little bit. At least it was that way for me.

INTERVIEWER: After you sensed this calling, what were your first actions? How did your life change immediately after your calling?

KEVIN HUGULEY: Honestly, most days it feels like I'm still living out my first actions. The ministry we have now with Rush of Fools is still in its infancy. We are in our third year of full-time ministry with regards to traveling as a worship band, and many days we are perplexed as to why God chose to use us in the first place. We are still trying to figure out what we're doing and why we're doing it sometimes, but nonetheless, we are seeking to be obedient to the gospel. With regards to how life has changed, it is as easy as understanding the concept of a fast-forward button. Things moved so quick for our ministry, and so it seems like God was that mean uncle that wanted us to learn how to swim as soon as we were in the pool for the first time. So like any good mean uncle would do, He just threw us in the deep end with our little orange arm floats already deflated.

INTERVIEWER: When did you get a vision for Rush of Fools?

KEVIN HUGULEY: With our story, the vision of our present ministry is unified as a whole, and yet it looks different for each of us involved. Even so, the vision is more than likely still shaping itself out on some of the more specific aspects of why we do what we do. It's difficult to flesh this idea out on paper, but it is easy to see that those of us God chose to be in this worship band are wired differently by God's design and purpose. Myself and one other Fool are the two songwriters/leaders, and I can honestly say that the two of us feel that we are the least musical out of the group. However, all of us on the road truly take ownership in the vision of what God has called us to do. The desire for our ministry and vision is to write biblical worship songs to encourage the Church, because we believe that Jesus has changed everything about us. Our vision to live out this ministry from a biblical perspective became clearer in the early stages of our road life, seeing some people around us make great decisions that seemed to be honoring to the Kingdom of God, as well as seeing people make decisions that we felt we could learn what *not* to do with regards to our ministry and calling.

INTERVIEWER: What has been the biggest shift as you look back on the landscape of your journey? How has your calling matured or evolved?

KEVIN HUGULEY: Our biggest shift might not look so big due to the short-lived journey so far. It is likely true that the only obvious shift has been in the evolution of our songwriting, and in our desire to push our own lyrical envelope. While all of our songs typically come back to us being the bad guys of the story, and Jesus being the hero, we have shaped *how* we say that as we grow artistically. On the first record we put much focus on our sin and thus need for grace, while the more recent album does that while tackling deeper issues like irresistible grace and suffering for God's glory. All the while, we have felt a shift, especially in the songs we are currently writing, to seek out how to grow to be more theological in depth but also more congregational melodically speaking, as we would love for God to use our songs in families of faith all over the world.

INTERVIEWER: Who have been the most influential people (*that you know personally*) in your journey? How did they influence or impact you?

KEVIN HUGULEY: Chad Sentell is one of my mentors, and in the more recent days has become my spiritual and physical mentor, 'cause this body isn't getting any younger. He was a student pastor for years and now serves as a chaplain for a hospice organization; talk about going from one side of the circle of life to the other . . . One of the greatest ways Chad has influenced my life is his willingness to let me see him on good days and bad. He will watch me fall and then give me the opportunity to learn how to fall more gracefully without just showing me how to get things right. There is also great humility that comes from guys like Chad, because he is knowledgeable of so much, yet so cautious with his use of words. Unfortunately for guys like me, we don't know much and want to talk about everything. His impact goes beyond being some guy that prays for me on Tuesday mornings. He has sacrificed many heartbeats of his days here to pour into me, and other guys God has placed on his path.

INTERVIEWER: What is the greatest single theological theme that seems to come out in your sermons and books?

KEVIN HUGULEY: Having grown up in the reformed circle of the church world, there has seemed to be a lack in songs that focus on anything much beyond God's greatness or mercy and grace. While I love those topics as much as the next guy, I feel that we can also worship with songs that go lyrically more to our core depravity and the sufficiency of the blood of Christ over our sinfulness. The absolute sovereignty of God is likely the most consistent theme within our worship songs, but we honestly just want to craft whatever songs (biblically based, of course) God wants for His bride to sing. That parenthetical statement now seems pretty redundant, but if it weren't there I wouldn't have been able to type this sentence.

INTERVIEWER: How have you stayed focused on what God has called you to do? What role have spiritual disciplines, such as Bible study, played in keeping that focus?

KEVIN HUGULEY: To assume I've stayed focused might be dangerous. There is not a doubt that I'm most grateful for my wife, who at the end of the day is not concerned with how many records we have sold or what number our song is on the charts. She is my helpmate and my highest priority right under Jesus, as God's first institution in Genesis is the family. Malerie has been able to be my focus point at the end of a bad day, and it's encouraging to know that she is always there. As regards to additional help, Don Whitney's book *Spiritual Disciplines of the Christian Life* was a great read for me years back in trying to understand basic biblical disciplines to live out as a disciple of Christ.

INTERVIEWER: What makes you laugh?

KEVIN HUGULEY: One of the most humorous things currently in my life is the fact that some people are under the impression that we (Rush Of Fools) are cool. We are so not cool. And when we see people that have been convinced of such a lie, there is great humor to be had. Conan O'Brien also makes me laugh, as well as *The Office*.

INTERVIEWER: What has been your greatest temptation?

KEVIN HUGULEY: To have been given any sort of platform causes something strange in one's self. With that said, one thing that comes with this calling is the excessive expression of affirmative words from others. Let me explain. We are constantly being told from people (with good intentions, I might add) that meet us on the road just how phenomenally amazing we are as guys who travel and do this sort of thing. And I think one of the scariest temptations for me in this line of work and ministry are those times that Satan is hoping that I'll begin to believe what those people are saying. God is absolutely clear in the Bible that I'm far from worthy of anything other than death and hell, so anytime I'm given the opportunity to believe that I'm awesome is a dangerous temptation that I pray I'll never fall into.

INTERVIEWER: What resource (book, ministry, place, etc.) has had the most significant impact on your life?

KEVIN HUGULEY: This is difficult to answer, because I know that the impact that heroes in the faith like Spurgeon, Luther, and Calvin have had goes so far, but I think I'll go with a living guy answer, just because it wraps up multiple resources for me. John Piper, ever since my first read of *Desiring God* so many years ago, has been the single most influential servant of Jesus in my life so far. His ability to communicate and articulate the gospel so well blows my mind, and makes me thankful to Jesus and His grace on Piper's life.

INTERVIEWER: If you were on a deserted island and allowed a certain number of books, what would be your top five?

KEVIN HUGULEY: This is just mean. I'll go from the easiest on: The Bible, Wayne Grudem's *Systematic Theology*, John Piper's *Don't Waste your Life*, Khaled Hosseini's *The Kite Runner*, and some really brilliant guy's manual on how to get off a deserted island alive.

INTERVIEWER: What is the single most influential piece of advice someone ever gave you (for better or worse)?

KEVIN HUGULEY: "Boast only in the Cross of our Lord Jesus." Piper's greatest Passion talk.

INTERVIEWER: Is there one particular quote that has always stuck with you?

KEVIN HUGULEY: "Everyone poops." Not so sure of the author.

INTERVIEWER: What concerns you most about the church right now?

KEVIN HUGULEY: False gospels have been prominent since Jesus, but Christian Smith's research on moralistic therapeutic deism is one of the most frightening things I've thought through lately. The amount of unregenerate church folk has been the greatest concern for me for about five years now.

INTERVIEWER: What encourages you most? What is the church doing right?

KEVIN HUGULEY: At the most recent SBC convention, a great guy and friend, Dr. Danny Akin from Southeastern Baptist Theological Seminary, gave a push for a Great Commission Resurgence. When the body of Christ is about the Great Commission, there is much to be encouraged about.

INTERVIEWER: When I say the word *accountability*, what or who comes to mind? Why?

KEVIN HUGULEY: Adam Lewis, my best friend. He is always willing (sometimes *too* willing) to tell me where I've jacked up.

INTERVIEWER: On the following subjects, what nuggets of wisdom come to mind that you would want to pass on to this next generation desiring to serve God, starting with marriage?

KEVIN HUGULEY: Live in the roles God has ordained. Read 1 Timothy and Titus.

INTERVIEWER: On raising children?

KEVIN HUGULEY: Teach them to love God and obey you.

INTERVIEWER: On finances?

KEVIN HUGULEY: Read any and all of Dave Ramsey's books.

INTERVIEWER: On living healthy?

KEVIN HUGULEY: Find a wife that will cook healthy junk.

INTERVIEWER: On communication?

KEVIN HUGULEY: Be honest.

INTERVIEWER: If you could give just one piece of advice to this generation, what would it be?

KEVIN HUGULEY: Live as Paul did in Philippians 3:1-12, and ask God to help you be willing to lose *everything* for the sake of knowing more of Jesus.

INTERVIEWER: With your permission I would like to ask some light questions that have some pretty short answers . . . beginning with what is your favorite sports team?

KEVIN HUGULEY: Auburn Tigers, War Eagle!

INTERVIEWER: Favorite movie?

KEVIN HUGULEY: *Luther*, or *That Thing You Do*.

INTERVIEWER: Greatest band ever?

KEVIN HUGULEY: The Beatles.

INTERVIEWER: Dream vacation?

KEVIN HUGULEY: Paris, France.

INTERVIEWER: Favorite hobby?

KEVIN HUGULEY: Reading or fishing.

INTERVIEWER: Favorite TV show as a kid?

KEVIN HUGULEY: *Saved by the Bell*.

INTERVIEWER: If your own child were graduating from high school, what would be the main piece of advice you would offer to them on graduation night?

KEVIN HUGULEY: Do what God is calling you to do, not what our culture is expecting you to do.

CHAPTER 39

A CONVERSATION WITH

Dr. Jay Strack

Lauded by Zig Ziglar as "entertaining, powerful, inspiring, and informative," Dr. Jay Strack is an established and highly sought-after communicator. He has authored several books and is acclaimed by leadership in government, business, education, and professional athletics. Jay is president and founder of Student Leadership University, an organization dedicated to equipping the world changers of tomorrow and offering a message of hope and inspiration for our future leaders. Jay and his wife, Diane, reside in Orlando, Florida, and are the parents of two daughters and grandparents of two grandchildren.

Dr. Jay Strack's interview was purposely placed last so that Brent and David could each add a personal note about the profound influence this man has had on both their lives.

A WORD FROM BRENT CROWE:

There is only one other man in my life, being my father, whom I have a deeper sense of respect for than Dr. Jay Strack. Early in my ministry, through a bizarre set of circumstances, our paths crossed and our futures were intertwined together. It is the great privilege of my ministry to serve the organization of Student Leadership University and work side-by-side with one of the great leaders of our time in equipping this generation to earn the right to be heard for the sake of the gospel. Anything great, be it an organization, a dream, or a movement, starts with a great idea. Fifteen years ago Dr. Jay Strack had such an idea with the conception of SLU which teaches thousands of students to think, dream and lead through a set of experiences that include taking them around the world to places like London, Paris, Oxford, Normandy, Rome, Jordan, Palestine and Israel. Every day I am grateful for an idea that evolved into a vision that birthed an organization that hopefully one day will lead a movement. I have learned so much of what I know about influence and ministry through my relationship with Jay and for that I am eternally grateful.

A WORD FROM DAVID NASSER:

Someone once told me to only pick dead heroes. That way you're sure they have finished well. Although this is a good rule, I have to break it when it comes to Dr. Jay Strack. Dr. Jay is a hero to me for several reasons. As a mentor, Dr. Jay has always taken time to invest in my life. When Dr. Jay speaks I listen intently knowing that his counsel has always proven itself to be incredibly valuable. His kindness and allegiance has taught me to be a better friend to others. His commitment to his family has also served as a model worthy to emulate. I love him as a father figure and consider it a blessing to have him in my life.

———

INTERVIEWER: Describe the experience or moment that helped your calling become evident to you.

DR. JAY STRACK: I believe that we're all called to do something once we become a child of God. I believe we're all called to be on mission whether we're a businessman or a doctor or a housewife or a schoolteacher or a student. It is what the Bible calls being a co-laborer with God. But having said that, not to split theological hairs, there is also a calling that can take place after one's salvation experience. Maybe it's because I had such a non-church background. I knew I was clueless about things of God. So when I heard the message of salvation, I was greatly overwhelmed by the love of God. The Lord just made it very clear to me that He had protected me. He showed me that where several of my friends didn't make it home from the party, didn't make it home from a certain fight or whatever the case may be, and yet somehow I did. So I had this sense of gratitude. I had this sense of being spared. So that was a very profound, traumatic experience for me. But it wasn't until I really began to study the Word of God, to be involved in making a difference in the lives of my friends, that I really began to get a sense of what God was calling me to do with the rest of my life.

INTERVIEWER: After you sensed this calling what were your first actions? How did your life change immediately after your calling?

DR. JAY STRACK: When I gave my life to Christ it was like what the Lord said to the disciples: "Go tell your family and friends what great things I've done for you." So, I did that for several years during the Jesus movement in the early '70s all along the beaches of Florida from Miami to Tampa. During that time, I had a job as a traveling salesman to sell various products. I would peddle the latest gadget, leave, and then like an hour and a half out of town I'd have to turn around and go, "I forgot to share with them about Jesus." And that's when the Lord really began to impress upon me, *I'm setting you apart. I want you to tell people about Me.* And so I got on my knees and told God I'll go anywhere and do anything. The next day I got a phone call from Fred Williams, who was in charge of missions for fifty or sixty churches all across Southwest Florida. He would become my father in the ministry, and he told me about a church in the small town of Immokalee, Florida, that needed a pastor. There were seventeen people who attended, and that was my first church, but the first year the Lord would allow us to baptize 106 people. Leading that church gave me a great sense of confirmation that the Lord had in fact called me.

INTERVIEWER: When did you get a vision for Student Leadership University?

DR. JAY STRACK: After a few years in the pastorate I would go on to spend close to thirty years conducting evangelistic crusades throughout the country, and during this time I was asked more and more to speak at universities and high schools. I noticed that the students would be so on fire for God in high school and then something would happen in college. Then I was asked to speak to the Air Force Academy on a repetitive basis observing the decline in morals and ethics among some of the elite students in the country. So after being with the Air Force Academy and on so many high school and college campuses, I began to realize that if our best and brightest are getting shot out of the saddle, what's happening to the average student? I felt God telling me, *Jay, I want you to start spending time trying to give kids the tools they need so they don't stop following Jesus in college. I want you to prepare them.* So I got about fifty youth pastors together that I thought were the best in the nation and asked them their thoughts on the issue. Overwhelmingly the response was that somebody needed to teach our kids Christian worldviews and what it means to be a leader. So SLU and all of our programs are designed so that a youth pastor can have a week with his students without a hundred interruptions to hear their dreams, hear their burdens, hear their failures, see their tears, and most of all help them understand how they were called, so that the students can recognize it themselves when God starts calling them.

INTERVIEWER: What has been the biggest shift as you look back on the landscape of your journey? How has your calling matured or evolved?

DR. JAY STRACK: I think the Lord tried to teach me that I was too committed to evangelism, meaning, it was evangelism versus discipleship. How stupid could we have been getting into all of these theological debates and fights, and at times not even fellowshipping with some people because they were just discipleship guys and we were evangelist guys? So the biggest shift came in my thinking and realizing that the Bible teaches that evangelism and discipleship complement and fuel each other.

INTERVIEWER: Who have been the most influential people in your journey? How did they influence or impact you?

DR. JAY STRACK: There would be three people who helped me become the man I am today. Dr. Williams taught me what it means to serve. He'd come over once a week and eat in our home with us. Later, I would go to the restroom in our little house. There'd be a twenty-dollar bill in the towels or he'd give me a book and inside the book about halfway through there'd be some money. So I mean there was just that constant love, support, and encouragement. Zig Ziglar taught me what it means to lead. He taught me the power of written goals and positive thinking. James Robison opened doors for me and gave me so many opportunities to preach. He wrote a letter for me recommending me to preach all over the country. Our answering machine would fill up each day with opportunities to come preach off of that one letter he wrote. Because of that, I was able to preach forty weeks a year!

INTERVIEWER: What is the greatest single theological theme that seems to come out in your sermons and books?

DR. JAY STRACK: In a sentence, *no matter who you are, no matter what you've done or where you've been, that if you're in Christ, somehow, some way, all things are possible.* I would say this theme stems from the blessed doctrine of justification by faith.

INTERVIEWER: How have you stayed focused on what God has called you to do? What role have spiritual disciplines, such as Bible study, played in keeping that focus?

DR. JAY STRACK: Obviously they play a huge role. The three disciplines in my life that have been the most significant are reading the Scriptures, fasting, and seeking wise counsel to confirm and help give confirmation in my spirit as I have moved forward on some of the big projects throughout my life.

INTERVIEWER: What makes you laugh or who are your top three comedians?

DR. JAY STRACK: When I was a kid there was Jonathan Winters, the guy who influenced Robin Williams. He was so amazing because he never used a script. He would just walk out there and make it happen. Also Red Skelton was my favorite comedian as a kid growing up. He was always clean. But I think my favorite comedian now, though he's got a problem with language so I can only watch him on television, is Ron White, one of the Blue Collar Comedy guys, because he's got the greatest sense of timing. I love people who can look at what you've looked at a hundred times, only to see something funny that no one else has. I love to laugh. I think if you help people laugh, they kind of lower their guard a little bit.

INTERVIEWER: What has been your greatest temptation?

DR. JAY STRACK: The three things I have struggled with the most and have had to push myself through are to never settle for immediate satisfaction; never settle for just being the shooting star; and to make sure that I live a life that's open, where people can look at any time and examine all that I have done.

INTERVIEWER: What resource has had the most significant impact on your life?

DR. JAY STRACK: The Bible, no question. Also, going digital has really helped me because I am a visual learner. I have to see it and with the technology, I can be reading about something in the Bible, such as Golgotha, and see it. I can see that it literally looks like a skull and it all becomes so real and clear.

INTERVIEWER: If you were on a deserted island and allowed a certain number of books, what would be your top five?

DR. JAY STRACK: The books that have changed my life I would say without question are:
1. *Screwtape Letters* by C. S. Lewis;
2. *In His Steps* by Charles M. Sheldon;
3. *See You at the Top* by Zig Ziglar;
4. *Cross of Christ* by John Stott; and
5. a tie between *Developing the Leader Within You* by John Maxwell and *Why I Preach That the Bible Is Literally True* by W. A. Criswell.

INTERVIEWER: What concerns you most about the church right now?

DR. JAY STRACK: One of my biggest concerns is that I'm afraid we've limited our vision of what orthodoxy is and how we do church. God uses different personalities and different styles. Look at Jesus' inner circle. There's John, the beloved disciple, who would walk six blocks out of the way to avoid being in a fight. Paul would cross the street to avoid being in a fight. Peter would cross the street to get in a fight. We see young leaders come along and they're doing it so differently and some of the older crowd in the church doesn't want to give them a chance.

INTERVIEWER: What encourages you most? What is the church doing right?

DR. JAY STRACK: I think the church is well connected to the fact that they care about the needs of people. I see so many churches that care about the environment, who care about the poor in their city, and who realize that we've got to take the gospel to every tribe, language, and nation.

INTERVIEWER: When I say the word *accountability*, what or who comes to mind? Why?

DR. JAY STRACK: I think of the unseen guest at every meal. I think of the power that Jesus is the only one that could really keep us accountable. And when you have that right you want to be accountable to others. There are only two days that matter . . . this day and that day.

INTERVIEWER: On the following subjects what nuggets of wisdom come to mind (these are designed to be short answers ranging from a phrase to a few sentences) that you would want to pass on to this next generation desiring to serve God, beginning with marriage?

DR. JAY STRACK: Well, to quote what the firemen teach, "You never leave your partner." It is, other than our commitment to Jesus, the single greatest most profound decision we will make. Also, choose wisely because it is the most significant and important relationship you will have in your lifetime.

INTERVIEWER: Raising children?

DR. JAY STRACK: You need to realize that there's nothing else you will do that is more important than touching the lives of your children. You need to model Christ in front of them, and they need to know beyond the shadow of a doubt that when the chips are down, you're on their side.

INTERVIEWER: Finances?

DR. JAY STRACK: The greatest piece of advice I ever got was to save 10 percent, give 10 percent. You may get to a point later in life when you can do more, but this is where you start. And, most important, live within your means!

INTERVIEWER: Communication (writing, teaching, preaching, etc.)?

DR. JAY STRACK: There are three things: First, what's inside is going to come out. Then, learn how to share and partake with others; discover common ground. And finally, Stephen Covey says that you must first seek to understand before you can be understood.

INTERVIEWER: With your permission I would like to ask some light questions that have some pretty short answers . . . beginning with what is your favorite sports team?

DR. JAY STRACK: Dallas Cowboys.

INTERVIEWER: Favorite movie?

DR. JAY STRACK: Raiders of the Lost Ark.

INTERVIEWER: Greatest band ever?

DR. JAY STRACK: Creedence Clearwater Revival.

INTERVIEWER: Dream Vacation?

DR. JAY STRACK: Skibo Castle in Scotland or somewhere in the Caribbean on a private beach.

INTERVIEWER: If you could give just one piece of advice to this generation, what would it be?

DR. JAY STRACK: I think that the answer is actually twofold: *He that hath the Son hath life* and *It's not how you start but how you finish.*

WEBSITES

Matt Redman	mattredman.com
Anne Graham Lotz	annegrahamlotz.com
Francis Chan	francischansblog.blogspot.com
Chaplain Barry C. Black	senate.gov/reference/common/person/barry_black.htm
Mark Hall	castingcrowns.com
Ed Young	edyoung.com
Louie Giglio	268generation.com
Vonette Bright	sistercircles.com
Mac Powell	thirdday.com
Scott Dawson	scottdawson.org
Chris Tomlin	christomlin.com
Dr. Johnny Hunt	johnnyhunt.org
Rick Stanley	rickstanleyministries.com
Alex and Brett Harris	therebelution.com
Dr. Jack Graham	jackgraham.org
Darren Whitehead	premierespeakers.com/christian/darren_whitehead
Ron Luce	ron-luce.com
Leeland Mooring	leelandonline.com
Pat Williams	speakersbureau.com/pat-williams.htm
Dr. Hank Hanegraaff	equip.org
Rebecca St. James	rebeccastjames.forefrontrecords.com
Tony Nolan	tonynolan.org
Dr. Ergun Caner	erguncaner.com
Kevin Huguley	rushoffools.com
Dr. Jay Strack	studentleadership.net